T0133959

ISO 9001:2000

for Software and Systems Providers

An Engineering Approach

OTHER COMPUTER BOOKS FROM AUERBACH AND CRC PRESS

The ABCs of IP Addressing
Gilbert Held
ISBN: 0-8493-1144-6

The ABCs of LDAP: How to Install, Run, and Administer LDAP Services
Reinhard Voglmaier
ISBN: 0-8493-1346-5

The ABCs of TCP/IP
Gilbert Held
ISBN: 0-8493-1463-1

Building an Information Security Awareness Program
Mark B. Desman
ISBN: 0-8493-0116-5

Building a Wireless Office
Gilbert Held
ISBN: 0-8493-1271-X

The Chief Security Officer: A Guide to Protecting People, Facilities, and Information
Ron Hale
ISBN: 0-8493-1952-8

The Complete Book of Middleware
Judith Myerson
ISBN: 0-8493-1272-8

Computer Telephony Integration, 2nd Edition
William A. Yarberry, Jr.
ISBN: 0-8493-1438-0

Creating Components: Object Oriented, Concurrent, and Distributed Computing in Java
Charles W. Kann
ISBN: 0-8493-1499-2

Database Design Using Entity-Relationship Diagrams
Sikha Bagui and Richard Karp
ISBN: 0-8493-1548-4

Electronic Bill Presentment and Payment
Kornel Terplan
ISBN: 0-8493-1452-6

Information Security Architecture: An Integrated Approach to Security in the Organization
Jan Killmeyer Tudor
ISBN: 0-8493-9988-2

Information Security Management Handbook, 5th Edition
Harold F. Tipton and Micki Krause, Editors
ISBN: 0-8493-1997-8

Information Security Policies, Procedures, and Standards: Guidelines for Effective Information Security Management, 2nd Edition
Thomas R. Peltier
ISBN: 0-8493-1958-7

Information Security Risk Analysis
Thomas R. Peltier
ISBN: 0-8493-0880-1

Interpreting the CMMI: A Process Improvement Approach
Margaret Kulpa and Kent Johnson
ISBN: 0-8493-1654-5

IS Management Handbook, 8th Edition
Carol V. Brown and Heikki Topi
ISBN: 0-8493-1595-6

Managing a Network Vulnerability Assessment
Thomas R. Peltier and Justin Peltier
ISBN: 0-8493-1270-1

Maximizing the Enterprise Information Assets
Timothy Wells
ISBN: 0-8493-1347-3

A Practical Guide to Security Engineering and Information Assurance
Deborah S. Herrmann
ISBN: 0-8493-1163-2

Server Disk Management in a Windows Environment
Drew Robb
ISBN: 0-8493-2432-7

Six Sigma Software Development
Christine B. Tayntor
ISBN: 0-8493-1193-4

Software Engineering Measurement
John Munson
ISBN: 0-8493-1503-4

A Technical Guide to IPSec Virtual Private Networks
James S. Tiller
ISBN: 0-8493-0876-3

Telecommunications Cost Management
Brian DiMarsico, Thomas Phelps IV, and William A. Yarberry, Jr.
ISBN: 0-8493-1101-2

Web Data Mining and Applications in Business Intelligence and Counter-Terrorism
Bhavani Thuraisingham
ISBN: 0-8493-1460-7

AUERBACH PUBLICATIONS
www.auerbach-publications.com
To Order Call: 1-800-272-7737 • Fax: 1-800-374-3401
E-mail: orders@crcpress.com

ISO 9001:2000
for Software and Systems Providers

An Engineering Approach

Robert Bamford and
William J. Deibler

CRC PRESS

Boca Raton   London   New York   Washington, D.C.

CMM is registered in the U.S. Patent and Trademark Office. Capability Maturity Model is a registered service mark of Carnegie Mellon University.

Rational Unified Process and RUP are registered trademarks or trademarks of Rational Software Corporation in the United States and/or other countries.

Library of Congress Cataloging-in-Publication Data

Bamford, Robert
    ISO 9001:2000 for software and systems providers : an engineering approach / by Robert Bamford and William J. Deibler.
        p. cm.
    Includes bibliographical references and index.
    ISBN 0-8493-2063-1 (alk. paper)
    1. ISO 9000 Series Standards. I. Deibler, William J. II. Title.

TS156.6.B36 2003
620′.0068′5—dc22   2003055803

This book contains information obtained from authentic and highly regarded sources. Reprinted material is quoted with permission, and sources are indicated. A wide variety of references are listed. Reasonable efforts have been made to publish reliable data and information, but the author and the publisher cannot assume responsibility for the validity of all materials or for the consequences of their use.

Neither this book nor any part may be reproduced or transmitted in any form or by any means, electronic or mechanical, including photocopying, microfilming, and recording, or by any information storage or retrieval system, without prior permission in writing from the publisher.

The consent of CRC Press LLC does not extend to copying for general distribution, for promotion, for creating new works, or for resale. Specific permission must be obtained in writing from CRC Press LLC for such copying.

Direct all inquiries to CRC Press LLC, 2000 N.W. Corporate Blvd., Boca Raton, Florida 33431.

Trademark Notice: Product or corporate names may be trademarks or registered trademarks, and are used only for identification and explanation, without intent to infringe.

Visit the CRC Press Web site at www.crcpress.com

© 2004 by CRC Press LLC
Auerbach is an imprint of CRC Press LLC

No claim to original U.S. Government works
International Standard Book Number 0-8493-2063-1
Library of Congress Card Number 2003055803
Printed in the United States of America 1 2 3 4 5 6 7 8 9 0
Printed on acid-free paper

INTRODUCTION

This volume incorporates more than a decade of experience with ISO 9001, a standard created by committees of volunteers working under the aegis of the International Organization for Standardization (ISO). This volume is intended for individuals who are responsible for using ISO 9001 to implement or revitalize systematic process improvement in engineering organizations.

Since 1989, the authors of this volume have assisted organizations in implementing ISO 9001–based processes. Their clients range from start-up organizations with fewer than ten people to multinational corporations with thousands of employees. The authors have worked with organizations in a wide variety of industries, from sheet metal shops and processed materials manufacturers to developers of semiconductor manufacturing equipment and stand-alone, commercial software products.

Although their focus has been on software, hardware, and systems engineering practices, they have worked extensively in all of the functions that deliver or support the delivery of value to customers—from sales, marketing, order processing, and legal, to engineering and manufacturing, to logistics and warehouse operations, to technical support, and to MIS, credit, finance and administration, and human resources.

This volume is based on the material in the authors' course, *A Detailed Introduction to ISO 9001*. This course, originally developed in 1990, based on the 1987 version of ISO 9001, reflects the authors' commitment to ensuring that client organizations develop the understanding necessary to maintain and improve their own processes. Based on their extensive experience with the no-nonsense Silicon Valley culture, without such systematic knowledge transfer, the authors' experience has been that when the consultant leaves, so does most of the improvement.

Systematic knowledge transfer is the only way to ensure that the improvement stays when the consultant leaves.

The course, which has evolved as the standard has evolved, from 1987 to 1994 to 2000, has been offered hundreds of times to thousands of students. It has been presented publicly, through various extension campuses of the University of California and California State University and through professional organizations, including the Audit and Software Divisions of the American Society for Quality and the Software Engineering Institute at Carnegie Mellon University. It has also been selected by numerous companies for on-site training of their ISO 9001 implementation teams.

The extended history of the course brings three benefits to the reader of this volume. The first benefit is that this volume weaves the information in ISO 9001 into a framework that has been proven to be of use to a broad audience. The concepts and presentation have been tested by and refined with input from participants with every level of prior experience—from individuals new to ISO 9001 to registrars' auditors and implementers with years of experience with this and other standards. These individuals have come from a wide variety of industries and specialties and have represented organizations ranging in size from under 200 to over 5,000 employees.

The second benefit is that the grounding in earlier versions of the standard provides readers with unique insights into the precedents that have formed the latest version of the standard. The effect of the lack of such a perspective is illustrated by the many Internet discussions in which previously exhausted issues reappear and are the subject of lengthy speculation and analysis.

The third benefit derives from the extensive validation the course has received. In addressing the diverse backgrounds of their students and consulting clients, the authors have taken each offering of the course to be an opportunity to test, expand, and refine their understanding of the many ways in which organizations can gain the greatest possible bottom-line business benefit from ISO 9001:2000.

WHAT'S IN THIS VOLUME

This volume is divided into three sections. The first section contains Chapters 1 and 2. This section presents an implementation and maintenance roadmap with suggested techniques for ensuring that the organization secures and continues to accrue the greatest possible benefit from adopting ISO 9001 as a global standard for its processes. The first section concludes with an unavoidable discussion of the acronyms, specialized terms, and concepts that inevitably insinuate themselves into any discussion of ISO 9001.

The second section provides a paragraph-by-paragraph analysis of ISO 9001. In this analysis, the paragraphs are presented, for the most part, in the order in which they appear in the standard. Because the paragraphs do not stand alone, paragraphs are also introduced where they fit logically. Each paragraph is examined to determine how its requirements might be effectively and efficiently satisfied by and to the benefit of an engineering organization. The goal of presenting the paragraphs from this perspective is to ensure that the reader understands not only the requirements encompassed in the paragraphs but also the relationship among the paragraphs—especially when that relationship is critical to efficient implementation. By taking a rigorous approach to the language in the standard, the authors of this volume build a foundation in fact that substantially reduces the effort an implementation team spends in resolving seemingly conflicting interpretations. In particular, it is intended that readers be able to identify various ways in which the requirements of the paragraphs can be—and in many cases are—satisfied in their organizations.

CONSIDER: The paragraphs do not stand alone.

Throughout this volume, one of the authors' goals is to establish and reinforce readers' understanding that ISO 9001:2000 is about good engineering practices. If a requirement in the standard does not appear to support a fundamental, relevant engineering practice or does not appear to offer any benefit, further study is indicated. It is the experience of the authors of this volume that an organization can demand that all of the requirements of ISO 9001 be implemented in ways that deliver value to the organization, its employees, and its customers. A value-based implementation takes effort and investment, but it is also the experience of the authors that adherence to a process or adoption of a new tool or methodology is proportional to the perceived value. A process that does not have any perceived value will not be followed for long—if at all.

CONSIDER: Demand value.

The third section comprises a number of appendices, referenced throughout the volume. These appendices provide background, examples, samples, and reference material.

The last page in this volume provides the information needed to submit comments and questions to the authors.

WHAT'S NOT IN THIS VOLUME (AND WHY AND HOW TO GET IT)

ISO 9001:2000 is not provided. First, it is a copyrighted document and would add unnecessarily to the cost of this volume for readers who already have a copy of the standard. Second, it is important that the reader become comfortable with the look and feel of ISO 9001:2000 in its published, official form, rather than as a section or series of extracts embedded in a printed or electronic book. In fact, the 32-page standard (as provided by the American Society for Quality) is the only source of information the reader can trust without reservation. Books about the standard (including this one), booklets, pamphlets, videotapes, movies, seminars, computer-based self-study courses, descriptions of previous experience, and Internet discussions are useful, but they require careful evaluation to determine whether they are credible and accurate and whether, if accurate, they are relevant to the reader's current circumstances. The bases for this careful evaluation are common sense and what is actually stated in ISO 9001:2000.

Although it is not necessary, consider obtaining a copy of ISO 9001:2000 before proceeding. In particular, to simplify word searches, consider purchasing a downloadable soft copy. Standards are available from:

- National standards bodies
  To find a list of national standards bodies, go to the ISO home page, at http://www.iso.ch, click on *Enter*, then click on *Members* and follow the instructions provided.

- ISO
  International Organization for Standardization, Central Secretariat
  1, rue de Varembé
  CH-1211 Genève 20
  SWITZERLAND
  TEL: 011-41-749-01-11 FAX: 011-41-22-733-34-30
  http://www.iso.ch

- ASQ
  American Society for Quality
  P.O. Box 3066
  611 East Wisconsin Avenue
  Milwaukee, WI 53201-3066
  TEL: 414-272-8575, 800-248-1946 FAX: 414-765-8661
  http://www.asq.org

Table of Contents

Section I
A Brief Orientation

ISO 9001:2000 FOR SOFTWARE AND SYSTEMS PROVIDERS

This section contains two chapters. The first chapter provides a roadmap for an organization to analyze and convert its existing practices into a set of consistent, effective processes that meets the requirements of ISO 9001:2000. This roadmap is inferred from PARAGRAPH 4.1 of ISO 9001:2000. The second chapter is a discussion of significant terminology, definitions, and concepts found in ISO 9001:2000.

Chapter 1
An Implementation Roadmap

PARAGRAPH 4.1 in ISO 9001:2000 contains a slightly disorganized list of steps for an implementation team to follow. Following the discussion of the list of steps, Exhibit 1-5 arranges the steps in a process.

PARAGRAPH 4.1 *a*: Identify the Processes

Exhibit 1-1 is an example of how an organization defines its core capabilities or processes. Five of the processes (on the left side of the Exhibit 1-1) relate directly to delivering product—from business acquisition (finding customers, obtaining orders) to service, maintenance, and support (all postdelivery activities). The four processes on the right of the exhibit support product delivery.

PARAGRAPH 4.1 *b*: Determine the Interactions

Exhibit 1-2 continues the example from Exhibit 1-1. The organization determines that all nine core processes interact to a lesser or greater extent with every other core process. Management reaches two conclusions. First, at the top level of the organization, divisions of responsibility and specialization intended to enhance control may inadvertently inhibit effectiveness, coordination, and cooperation. Second, in determining whether to make changes to a process, the potential effect on all of the other core processes is considered to prevent suboptimization—where the gain realized in one process is more than offset by the inadvertent degradation of other processes.

PARAGRAPH 4.1 *b*: Determine the Sequence of Processes

Exhibit 1-3 continues the example as the organization creates a high-level process map to capture the sequence of activities. Teams are assigned to create a succession of more detailed maps that describe the high-level activities. In these maps, sequence does not preclude the reality of overlapping, parallel, or iterative processes. In Exhibit 1-3, although the steps occur in a rough sequence, they also overlap. Designing, developing, and testing begins while the contract and requirements of business acquisition are still being prepared. Some production occurs while designing, developing, and testing is still underway (e.g., preproduction and beta product). Delivery (of beta product) occurs while designing, developing, and testing is still in process, but service and support do not start until after designing,

3

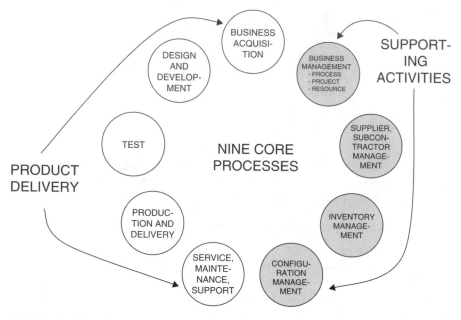

Exhibit 1-1. Identify the processes.

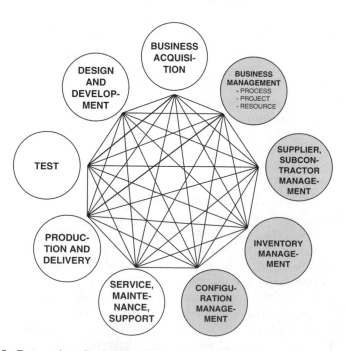

Exhibit 1-2. Determine the interaction.

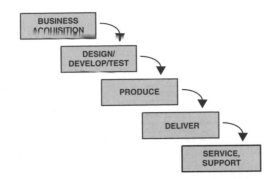

Exhibit 1-3. Determine the sequence.

developing, and testing are complete (e.g., beta test support is provided by engineering, outside the normal support processes).

In addition to overlapping, although it is not shown, product can go through processes multiple times. For example, the sequence of designing, developing, and testing; producing; and delivery described above can be repeated as increments of functionality are added to the product. The final cycle represents the planned delivery of completed, tested product for general availability.

Identifying the processes and establishing the interactions creates a model of the organization's behavior as it relates to delivering products and services to its customers.

PARAGRAPH 4.1 *c*: Map the Organization's Processes against the Standard

PARAGRAPH 4.1 c describes requirements for determining the criteria and methods needed to ensure that both the operation and control of these processes are effective. These criteria and methods include both success criteria (e.g., statements of goals, objectives, performance criteria, and requirements) and descriptions of how management intends to ensure that those criteria are being met.

The essential tool for ensuring that the organization's processes meet the requirements of ISO 9001:2000 is a document that describes the relationship between the identified processes and the requirements of ISO 9001:2000. This document ensures that existing or planned processes achieve full coverage of the requirements of the standard. It also alerts implementers to the relevant requirements of ISO 9001. The mapping is an invaluable reference for internal auditors and, if appropriate, for customers and for registrars' auditors. Exhibit 1-4 suggests a method for graphically representing the relationship. In Exhibit 1-4, the life cycle phases appear across the top, and the paragraphs of ISO 9001:2000 appear below the phases to which they apply.

BUSINESS ACQUISITION	DESIGN/ DEVELOP/TEST	PRODUCE	DELIVER, INSTALL	SERVICE, SUPPORT

4 QUALITY MANAGEMENT SYSTEM

5 MANAGEMENT RESPONSIBILITY

6 RESOURCE MANAGEMENT

7 PRODUCT REALIZATION

7.1 PLANNING OF REALIZATION PROCESSES

7.2 CUSTOMER-RELATED PROCESSES

7.3 DESIGN AND DEVELOPMENT

7.4 PURCHASING

7.5.1 CONTROL OF PRODUCTION AND SERVICE PROVISION
7.5.2 VALIDATION OF PROCESSES FOR PRODUCTION AND SERVICE PROVISION

7.5.3 IDENTIFICATION AND TRACEABILITY
7.5.4 CUSTOMER PROPERTY
7.5.5 PRESERVATION OF PRODUCT

7.6 CONTROL OF MEASURING AND MONITORING DEVICES

8 MEASUREMENT, ANALYSIS, AND IMPROVEMENT

Exhibit 1-4. High-level mapping.

More-detailed maps evolve from the top-level map to elaborate on the relationship between the organization's processes and the requirements of ISO 9001:2000.

PARAGRAPH 4.1 *d*: Planning and Communication

Implementing processes to meet the requirements of ISO 9001:2000 requires the same degree of management as any other project to develop a product that meets customer or market requirements. Following the direction in PARAGRAPH 4.1 *d*, the implementation team prepares and manages a plan that ensures the availability of resources and information necessary to support the implementation. Responsibility and timing are clearly defined, and the plan is the basis for reporting progress and making any necessary adjustments to ensure the successful completion of the implementation.

PARAGRAPH 4.1 *e*: Monitor and Measure

PARAGRAPH 4.1 *e* specifies requirements for monitoring, measuring, and analyzing processes. Monitoring and measurement occur at three stages of the implementation. At the beginning, an assessment comparing the current state of the organization with the model provides the organization with a measure of the extent of the work needed to achieve compliance with ISO 9001:2000.

During the implementation, periodic self-assessments (internal audits, required by ISO 9001:2000) and progress reviews measure actual progress and provide the factual basis for making the inevitable adjustments to the implementation plan.

Finally, periodic, planned self-assessments continue after the complete set of processes has been implemented to ensure the continuing integrity of the processes. In addition, if the organization seeks an official certificate to confirm its continuing adherence to the requirements of ISO 9001:2000, an accredited third party, called a registrar, performs periodic assessments and reassessments. Registrars and registration are discussed below in "To Register or Not To Register" and "Selecting a Registrar."

PARAGRAPH 4.1 *f*: Execution

PARAGRAPH 4.1 *f* reminds the implementation team to implement actions necessary to achieve planned results and continual improvement of these processes. The success of the implementation team requires the active participation and support of every member of the organization. No amount of well-intentioned investment in planning, process definition, tools acquisition, and training is sufficient if the organization is not committed to the realization of those plans and processes.

Representing the Implementation Process

Exhibit 1-5 represents the implementation process as it is suggested by PARAGRAPH 4.1. The three activities represented at the top of Exhibit 1-5 occur throughout the implementation process. As processes are implemented, the team plans and manages the implementation as if it were a revenue project and, to prevent speculation and minimize unnecessary stress, communicates with the organization.

The five numbered steps form a cycle that begins with 5. MEASURE. As described in Chapter 4, "The Gap Assessment," an assessment is frequently the first activity funded by management following the initial commitment to seek ISO 9001 compliance. The information from the gap assessment provides input for the first four steps:

1. Identify processes needed.
2. Determine interactions.
3. Determine sequence.
4. Map the standard.

As processes are defined and implemented, internal audits as part of 5. MEASURE determine the effectiveness of the processes and ensure that adjustments do not inadvertently affect ISO 9001 compliance.

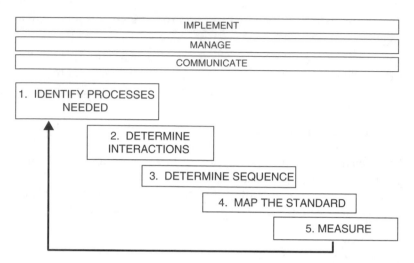

Exhibit 1-5. Recommended implementation road map.

Appendix F describes in detail proven methods for planning and managing the implementation of processes.

Charting an Alternate Path through the Paragraphs

Because the paragraphs of ISO 9001:2000 do not stand alone, the paragraph-by-paragraph analysis is filled with references—forward and backward—to other paragraphs. In Exhibit 1-6, the paragraphs are placed in concentric circles based on the number of references. The paragraphs in the center circle are referenced the most; those in the outer circle, the least.

This picture suggests a strategy for partitioning the work of the implementation team. The whole team needs to be aware of all aspects of the standard from the beginning of the implementation, and all team members need to be involved in analyzing the paragraphs that lie in the innermost circle. These tend to be the paragraphs that address processes directly associated with products and customers.

Subteams can focus simultaneously on the paragraphs in the second and third circles, conveying information to and coordinating with the whole team.

Recommendations for Implementers: Establishing ISO 9001 as a Framework

ISO 9001:2000 PARAGRAPH 3 *Fundamentals of quality management systems* presents valuable background information on the principles underlying the adoption of systematic business and engineering practices. In practice, there are three overriding principles that can guide implementers in software engineering organizations.

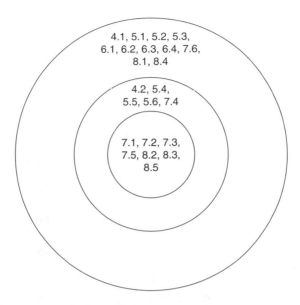

Exhibit 1-6. Alternate path through the paragraphs.

Principle 1: ISO 9001:2000 Is a Requirements Specification

The first key principle for implementers to follow the often-overlooked guidance in ISO 9001:2000 PARAGRAPH 0.1 *General*:

> *The adoption of a quality management system should be a strategic decision of an organization. The design and implementation of an organization's quality management system is influenced by varying needs, particular objectives, the products provided, the processes employed, and the size and structure of the organization.*
>
> *It is not the intent of this International Standard to imply uniformity in the structure of quality management systems or uniformity of documentation.*

This translates into a recommendation to focus on the definition of development practices that suit the organization. In the implementation, the standard serves as a checklist for assessing how well the organization's current practices already meet the criteria for compliance.* The implementer's assignment is to address any omissions identified in the assessment in a manner that enhances the ability of the organization to meet its business objectives.

To ensure that the organization achieves full coverage of the requirements in ISO 9001:2000, the implementer studies the standard, digests the

---

* It is the experience of the authors of this volume that a well-defined, reasonably efficient, effective set of software development practices satisfies most, if not all, of the requirements of ISO 9001:2000.

results of the assessment, and maps the organization's policies, procedures, and practices to the requirements of ISO 9001:2000. This mapping may be maintained by the management representative and internal auditors as part of the process for ensuring that compliance with ISO 9001:2000 is achieved and maintained as the quality system and organization evolve. This mapping can also be made available to the registrar's auditor. Based on experience with ISO 9001:1994, this mapping is typically part of the quality manual, as described in ISO 9001:2000 PARAGRAPH 4.2.2 *Quality manual.*

The key processes for implementers to address are the processes that have always challenged systems providers:

- Requirements engineering
- Project planning and management—including estimating effort and coordinating team activities
- Configuration management, including the hand over to manufacturing and distribution
- Testing
- Bug reporting and tracking, including coordination among engineering, in-house support, and field support organizations
- Managing third-party development.

About Registrars and Their Auditors

The registrar's auditor's first responsibility is to examine the quality manual to verify the completeness of the organization's quality system in satisfying the requirements of the standard. The verification of completeness is based solely on the content of ISO 9001:2000 and ISO 9000:2000. Because each organization's quality system is potentially unique, the registrar's auditor's job is to recognize compliance based on the information in the quality manual—not enforce some industry standard practice or conventional wisdom that is established outside the two standards.

If the registrar's auditor cannot determine how the organization is addressing a particular requirement of ISO 9001:2000, additional information is requested. Internal inconsistencies or omissions may result in an update to the quality manual during this review.

The registrar's auditor's second responsibility is to verify through on-site inspection and interviews that

- The system of policies, procedures, and practices defined in the quality manual is implemented throughout the portion of the organization that falls within the scope of the registration.
- The evidence provided by the organization demonstrates that these policies, procedures, and practices are effective in producing the planned results.

Principle 2: It Is Easier To Achieve Compliance Than To Maintain Compliance

The second key principle for implementers is to ensure that the set of policies, procedures, and practices remain current as the organization evolves. During the initial implementation, the implementation team ensures that the set of policies and procedures is sufficiently scaleable and flexible to address all of the product development activities within the organization as they currently occur. For efficiency, the implementation team also ensures that the policies and procedures address new or evolving activities as they will occur in the immediate future. The policies and procedures represent a foundation for sustaining an organization's culture during periods of high employee turnover and growth.

After the initial implementation has achieved compliance, it is the responsibility of management to ensure that the policies and procedures remain valuable assets and are revised as the organization and its practices evolve (PARAGRAPH 5.4.2 *b*). The systematic evolution of these policies and procedures, with the associated commitment of resources, is a continuing demonstration of management's priority for meeting the needs of customers and employees.

The internal audits (PARAGRAPH 8.2.2), management review (PARAGRAPH 5.6), and corrective (PARAGRAPH 8.5.2) and preventive action (PARAGRAPH 8.5.3) are the mechanisms built into ISO 9001:2000 to ensure that compliance is maintained. Periodic surveillance audits (typically twice a year) are an additional mechanism for the organization that obtains formal registration as further confirmation of compliance.

Looking beyond ensuring compliance, the system of audits, management review, preventive and corrective action, and employee training (PARAGRAPH 6.2.2) can be a significant asset to the organization.

Principle 3: Manage the Implementation as if It Were Product Development

Although ISO 9001 compliance is easier to achieve than maintain, it is not trivial to achieve. A detailed plan and ongoing project management are critical factors in achieving ISO 9001 compliance in a cost-effective and timely manner. The organization's commitment to the ISO project is reflected in its priority relative to all of the other projects in the organization and in its continuing progress, even as adjustments are made. Without careful, obvious attention from all levels of management, the ISO project can falter, signaling the organization that it must shift its attention and resources to the projects that do matter to management.

Appendix F describes in detail proven methods for planning and managing the implementation of processes.

Recommendations for Maintainers: Addressing the Changes in ISO 9001:2000

For anyone who is required to be familiar with the requirements of ISO 9001, the transition from the 1994 version to the 2000 version is significant. These individuals are faced with a completely new structure and approach. Familiar terms, such as "receiving inspection" and "in-process inspection," are replaced with requirements for measurement and monitoring. In some cases, terms are used with a more narrow definition (e.g., "design and development" and "design review").

The members of ISO, who represent the interests of national industries, imposed requirements that

> *The revision of the ISO 9000 standards will not require the rewriting of an organization's quality management system documentation.*
>
> *The 20 elements in the current ISO 9001 will be clearly identifiable in the new process-based structure.*
>
> *Organizations that have implemented the current ISO 9000 standards will find it easy to transition to the revised standards.*[1]

Based on this stated goal, on the mapping of ISO 9001:2000 to ISO 9001:1994 contained in ISO 9001:2000, and on more-detailed mappings created in studying the drafts, it is our conclusion that the revision neither adds nor removes requirements.

However, because of past inconsistent interpretation of the standard and variability in the effectiveness of registrar's audits, the revision may bring clarification or add emphasis that requires some level of change.[2]*

Points To Focus on for Maintainers

The following are some areas that the authors of this volume identify as likely to require fine-tuning of an organization's quality management system. Appropriate individuals in each organization will have to study and understand the new version of the standard to ensure continuing compliance.

In implementing any changes, consider the same principles listed for implementers of new quality management systems. Implement any changes in a manner that enhances the ability of the organization to meet its business objectives.

---

* The issue of variability in the effectiveness of registrar's audits has been addressed by ISO in documenting requirements for the operation of accreditation bodies and registrars (see ISO Guide 61 *General requirements for assessment and accreditation of certification/registration bodies* and ISO Guide *General requirements for bodies operating assessment and certification/registration of quality systems*) and in facilitating the establishment of the International Accreditation Forum (IAF) as an agency for ensuring that these requirements are adopted and implemented.

Exhibit 1-7 presents a number of key points of interest to individuals responsible for maintaining or upgrading an existing registration. The points are presented in no particular order, however, in our view, points 3, 7, 10, and 15 represent the areas of highest risk and offer the most opportunity for leveraging the revision to improve processes.

Selecting a Scope

Setting aside the issues of what exclusions are permitted by PARAGRAPH 1.2, the most benefit is derived from including all of the organizational units that participate in the chain of activities that make up product realization. It is reasonable to refine the scope to focus on particular products or market segments. Within the selected scope, as with any project, the plan associated with the implementation structures the work into manageable pieces, to address dependencies, critical needs of the organization, and the availability of resources.

For organizations that are pursuing a new or expanded registration, the only issue is whether and how the registrar can recognize and certify completion of the implementation in parts of the organization (e.g., manufacturing is ready; service and engineering are not; engineering and manufacturing are ready, service is not; service is ready, engineering and manufacturing are not). This is a topic for discussion with the registrar.

To Register or Not To Register?

From a process improvement perspective, the organization realizes the majority of the benefits when it achieves and maintains compliance: effective processes are implemented and managed; process operation and results are measured, monitored, and periodically audited; and improvement opportunities are systematically considered.

Registration is an add-on that offers several potential benefits:

- Registration is sometimes the price of admission to a market or to the pool of suppliers selected to receive a request for proposals.
- The registrar's auditors are able to validate the implementation and, at times, identify omissions that, when addressed, strengthen the organization's processes.
- The public commitment and the regular visits by the registrar's auditors keep management focused on maintaining and improving processes and prevent occasional backsliding, which is almost inevitable as managers respond to day-to-day pressures with decisions regarding priorities and trade-offs.

In comparison to the costs of implementing ISO-compliant processes (e.g., acquiring tools, training personnel, developing, and, as required, documenting processes), the incremental cost of registration is relatively

Exhibit 1-7. Points to focus on for maintainers.

Number	Point
Point 1	Provide training and support for all individuals who are required to understand the new standard.
Point 2	Part of the internal audit process (Paragraph 8.2.2) is to verify compliance with ISO 9001:2000. If internal auditors have previously been auditing against procedures, the organization needs to determine how this new requirement is to be satisfied (e.g., train some or all internal auditors in the standard, use outside resources).
Point 3	Ensure that mechanisms for measuring customer satisfaction and taking appropriate action are well defined and consistently understood and implemented, and that the data is analyzed. See Paragraphs 8.2.1 and 8.4(a).
Point 4	For corrective action (Paragraph 8.5.2), ensure that the organization records the results of the action. In ISO 9001:1994 Paragraph 4.14.2, the requirement is to record the results of the investigation.
Point 5	Ensure that the organization's policy for quality (however it is expressed) addresses the specific elements in Paragraph 5.3, particularly as it relates to continual improvement.
Point 6	ISO 9001:2000 Paragraph 8.5 *Continual improvement* is specific in identifying associated practices, many of which should already be in place for ISO 9001:1994: quality policy, quality objectives, audit results, analysis of data, corrective and preventive action, and management review. Ensure that they are all in place—preventive action and measurement in particular (see point 7).
Point 7	Ensure that appropriate monitoring, measurement, and data analysis are in place. For organizations seeking to maintain registration, objective evidence of systematic monitoring, measurement, and analysis is a potential new focal point for registrars' auditors.
Point 8	Ensure that the management review process incorporates the detailed inputs listed in Paragraph 5.6.2 *Review input* and produces the outputs listed in Paragraph 5.6.3 *Review output.*
Point 9	As part of training (Paragraph 6.2.2), ensure that the organization defines mechanisms for evaluating the effectiveness of training (6.2.2 *c*). This can be as simple as participant evaluations at the completion of a course and periodic solicitation by the training group of management input on training effectiveness. In addition, the organization is required to establish a mechanism for examining this data (Paragraph 8.4).
Point 10	As required by Paragraph 7.3.3 *b*, ensure that design and development processes provide the information required for downstream processes.
Point 11	Ensure that the management representative carries out the new responsibility to promote awareness of customer requirements. See Paragraph 5.5.2.
Point 12	Ensure that there are processes in place to address handling of confidential information supplied by customers, as specified by Paragraph 7.5.4.
Point 13	Although there is a new list of quality records (identified by "see 4.2.4"), they correspond to the ISO 9001:1994 quality records, except for Paragraph 8.5.2 *Corrective action* and 8.5.3 *Preventive action*. Both paragraphs require that the organization "record the results of action taken." See also point 4.

Exhibit 1-7. (continued)   Points to focus on for maintainers.

Number	Point
Point 14	Ensure that software used for testing is verified before it is put into use by engineering, manufacturing, or support. See PARAGRAPH 7.6.
Point 15	Monitor additional clarification and discussion of the issue of permissible exclusions. See PARAGRAPH 1.2.

Exhibit 1-8. A completed budgetary worksheet.

Audit cost components			Subtotal
One auditor day per 50 employees in scope	Six days	$1,000/day	$6,000
Local expenses per auditor day	Six days	$190/day	$1,140
Fees	—	—	$1,000
Preparation	—	—	$1,000
			—
Travel per auditor	Two auditors	$500/auditor	$1,000
TOTAL			$10,140

small. For example, Exhibit 1-8 represents a worksheet completed to prepare a budgetary estimate of the costs of registering a 300-person organization. The worksheet is based on the assumption that the registrar's auditors interview 10 to 15 percent of the organization's employees, that the auditors interview six or seven individuals per day, and that the decision is made to send two auditors on-site for three days.

On the basis of the assumption that the registrar reaudits portions of the organization every six months, the annual cost is approximately 60 percent of the cost of the initial registration audit. In the above example, the estimated annual budget for ongoing audits by the registrar is 60 percent of $10,140, or $6,084.

The costs and fees included in Exhibit 1-8 represent a conservative (high-end), but not unreasonable, basis for a budgetary estimate based on our experience. As you interview candidate registrars, you will be able to obtain actual costs.

Do Not Expect Too Much; Do Not Demand Too Little. As a rule of thumb, the internal audits find ten times the number of problems the registrar's auditors find. The registrar's auditors will typically find a few items that require correction, but their overall contribution is in validating the integrity and compliance of the organization's quality management system.* It is useful to keep in mind the standard disclaimer that accompanies every audit report. The disclaimer states something like the following:

---

* For a discussion of the institutional pressures that affect registrars' performances, see Reference 3.

*This report is based on a sample of the organization's personnel, pro-
cesses, and procedures. As such, while the auditors undertake their best
efforts to ensure that every assessment is through and correct, there may
be nonconformities in areas that are not represented in the sample. The
lack of reported nonconformities is not to be construed as indicating an
absence of nonconformities, which may be identified in subsequent
audits. Likewise, successful correction of identified nonconformities does
not prevent additional nonconformities from being found in subsequent
audits.*

Although this may seem almost as complete a denial of responsibility as
is found in many commercial software packages, it accurately characterizes the results of any single assessment. The strength of the internal audit
process and the registration audit process is in its iterative nature.

Selecting a Registrar

Selecting a registrar is like selecting any other supplier. Although all registrars follow the rules of the International Accreditation Forum (IAF) and of
ISO Guide 62,[4] there is unfortunately significant variation in registrars'
interpretations of ISO 9001. The objective of the registrar selection process
is to find a registrar whose views on the standard are compatible with
those of the organization. The relationship with the registrar is potentially
long, so time invested in evaluating registrars is well spent. If the relationship does not mature as expected, the organization always has the option
of changing registrars. Unless there are extenuating circumstances, the
new registrar will typically pick up at the point the previous registrar
stopped.

About Accreditation

Registrars are businesses that assess and certify an organization's compliance with the requirements of ISO 9001. Registrars are accredited by
national accreditation bodies, which are either part of or are associated
with national governments. Accreditation bodies are the authority under
which a registrar operates; the certificates issued by a registrar indicate
the registrar's accreditation. For example, in the United States, the

*National Accreditation Program (NAP) is jointly operated by [Registrar
Accreditation Board] RAB and American National Standards Institute
(ANSI). NAP programs cover the accreditation of Environmental Management Systems ISO 14001 and Quality Management Systems ISO 9000
registrars and auditor training course providers. Representatives of industry, government, environmental, and quality organizations, as well as
auditing professionals and other EMS and QMS stakeholders developed
all NAP programs through a consensus process.* *

---

* The Registrar Accreditation Board was originally established by the American Society for Quality but is now an independent organization. Information is found at http://www.rabnet.com/.

Exhibit 1-9. Two scope categories from the Registrar Accreditation Board list.

Scope category 33: information technology	Scope category 19: electrical and optical equipment (manufacture)
Hardware consultancy	Office machinery and computers
Software consultancy and supply	Electric motors, generators, and transformers
Software development (writing code and testing)	Electricity distribution and control apparatus
	Insulated wire and cable
	Accumulators, primary cells, and primary batteries
Data processing	Lighting equipment and electric lamps
Database activities	Other electrical equipment n.e.c. (including for engines and vehicles n.e.c.)
Maintenance and repair of office, accounting, and computing machinery	Electronic valves and tubes and other electronic components
	Television and radio transmitters and apparatus for line telephony and line telegraphy
Other computer-related activities	Television and radio receivers, sound or video recording, or reproducing apparatus and associated goods
	Instruments and appliances for measuring, checking, testing, navigating, and other purposes, except industrial process control equipment
	Industrial process control equipment
	Optical instruments and photographic equipment
	Watches and clocks

National accreditation bodies assess and monitor registrar performance and provide an independent channel for complaints from registrars' customers. National accreditation bodies also maintain public lists of the registrars they accredit, with some indication of the types of organizations the registrar is accredited to assess. For example, the RAB maintains a list of registrars it accredits and indicates the scope categories that the registrar is accredited to assess.* The scope categories indicate types of industries and technologies. Two scope categories from the RAB list are listed in Exhibit 1-9. These scope categories are the European Accreditation of Conformity industry classifications, in use by many accreditation bodies and registrars.** As the examples illustrate, these classifications provide a vague indicator of whether a registrar may be able to service a particular organization.

To ensure that ISO certificates are a consistent indicator of the effectiveness of an organization's quality management system, many accreditation bodies are members of the IAF and conform to the requirements of ISO Guide 61.[5]

---

* The list is found at http://www.rabnet.com/rab/presearchReg.do?command-QMS (9 Oct. 03).
** The EAC codes are currently the responsibility of an organization called the European Accreditation (EA). The organization's Web site is http://www.european-accreditation.org (9 Oct. 03). The codes are published by the International Accreditation Forum in *Annex 1* of IAF-PL-01-014, IAF Guidance on the Application of ISO/IEC Guide 62:1996, 4-Dec-2001, available at http://www.iaf.nu, under Documentation (9 Oct. 03).

Although accreditation allows a registrar to operate anywhere in the world, it is not unusual for a registrar to maintain multiple accreditations to make its services more marketable.

Selection Criteria

Although all ISO registrations are theoretically equal (a theory that has gained increased validity and acceptance as ISO has become more involved in ensuring the uniformity of assessments), the first step for an organization is to determine whether there are any significant customer or market preferences that should be considered in developing a short list of candidate registrars.

Because the detailed evaluation of a candidate registrar is time consuming, a short-list of three or four candidates can be developed based on information available on the Internet, on the results of a preliminary questionnaire filled out by the registrar, and on reference checks with existing customers (for whom contact information is provided by the registrar). A sample questionnaire is provided in Appendix H.

The topics to explore in detail with candidate registrars are accreditation, experience in assessing similar organizations, any critical issues regarding interpretation, and the elements of the business relationship. The particular issues related to the business relationship go beyond cost to include:

- Criteria for assigning auditors (maintaining continuity, building experience)
- Use and management of subcontractors as auditors
- Registration process—activities, duration, schedule requirements, and costs
- Surveillance process—activities, duration, schedule requirements, and costs
- Client management—continuity and management support

Because the relationship with the registrar will potentially remain in place as long as the organization maintains its registration, the organization can insist that registrars' auditors participate in the final selection interviews and presentations.

About Preassessments. In addition to the registration and regular surveillance audits, registrars offer a one-time preassessment service. A preassessment is conducted as if it were a standard audit (i.e., nonconformities are identified, no solutions are offered). In the case of a preassessment, the organization is able to specify areas to be audited. The results of the preassessment are useful for building confidence that the organization is ready for the assessment and for motivating groups that may not be fully supportive of the implementation. An impending audit is an effective wake-up call for any individuals who may have gambled or assumed that management would lose interest before anything significant actually had to be done.

About Consulting. To avoid conflict of interest, registrars' auditors are strictly forbidden to consult and to provide solutions and advice regarding the nonconformities they find. The auditor's only job is to compare all aspects of the organization's quality management system to the requirements in ISO 9001, to identify nonconformities, and, when appropriate, to issue a certificate of registration.

To ensure that this happens, the registrar's auditor is accompanied at all times by a guide from the organization. The guide helps with administration (e.g., where to go and how to get there) and also serves to keep the registrar's auditor on track. Guides who are knowledgeable in the standards and in the organization's processes can develop a rapport with the auditor, which allows for the guide to provide occasional assistance. For example, with the auditor's permission, the guide can help clarify confusion when an auditor's question does not match the terminology of the organization. The guide can indicate that an inappropriate question has been asked (e.g., the department is not responsible for the item in question). The guide or the management representative can also question an auditor's interpretation of the standard or of the evidence (in a professional, nonconfrontational way).

References

1. PARAGRAPH 1.5 *Structure of the Revised Standards,* ISO/CD1 9001:2000 and ISO/CD1 9004:2000, ISO/TC 176/SC 2/N 415, International Organization for Standardization, Geneva, Switzerland, July 30, 1998.
2. PARAGRAPH 1.3 *Structure of the Revised Standards,* ISO/CD1 9001:2000 and ISO/CD1 9004:2000, ISO/TC 176/SC 2/N 415, International Organization for Standardization, Geneva, Switzerland, July 30, 1998.
3. Bamford, Robert and Deibler, William J., Third-party registrars' audits—for better or for worse? in *Quality New Zealand,* New Zealand Organisation for Quality, May 1996, vol. 27, and in *Proceedings of SEPG 98,* Software Engineering Institute, Carnegie Mellon University, Chicago IL, 1998.
4. International Organization for Standardization, *ISO/IEC Guide 62, General Requirements for Bodies Operating Assessment and Certification/Registration of Quality Systems,* 1st ed., International Organization for Standardization, Geneva, 1996.
5. International Organization for Standardization, *ISO/IEC Guide 61, General Requirements for Assessment and Accreditation of Certification/Registration Bodies,* 1st ed., International Organization for Standardization, Geneva, 1996.

Chapter 2
Terminology and Definitions

The following terms and concepts are used throughout this volume. They are presented here to ensure that readers have a common understanding of terms that may be unfamiliar (such as quality management system) or ambiguous (such as ISO 9000 and should). They are presented in an order that is intended to answer questions as they occur to the reader.

What Is in a Name: ISO 9000 and Standard

The first terms that require explanation are *ISO 9000* and *standard*. The ISO 9000 family of standards currently includes four principal documents—all labeled as International Standards.* The four documents are

- ISO 9000:2000 Quality management systems—fundamentals and vocabulary, which is normative (must be followed).
- ISO 9001:2000 Quality management systems—requirements, which is normative (must be followed).
- ISO 9004:2000 Quality management systems—guidance for performance improvement, which provides guidance on process improvement for organizations that wish "to move beyond the requirements of ISO 9001:2000 in pursuit of continual improvement of performance."**
- ISO 9000-3, Quality management and quality assurance standards—guidelines for the application of ISO 9001 to the development, supply, installation, and maintenance of computer software.

---

* ISO publishes a standard identified as an International Standard. National standards bodies adopt these standards on behalf of their respective countries and, in some cases, rebadge and sell the standard as a national standard. For example, in the United States, ISO 9001 is identified as ANSI/ISO/ASQ Q9001 and labeled as an American National Standard. Other than appropriate language changes, the content is preserved.

** ISO 9001:2000 Paragraph 0.3 explicitly defines the relationship between ISO 9001:2000 and ISO 9004:2000:

> *ISO 9004:2000 gives guidance on a wider range of objectives of a quality management system than does ISO 9001. ... [It] is not intended for certification or for contractual purposes.*

ISO 9004:2000 Paragraph 0.3 precisely echoes ISO 9001:2000 when it states that ISO 9004:2000 is "not intended as guidance for compliance with ISO 9001:2000." These coordinated statements directly address the frequently expressed misconception that an organization has to provide justification for not implementing guidance found in ISO 9004-1:1994.

ISO 9000-3:1997 is to be revised and reissued as ISO 90003 by December 2003.

Unfortunately, the authors of the standards have chosen to use ISO 9000 to designate both the family of documents and one specific member of the family. Two of the four standards, ISO 9004 and ISO 9000-3, provide guidance and amplification, rather than requirements for which the organization is accountable if it claims conformance with ISO 9001. A third standard, ISO 9000, is a glossary of terms used throughout the ISO 9000 family. Only ISO 9001 contains explicit requirements that an organization can apply to its processes.

The committee responsible for ISO 9000, ISO 9001, and ISO 9004* also provides a number of guidance documents that are intended to directly support ISO 9001:2000. This set of documents includes standards and Technical Reports (TRs): **

- ISO 10005:1995, Quality management—guidelines for quality plans
- ISO 10006:1997, Quality management—guidelines to quality in project management
- ISO 10007:1995, Quality management—guidelines for configuration management
- ISO 10011:1990, Guidelines for auditing quality systems (parts 1, 2, and 3)***
- ISO 10012:1992, Quality assurance requirements for measuring equipment (parts 1 and 2)
- ISO 10013:1995, Guidelines for developing quality manuals
- ISO/TR 10014:1998, Guidelines for managing the economics of quality
- ISO 10015:1999, Quality management—guidelines for training
- ISO/TR 10017:1999, Guidance on statistical techniques for ISO 9001:1994
- ISO/DIS 19011:2001, Guidelines for quality or environmental management systems auditing****

---

* These standards are the responsibility of Technical Committee 176 (TC 176). For a full list of the committees, their subcommittees, and the standards documents for which they are responsible, from the ISO home page, at http://www.iso.ch, click on Enter and then select List of Technical Committees under Standards development.
** Documents designated by ISO/TR are Technical Reports, which undergo a less demanding review and approval cycle than documents designated as standards. In some cases, Technical Reports test industry interest and, if the response is favorable, become standards in a subsequent revision.
*** ISO 10011 is being replaced by ISO 19011, which consolidates auditing guidelines for ISO 9001 and ISO 14001 (environmental systems).
**** At the time this volume is being written, ISO 19011 is only available as a draft international standard (DIS).

A number of other ISO standards that are more or less coordinated with ISO 9001 focus on the specialized needs of software engineering organizations and systems providers.* These standards include:

- ISO/IEC 9000-3, Quality management and quality assurance standards, part 3: Guidelines for the application of ISO 9001 to the design, development, supply, installation, and maintenance of computer software, International Organization for Standardization, Geneva, Switzerland, scheduled for release as ISO 90003 in December 2003**
- ISO/IEC 12207:1995, Information Technology—software life cycle processes*** and ISO/IEC TR 15271:1998, Information technology—guide for ISO/IEC 12207 (Software Life Cycle Processes)
- ISO/IEC 15288: Information Technology—Life cycle management—System life cycle processes, currently in preliminary draft, scheduled for publication in October 2002
- ISO/IEC/TR 15504 Software Process Assessment, parts 1 through 9

The contents of these specialized standards and technical reports are referred to throughout this volume to define the core competencies associated with systems design and development.

Exhibit 2-1 summarizes the relationships among the documents listed above.

Quality and Quality Management System

The definitions of *quality* and *quality management system*, used throughout ISO 9001, are found in ISO 9000. *Quality* is "the degree to which a set of inherent characteristics fulfils requirements." A *quality management system* is defined as "the set of interrelated or interacting elements to direct and control an organization with regard to quality." In practice, a quality management system includes the organizational structure, people, processes, documentation, and other resources applied to fulfilling the requirements

---

* These standards are the responsibility of Joint Technical Committee 1 (JTC 1), co-sponsored by the International organization for Standardization (ISO) and by the International Electrotechnical Commission (IEC).

** The two previous verions of ISO 9000-3, ISO 9000-3:1991, and ISO 9000-3:1997 were the responsibility of Technical Committee 176, also responsible for quality assurance standards, including ISO 9001. As of April 2001, through the approval of TC176 resolution 174, responsibility was transferred to Joint Technical Committee (JTC 1), which is the committee responsible for Information Technology standards, including software standards.

*** Under the auspices of the American National Standards Institute (The U.S. representative to ISO), the Institute of Electrical and Electronics Engineers, Inc. (IEEE), and the Electronics Industry Association (EIA) issued a three-part version of ISO/IEC 12207. The three parts are:

- IEEE/EIA 12207.0:1996 (Part 0) is ISO/IEC 12207.
- IEEE/EIA 12207.1:1997 (Part 1) provides guidance on the various documents (e.g., data items) specified in IEEE/EIA 12207.0:1996.
- IEEE/EIA 12207.2:1997 (Part 2) provides paragraph-by-paragraph implementation guidance for the processes specified in IEEE/EIA 12207.0:1996.

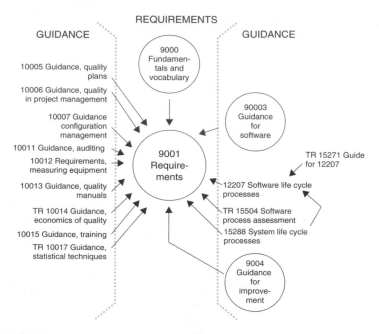

Exhibit 2-1. ISO standards and technical reports.

of customers and any other interested parties (e.g., shareholders, investors, employees, and governments).

Shall, Should, and Other Formalities

By convention,[1] *shall* signals a requirement in ISO 9001. For example, PARAGRAPH 6.2.2 states that the "The organization shall … determine the necessary competence for personnel performing work affecting product quality." Any organization that claims that it conforms to the requirements of ISO 9001 can describe how it meets this requirement.

Should, used most often in guidance standards, indicates a suggestion, a way in which an organization might satisfy a requirement in ISO 9001. For example, PARAGRAPH 0.1 in ISO 9001 states that the "adoption of a quality management system should be a strategic decision of an organization." Although a strategic, organizationwide approach can be effective, the decision to implement an ISO 9001-compliant quality management system is often initiated in the short term because of a particular business opportunity or market requirement. Alternatively, a quality management system can grow from a series of small decisions, prompted by an evangelist who works behind the scenes to educate and influence management in various portions of the organization.

Exhibit 2-2. Examples of *appropriate* and *suitable*.

Paragraph	Example
5.5.3	Top management shall ensure that *appropriate* communication processes are established within the organization and that communication takes place regarding the effectiveness of the quality management system.
7.3.4	At *suitable* stages, systematic reviews of design and development shall be performed in accordance with planned arrangements.

May and *can* serve the same purpose as should. They denote suggestions. An organization may, or it may choose not to do something. With *may*, it can do something, but it does not have to.

Notes appear at the end of various paragraphs in ISO 9001 (e.g., PARAGRAPHS 4.1, 4.2.1, and 7.2.2). By convention, notes in ISO standards represent suggestions. However, an apparent exception to this self-imposed rule is the note at the end of PARAGRAPH 4.2, which states that,

> NOTE 1 Where the term "documented procedure" appears within this International Standard, this means that the procedure is established, documented, implemented and maintained.

This note does not contain *shall*, but the authors of ISO 9001 clearly intended that it be treated as a requirement.

Finally, ISO 9001 contains phrases that include *appropriate* and *suitable*. Exhibit 2-2 provides examples of the use of these terms.

The use of *appropriate* and *suitable* builds necessary flexibility into the standard. Their presence throughout the standard compels the organization to consider, design, and enact processes that are appropriate and stages that are suitable for the organization's unique combination of people, products, and technologies.

Requirements versus Design: How Flexible Is the Standard?

ISO 9001 contains functional requirements. Like a good product requirements specification, ISO 9001 should describe verifiable, functional attributes of an organization that places a high priority on satisfying its customers. Although the standard is a high-level, relatively brief document, it thoroughly describes what a customer- and quality-focused organization accomplishes. ISO 9001 does not describe how the organization satisfies those requirements, which is consistent with the intent of the standard, stated in PARAGRAPH 1.2 as,

> All requirements of this International Standard are generic and are intended to be applicable to all organizations, regardless of type, size and product provided.

Even when *shall* is used, as discussed above, it is the responsibility of the organization to determine how to meet the requirement.

Exhibit 2-3 provides examples that illustrate the degree of flexibility found in ISO 9001.

Effective

Effective appears 24 times in ISO 9001 and is one of the criteria against which the success of an organization in meeting the requirements of ISO 9001 is measured. Effective is defined in PARAGRAPH 3.2.14 of ISO 9000:2000 as the "extent to which planned activities are realized and planned results achieved."

When the planning, operation, and control of an organization's processes are effective, the engineering organization "builds the right product (planned results achieved) and "builds the product right" (planned activities realized, where realized is used to mean "made real"). A particular focus of *planned activities realized* is on plans for verification and validation, which tend to be abandoned or curtailed when time runs short as a deadline approaches. The planned activities and defined processes are a baseline that has a proven capability (strengths and weaknesses) and that can be improved over time by eliminating causes of defects, by reducing risk, and by improving the efficiency of processes that are already effective.

Efficiency is defined in ISO 9000 PARAGRAPH 3.2.15 as the "relationship between the result achieved and the resources used." *Efficiency* does not appear in any of the requirements in ISO 9001. However, in the authors' experience, individuals find ways to streamline inefficient processes— especially if the inefficiency appears to be without value (from the individuals' perspectives) and if it prevents them from doing their jobs and meeting their objectives. If opportunities for improving efficiency are not systematically addressed, the way work is actually done drifts away from the documented procedures, which creates an ISO 9001 compliance problem. More important, unsystematic streamlining can inadvertently create significant quality and efficiency problems for subsequent processes.

The first responsibility of implementers and maintainers of the policies, procedures, and standards that make up the quality management system is to create and maintain a system that is effective and that addresses all of the requirements of ISO 9001. The second responsibility challenges implementers and maintainers to go beyond the requirements of ISO 9001:2000 to create and maintain a system that is efficient and robust and that incorporates:

- Market requirements
- Emerging and available technology for both product and process, including the plethora of industry, product, and technology-specific

Exhibit 2-3. Examples of flexibility.

Example 1   *Flexibility in ensuring competence*
A quality-focused organization ensures that its people are able to perform the tasks assigned to them. In PARAGRAPH 6.2.2, ISO 9001 states

> *6.2.2 Competence, awareness and training*
>
> *The organization shall*
>
> *a) determine the necessary competence for personnel perform-ing work affecting product quality,*
>
> *b) provide training or take other actions to satisfy these needs,*
>
> *c) evaluate the effectiveness of the actions taken,*
>
> *d) ensure that its personnel are aware of the relevance and importance of their activities and how they contribute to the achievement of the quality objectives, and*
>
> *e) maintain appropriate records of education, training, skills and experience (see 4.2.4).*

PARAGRAPH 6.2.2 describes *what* the organization has to do. To the detriment of organizations looking for a quick and easy cookbook ("Just tell me the least that I have to do ... so I can get the contract and go about business as usual"), ISO 9001 does not give a hint as to *how* anything is to be done. Job descriptions are a ubiquitous method for (a) determining necessary competence. Classroom instruction, seminars, one-on-one mentoring, and self-study programs are all ways to (b) satisfy needs. Final examinations, observation during a probationary period, and participant course evaluations are methods for (c) evaluating the effectiveness of training. An annual e-mail from the CEO to all employees can (d) ensure awareness. Records (e) can be individual pieces of paper in an employee's file in Human Resources or in the department, e-mails in an employee's electronic Human Resources file, or entries in a companywide skills database.

Example 2   *Flexibility in defining engineering practices*
A quality-focused organization ensures that people understand what tasks are assigned to them. In PARAGRAPH 7.3.1, ISO 9001 requires that the organization determine, first, the design and development stages, second, the associated verification and validation, and third, who is responsible for design and development.

ISO 9001:2000 can be applied with equal effectiveness to any combination of paradigms, methods, or models, including those associated with Agile Methods, Joint Application Development, Rapid Application Development, Concurrent Engineering, Integrated Product Teams, the Rational Unified Process, the V Model, and the Spiral Model.

The organization determines the extent to which specific activities are defined and documented, subject to the requirements stated in PARAGRAPHS 4.1 and 4.2. PARAGRAPH 4.1 states that the organization shall

> *c) determine criteria and methods needed to ensure that both the operation and control of these processes are effective*

Exhibit 2-3. (continued)   Examples of flexibility.

PARAGRAPH 4.2 states that the quality system documentation shall include

d) documents needed by the organization to ensure the effective planning, operation and control of its processes

---

Exhibit 2-4. Implementer's checklist.

Required by ISO 9001:2000:
Effective
Address all ISO 9001 requirements

Recommended for long-term success:
Efficient
Robust
Market and technology focused

---

standards, including the Capability Maturity Model and CMM-Integration from the Software Engineering Institute at Carnegie Mellon University, and ISO 12207 and ISO 15504

Exhibit 2-4 provides a checklist that summarizes the responsibilities of implementers.

Ensure

Ensure appears 31 times in the standard, most frequently in association with a responsibility for the organization, for top management, or for management. Ensure also appears in requirements for activities implemented as part of the quality management system. Ensure is not defined in ISO 9000:2000 or in the supplementary guidance on vocabulary.[2] The supplementary guidance, however, directs the reader to the *Concise Oxford Dictionary*,[3] which defines ensure as, among other things, to "make certain that (something) will occur or be so."

Top management and the organization ensure that activities occur through a combination of various other activities for which requirements are provided in other paragraphs of ISO 9001. These activities fall into two categories. The first category includes management activities that enable the desired activities to occur:

- Establishing the process requirement (e.g., telling people that they are required to do certain things, issuing policies; PARAGRAPHS 4.1 and 4.2.1)
- Establishing a process, if necessary (e.g., telling people how to perform certain tasks, issuing a procedure; PARAGRAPHS 4.1 and 4.2.1)
- Providing necessary resources (e.g., planning the activities, providing trained personnel, equipment, facilities; PARAGRAPHS 4.1 and 6)

The second category includes management activities that confirm that the desired activities actually do occur:

- Following-up through management processes for monitoring and measuring and through management review, particularly through the internal audits (PARAGRAPHS 5.6, 8.2, and 8.2.2)
- Taking appropriate action if the appropriate actions do not take place or the desired results are not achieved or if there is a significant likelihood that that will happen (PARAGRAPHS 8.5.2 and 8.5.3)

Once clear expectations and process requirements are expressed in policies, procedures, and plans, progress reporting and internal audits verify that intended activities take place. For example, to ensure that documents are reviewed and approved before release, review and approval are included in the appropriate policies, procedures, and plans. To verify that the activities actually take place, progress reports go beyond listing released documents to include appropriate information on completed reviews. Internal audits confirm the accuracy of the progress reports through sampling and examination of review results and through interviews with participants. In another example, tools that automate workflow can ensure both that review and approval steps are built into processes and that the activities actually take place.

The Purpose of ISO 9001

PARAGRAPH 1.1 states that ISO 9001

> *specifies requirements for a quality management system where an organization*
>
> *a) needs to demonstrate its ability to consistently provide product that meets customer and applicable regulatory requirements, and*
>
> *b) aims to enhance customer satisfaction through the effective application of the system, including processes for continual improvement of the system and the assurance of conformity to customer and applicable regulatory requirements.*

To address the need to demonstrate ability, ISO 9001 defines a set of global requirements against which an organization's processes can be assessed and claims of compliance objectively verified by the organization itself, by a customer, or by a third-party auditor.

The assessment and objective verification of claims of compliance is only half the stated purpose. Enhancing customer satisfaction through continual improvement and meeting requirements is the more important. Customer satisfaction is defined in ISO 9000 PARAGRAPH 3.1.4 as the "customer's perception of the degree to which the customer's requirements (3.1.2) have been fulfilled." Customer satisfaction appears in eight locations throughout ISO 9001. Continual improvement is a primary focus of management responsibility (ISO 9001 PARAGRAPH 5) and of measurement and monitoring (ISO 9001 PARAGRAPH 8). Improvement has its own section (ISO 9001 PARAGRAPH 8.5).

In contrast, the most common method for demonstrating compliance with the requirements of ISO 9001, third-party registration or certification, receives only an indirect mention in a note following ISO 9001 PARAGRAPH 5.5.2. This note comments that a management representative may also liaise with external parties on matters relating to the quality management system.

Registrars and Registration Revisited

As noted in Chapter 1, a registrar is an objective third party (neither the customer nor the organization itself) whom the organization hires to perform an audit and certify that the organization's processes satisfy the requirements of ISO 9001. On successful completion of the audit, the registrar issues a certificate to the organization. The registrar's auditors return periodically (typically twice a year) to reaudit the organization and confirm that the compliant processes are still in place and that any new or revised processes are also in compliance with the requirements of ISO 9001.

Registrars are accredited by one or more national accreditation bodies (e.g., the Registrar Accreditation Board in the United States and the United Kingdom Accreditation Services in the United Kingdom) and operate throughout the world. The certificate issued by the registrar indicates the applicable accreditation.

A registration certificate may be required by a customer as part of a contractual agreement, it may be the price of admission to a market, or it may be viewed as a way to keep management committed to processes and customer satisfaction as time passes and business conditions change.

The registrar's auditors examine the organization's business practices and determine whether they satisfy the requirements of ISO 9001. Although registration can be a tactical response to a customer or market requirement, in the experience of the authors of this volume, successful registration can also be a by-product of putting effective processes in place and satisfying customers.

References

1. International Organization for Standardization, *ISO/IEC Directives: Part 3, Rules for the Structure and Drafting of International Standards,* 3rd ed., 1997, http://isotc.iso.ch/livelink/livelink/fetch/2000/2123/SDS_WEB/sds_dms/dir3e_97.zip.
2. International Organization for Standardization, *Guidance on the Terminology Used in ISO 9001:2000 and ISO 9004:2000,* Document ISO/TC 176/SC 2/N 526R, May 2001, International Organization for Standardization, Geneva, http://www.iso.
3. Pearsall, Judy, Ed., *The Concise Oxford Dictionary,* 10th ed., Oxford University Press, Oxford, 1999.

Section II
ISO 9001: A Paragraph-by-Paragraph Analysis

This section contains six chapters that explore the effects, benefits, and various alternative methods for meeting the requirements of each paragraph in a software development organization. Chapter 3 reviews the structure of ISO 9001:2000. Each of the subsequent chapters explores the requirements of the corresponding paragraph of ISO 9001:2000:

- Chapter 4 covers the requirements of PARAGRAPH 4
- Chapter 5 covers the requirements of PARAGRAPH 5
- Chapter 6 covers the requirements of PARAGRAPH 6
- Chapter 7 covers the requirements of PARAGRAPH 7
- Chapter 8 covers the requirements of PARAGRAPH 8.

In this section, the paragraphs of ISO 9001 are examined in the order in which they appear in the standard. As noted above, because the paragraphs do not stand alone, paragraphs are introduced where they fit logically to simplify and improve the efficiency of the implementation. Alternative solutions are presented as a nonexhaustive set of examples. These examples are intended to provide information from which readers can identify current practices that satisfy the requirements of ISO 9001 and, as required, can construct reasonable solutions appropriate to their organizations' unique circumstances and needs.

Chapter 3
The Structure of ISO 9001

As illustrated in Exhibit 3-1, ISO 9001:2000 contains five first-level paragraphs that contain requirements. The 138 "shall"s in ISO 9001 are distributed among 23 second-level paragraphs (e.g., PARAGRAPH 4.1 and PARAGRAPH 7.3). However, to state that there are 138 requirements is misleading. Although ISO 9001 is an excellent standard, particularly notable for its brevity, it is like many succinct market and customer requirements definitions and statements, written by a committee.

- There are compound statements—a single "shall" precedes a list of discrete activities. For example, PARAGRAPH 4.1 contains five "shall"s and 23 distinct requirements.
- There is redundancy—the requirements in one paragraph duplicate or are decomposed into requirements in another paragraph. For example, PARAGRAPH 7.1 requires that all product realization activities be planned; PARAGRAPH 7.3 requires that design and development activities (which are part of product realization) be planned. As a second example, of the 23 requirements in PARAGRAPH 4.1, only two are not completely addressed in other paragraphs.
- There is factoring—the requirements in one paragraph apply to any solution for the requirements in one or more other paragraphs. Factoring streamlines the requirements but challenges implementers to ensure that the global requirement is addressed in all the instances to which it applies. For example, the document control requirements in PARAGRAPH 4.2.3 are implicitly repeated each time a documented procedure (or plan or other work product) is referenced in the quality management system.
- There are misplaced requirements. PARAGRAPH 7.5 is titled production and service provision, which is part of product realization. PARAGRAPHS 7.5.1 and 7.5.2 contain requirements for production and service provision. Surprisingly, PARAGRAPHS 7.5.3, 7.5.4, and 7.5.5 specify requirements that apply throughout product realization.

Exhibit 3-2 lists the first- and second-level headings in ISO 9001. PARAGRAPHS 4, 5, and 6, in the left column, deal with requirements for the organizational infrastructure. In the right column of Exhibit 3-2, PARAGRAPH 7 addresses requirements for the implementation of processes for business acquisition

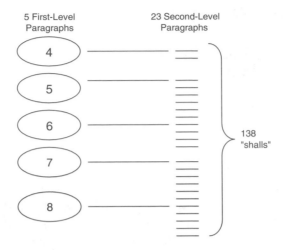

Exhibit 3-1. The first- and second-level headings.

and product delivery (including postdelivery service). PARAGRAPH 8 contains additional requirements for business acquisition and product delivery and for organizational infrastructure. The first-level paragraphs are placeholders, followed by second-level paragraphs that contain the requirements.

Product realization in PARAGRAPH 7 is the only term that is not relatively self-explanatory. *Product realization* is referred to in ISO 9000, ISO 9001, ISO 9004, and ISO 9000-3, but it is never defined. In addition, it does not appear in ISO 12207 or ISO 15504. For the purposes of this volume, the definition of product realization is derived from the various paragraphs in PARAGRAPH 7. Product realization comprises the processes that directly contribute to business acquisition and product delivery (e.g., proposal preparation, requirements gathering, design and development, manufacturing, and service and support) and a number of essential supporting processes—project management and purchasing.

A simplistic version of the relationship among the top-level paragraphs, similar to Deming's PDCA cycle, is described in PARAGRAPH 0.2 and portrayed in Exhibit 3-1 in ISO 9001, which is reproduced below, with the numbers of the paragraphs of ISO 9001 added, in Exhibit 3-3.

Management responsibility (PARAGRAPH 5) drives the management of resources (PARAGRAPH 6), which are used to operate the product realization (PARAGRAPH 7) processes. Product realization, in turn, provides the data and information needed to measure, analyze, and improve the organization's performance. The data is provided to management to operate the business (closing the loop to PARAGRAPH 5) and branches out to continual improvement, which is the subject of PARAGRAPH 8.

Exhibit 3-2. The first- and second-level headings in ISO 9001.

Infrastructure		Implementation	
Paragraph	**ISO 9001:2000**	**Paragraph**	**ISO 9001:2000**
4	Quality management system	7	Product realization
4.1	General requirements	7.1	Planning of product realization
4.2	Documentation requirements	7.2	Customer-related processes
		7.3	Design and development
		7.4	Purchasing
5	Management responsibility	7.5	Production and service provision
5.1	Management commitment	7.6	Control of monitoring and measuring devices
5.2	Customer focus		
5.3	Quality policy		
5.4	Planning	8	Measurement, analysis, and improvement
5.5	Responsibility, authority, and communication	8.1	General
5.6	Management review	8.2	Monitoring and measurement
		8.3	Control of nonconforming product
6	Resource management	8.4	Analysis of data
6.1	Provision of resources	8.5	Improvement
6.2	Human resources		
6.3	Infrastructure		
6.4	Work environment		

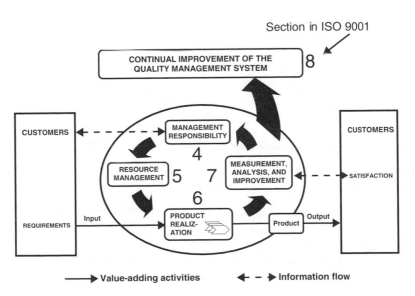

Exhibit 3-3. Modified version of Exhibit 3-1 from ISO 9001: the process approach to quality.

In the value stream, represented in Exhibit 3-3 by the horizontal, solid arrows, customers provide requirements and receive product. In addition, customers exchange information with the organization's management and provide input on satisfaction.

Chapter 4
PARAGRAPH 4 *Quality Management System*

PARAGRAPH 4 is presented in two paragraphs that serve as a framework for the rest of the paragraphs in ISO 9001.

PARAGRAPH 4.1 *General Requirements*

As noted earlier, once the lists preceded by "shall" and the numerous "and"s are taken into consideration, PARAGRAPH 4.1 contains 23 distinct, high-level requirements.* PARAGRAPH 4.1 is an excellent distillation of the requirements in ISO 9001:2000. Unfortunately, although 21 of the 23 requirements are satisfied as a result of collectively satisfying requirements in other paragraphs, two of the requirements appear only in PARAGRAPH 4.1. The two requirements unique to PARAGRAPH 4.1 are

(a) *Identify the … application [of the processes needed for the quality management system] throughout the organization*

(b) *Determine the sequence … of these processes.*

PARAGRAPH 4.1 *b* also refers to interactions, which are thoroughly discussed in conjunction with PARAGRAPH 4.2.2 *c*.

Implementation Considerations

Although the information in PARAGRAPH 4.1 is valuable for setting expectations and attitudes, there are two challenges in implementing processes to satisfy the requirements of PARAGRAPH 4.1. The first challenge is to identify and preserve the requirements that are unique to this paragraph. The second challenge is to avoid the frustrating exercise of constructing solutions for which clear, detailed requirements are provided later. Dealing with PARAGRAPH 4.1 can be like an inefficient review of a document, in which a great deal of time and energy spent on arguing about and analyzing the first paragraphs is made unnecessary by later portions of the document.

Eliminate Duplication. In keeping with the comments in Section 1 of this book about carefully evaluating all comments about the standard, Appendix C provides the justification for deferring almost all of the requirements stated in PARAGRAPH 4.1. However, because of the number of other paragraphs in which requirements of PARAGRAPH 4.1 are addressed, it is recommended

---

* The authors' detailed analysis of PARAGRAPH 4.1 is contained in Appendix C.

that Appendix C be read after completing this volume or otherwise gaining familiarity with all of the requirements in ISO 9001.

The two requirements unique to PARAGRAPH 4.1 are important and rarely receive the emphasis that they should. They offer significant benefits to the organization as principles to guide the organization's efforts. The gap assessment is a key activity in addressing these two requirements.

The Gap Assessment. Because the typical implementation occurs in an established organization, the initial management decision to adopt ISO 9001:2000 is followed by a gap assessment. The gap assessment identifies the work required to implement that management decision and becomes the basis for the plan and for renewing management's commitment to adopting ISO 9001 as a model for process implementation. The gap assessment encompasses two phases: inventory and analysis.

The first phase of the gap assessment produces a high-level "as-is" model of the organization—an inventory of the activities that occur in the organization. The larger and more complex the organization, the more challenging conducting this inventory becomes.

This inventory is a critical and time-consuming activity in large, successful organizations—such as automobile manufacturers and semiconductor equipment manufacturers—that regard their core engineering competencies as hardware related but that are, in fact, completely dependent on software and firmware. In these hardware-driven organizations, software development is often treated as a service group—not necessarily well integrated, effectively managed, or optimized from an organizational perspective. See Exhibit 4-1 for examples of inventory-related discoveries.

In the second phase of the gap assessment, the results of the inventory are compared with the standard to identify processes that:

- Are subject to the requirements of the standard
- Already meet requirements of the standard
- Are missing or are deficient

The information from the gap assessment is an input for creating or validating an organization's quality manual (see PARAGRAPH 4.2.2 *Quality manual*) and procedures and is the basis for identifying and sizing the work to address the requirements of the standard.

The Requirements Unique to PARAGRAPH 4.1. By looking at all aspects of the standard, the gap assessment, and the actions planned to correct omissions and deficiencies, provide the information necessary to identify where in the organization the various processes are being performed (the application of the processes), the processes that supply inputs to each

Exhibit 4-1. In our experience: surprises.

Surprise 1: In defining the focus of ISO 9001 introductory training for the implementation team, the implementation manager stated that the organization did not develop software. The executive management sponsor agreed. Two firmware engineers who attended the training vehemently disagreed.

Surprise 2: In an ISO 9001 gap analysis, the assessors found:

- Software engineers in the operations organization who were creating configuration utilities and diagnostic tools that were shipped with systems to customers and that were used by customers. This organization did not consider software development as one of its competencies—or software as one of its products.
- Software engineers in two different projects who were developing functionally identical algorithms for different customer applications intended to run in the same target environment. Neither project was aware of the other. Although both projects used the same development platform and were applying object-oriented (OO) methods, they used different development and configuration management tools. One project team had trained its engineers in OO techniques and had done several OO projects. The other team had sent two of its engineers to a 5-day C++ seminar and was hoping for the best.
- Managers who consistently asserted that projects were always late and over budget. At the same time, there was no process for controlling changes to project requirements, no measurement of actual effort expended in projects, and consequently, no adjusted baseline against which to measure on-time performance.

Surpise 3: The retiring CEO and founder of an established Silicon Valley company (which enjoyed an 80 percent share of a sizable, worldwide market) commented that it had come as a great surprise that 80 percent of the research and development budget went to software and 20 percent to hardware. Software accounted for 20 percent of the company's revenue; hardware, 80 percent.

---

process, and the processes that receive the outputs of each process (the sequence and interactions of the processes).

In the statement of the second unique requirement, "determine the sequence ... of these processes," both meanings of "determine" pertain. The first, to discover, is part of the inventory. The second meaning, to cause or regulate, applies when confusion or inconsistent understanding uncovered in the inventory is corrected by management.

The inventory or gap assessment also investigates process interactions (to be described in the quality manual, see PARAGRAPH 4.2.2 c), and the definition and communication of responsibility and authority (to be defined and communicated, see PARAGRAPH 5.5 *Responsibility and authority*).

The simplest way to address these requirements is through operational procedures that capture not just the steps to be taken, for example, "all unit tested modules are promoted to the Integration state," but also those that describe:

- Who is responsible
- What approvals are required and limits are imposed (e.g., authority)
- What inputs and outputs are expected
- What processes supply inputs to the process described in the procedure and what processes expect outputs from the process described in the procedure (e.g., interactions)

The quality manual (which may be a collection of documents) serves as the glue that organizes and links the procedures (and the associated processes) together.

Other requirements of ISO 9001:2000, such as documenting the disposition of records, can also be integrated into the operational procedures. A recommended template for procedures is included in Appendix D in this volume.

About Establish. One word that appears in PARAGRAPH 4.1 has a particular affect in engineering organizations: *establish*. In ISO 9001:2000, *establish* is defined as "set up on a firm or permanent basis."* The implied elements of permanence and controlled evolution are frequently reinforced by the use of the catchphrase, "establish and maintain." In the language of the Capability Maturity Model, the equivalent term is "institutionalize."

In the experience of the authors of this book, there is a tendency in engineering organizations to assume that a published procedure will be used or that a tool that has been made available and on which the organization has been trained will be used. This assumption leads frustrated managers to ask questions such as, "Why don't they use the (expensive) new Configuration Management tool?" and "Why do they keep changing requirements after code freeze?" Frequently, the answers to these questions lead back to the same managers. "They" do not use the tool or follow the procedure because:

- No manager told them they have to.
- There is no perceived benefit to following the procedure or using the tool.
- Not following the procedure or using the tool has no consequence.

Several comments can be made about the contribution of *benefit* and *consequence* to a successful implementation.

With regard to benefit, the operative word is "perceived." Individuals follow a procedure or use a tool if they understand the benefit to themselves or to others in the organization and if management permits them to. Management permission leads to the concept of consequence as a management responsibility.

---

* In this case, Reference 1 directs the reader to the definition in Reference 2.

In an effective and efficient system, consequence is logical rather than punitive. If the procedure is not followed or the tool is not used, something desirable does not happen or something undesirable does happen. For example, if the code is not checked in to the correct library in the configuration management system, it is not included in the product build (desirable) and tests fail (undesirable). In intellectually competitive professions, like hardware and software engineering, professional pride and real or imagined peer pressure drive the best engineers to avoid causing undesirable outcomes. Breaking the nightly build, creating the most defects found in test, and delaying the release of a product are humiliating, never-to-be-repeated achievements.

There are however, circumstances in which the consequence is delayed. For example, a clever (but unapproved) shortcut may not cause problems until an enhancement requires that another engineer modify the code. Or the consequence may be cumulative. For example, in an embedded system, if one component uses just a few more than its allocated CPU cycles, there may not be any problem. If, however, a number of components use just a few more cycles than anticipated, the net effect can be significant, jeopardizing the system's ability to meet customer requirements for reserve CPU capacity. In these cases, it is essential that management provides encouragement, pays attention, and demonstrates interest and concern. Management inattention is reflected in cases where no manager notices when a procedure is not followed or a tool is not used. No manager asks, "Why?"

Management can inadvertently or deliberately create consequences that undermine efforts to implement effective, efficient, and repeatable processes. An example of this extreme case is when individuals who ignore procedures and tools are identified as heroes and rewarded by management for extraordinary achievement. Such recognition reinforces a culture that focuses solely on immediate results and disregards procedures and tools, which are the basis for long-term results. A variation on the hero scenario is one in which the procedures actually do not provide any benefit. This can occur when management does not systematically maintain procedures. Experienced members of the organization know what needs to be done and do it. Although reliance on collective experience can be effective in the short term, performance erodes when experienced members leave or new members are added and when significant process changes are necessary. The establishment of processes is a critical factor in securing the ability of an organization to perform, improve, and evolve.

About Outsource. The final paragraph of PARAGRAPH 4.1 introduces the concept of outsourcing:

> *Where an organization chooses to outsource any process that affects product conformity with requirements, the organization shall ensure control*

over such processes. Control of such outsourced processes shall be identi-fied within the quality management system.

Because outsource is defined to be synonymous with subcontract,[1] and as this paragraph contains a "shall" statement that has significant cost implications, it is essential that the organization's implementation team determine the precise activities to which this "shall" applies. To make this determination, it is necessary to explore the relationship among the requirements of this paragraph and those in PARAGRAPH 7.4 *Purchasing.*

The document that offers the best available guidance is ISO/TC 176/SC 2/N 524R2, *Introduction and Support Package—Guidance on ISO 9001:2000 clause 1.2 'Application',* published in March 2001.[3] In PARAGRAPH 6, this ISO document states at length,

> *Where the overall responsibility for product realization belongs to an orga-nization, the fact that a specific product realization process (such as prod-uct design and development or manufacturing) is outsourced (or "sub-con-tracted") to an external organization is not an adequate justification for the exclusion of this process from the QMS [quality management system].* **Instead, the organization has to be able to demonstrate that it exer-cises sufficient control to ensure that such processes are per-formed according to the relevant requirements of ISO 9001:2000** *[emphasis added]. The nature of this control will depend on the nature of the outsourced process and the risk involved. It may include, for example, the specification and/or validation of processes as part of the contractual agreement with the supplier, requirements for the supplier's QMS, on-site inspections or verifications, and/or audits. ISO 9001:2000 clause 7.4 Pur-chasing should be applied to monitor the output of these outsourced or subcontracted processes.*
>
> *In these circumstances, the organization should include such processes in the scope of its QMS and make it clear in its Quality Manual and any other publicly available documents that the QMS covers the management of these outsourced or subcontracted activities for which the organization retains overall responsibility.*

No matter how the organization chooses to address the requirements associated with outsourced processes, there are potentially significant costs. The simplest way for an organization to satisfy these requirements is to require that suppliers of outsourced processes be ISO 9001:2000 reg-istered. Although this approach is a favorite of registrars, it may limit the pool of suppliers the organization can consider, and it may result in increased costs as the supplier passes along the overhead costs associated with registration. The alternative is for the organization to assume respon-sibility for ensuring that the supplier's processes satisfy the relevant requirements of ISO 9001:2000. In choosing this alternative, the organiza-tion assumes more of the cost directly and potentially reduces the amount of overhead cost for the supplier. In either case, as noted above, it is essential that the organization's implementation team determine the precise activities that fall within the definition of outsourced processes.

At the extremes, identifying outsourced processes is straightforward. If an organization purchases an off-the-shelf product (e.g., a font, an algorithm, or a board with firmware) from a supplier, it is not an outsourced process. The organization is required only to apply the requirements of PARAGRAPH 7.4 *Purchasing* to the relationship with the supplier. If an organization subcontracts first-line customer technical support or manufacturing, it is an outsourced process. In this second example, the organization takes additional steps necessary to ensure that the relevant requirements of ISO 9001:2000 are satisfied by the supplier's processes.

Shadows begin to form when subprocesses are outsourced and registrars and implementation teams attempt to interpret the guidance. The following two examples illustrate circumstances in which, based on the guidance cited above from N524R2, an organization can justify classifying the activity as purchasing a product that happens to be a service rather than outsourcing a process.

- A development organization sends its software and hardware to a third-party compatibility testing service that is certified by the providers of the specified target operating systems. The result is a report and a certificate.
- A software development organization employs a local production shop to burn several hundred copies of its software product onto CDs (a manufacturing process). The organization specifies appropriate requirements for virus protection, media, handling, testing, first-article inspection, and packaging.
- A software development organization employs an independent, Web-based service to deliver its products electronically. The software organization has reviewed and is satisfied with the service provider's procedures for the protection of the integrity of the product and for updating the deliverable product.
- An organization sells a system that includes developed software and off-the-shelf hardware components. The organization employs a sheet-metal shop to fabricate custom enclosures according to a specification provided by the organization. The organization sends the enclosures and purchased hardware components to another shop that assembles and boxes the completed systems. Handling, assembly, and packaging instructions are provided by the organization, and completed systems are inspected when the software is loaded. The organization periodically visits the assembly supplier to ensure that any special handling procedures are being followed.

In these examples, it appears that controls can be identified in conjunction with PARAGRAPH 7.4.2 *Purchasing information* and PARAGRAPH 7.4.3 *Verification of purchased product* and that there is no requirement to take the additional steps and incur the additional cost to ensure that those processes are "performed [by the subcontractor] according to the relevant requirements of ISO 9001:2000." As a caution, based on several interviews, the registrar community is struggling with defining the line between purchased product (when the product is a service) and outsourced processes. If it is relevant, it is strongly recommended that outsourced processes be discussed during the registrar selection process and during the review of the quality manual before a preassessment or the registration audit.

PARAGRAPH **4.2** *Documentation Requirements*

In PARAGRAPH 4.2, ISO 9001:2000 presents a much more flexible (and useful) approach to documentation than has been explicit in its earlier versions.* PARAGRAPH 4.2.1 lists the required documents. PARAGRAPH 4.2.2 provides detailed information about one of the required documents—the quality manual. PARAGRAPH 4.2.3 contains detailed requirements for the control of all documents except records. PARAGRAPH 4.2.4 contains the detailed requirements for the control of records.

PARAGRAPH *4.2.1* General [Requirements for Documentation]

The list of five items in PARAGRAPH 4.2.1 *General* contains a mixture of specific documents and types of documents.

Before looking at the various documents and types of documents, it is particularly worthwhile to examine the notes in PARAGRAPH 4.2.1, which are rich in information and that verge on violating the ISO convention that notes are guidance. These notes are presented in Exhibit 4-2.

The Required Documents. Four of the five items listed in PARAGRAPH 4.2.1 refer to one or more specific documents the organization is required to produce and maintain in a suitable form. Detailed requirements for these documents are supplied elsewhere in the standard. Two of the five items refer to additional documents defined by the organization.

---

* This is a significant departure from ISO 9001:1994, which specified documented procedure in 18 paragraphs: 4.3.1 (for contract review), 4.4.1 (for design control), 4.5.1 (for document and data control), 4.6 (for purchasing), 4.7 (for customer-supplied product), 4.8 (for product identification, for traceability), 4.10.1 (for inspection and testing), 4.11.1 (for inspection, measuring, and test equipment), 4.16 (for quality records), 4.9 (for production, installation, and servicing), 4.17 (for internal audits), 4.13.1 (for nonconforming product), 4.14.1 (for corrective action), 4.14.1 (for preventive action), 4.15.1 (for handling, storage, packaging, preservation, and delivery), 4.18 (for training), 4.19 (for servicing), and 4.20.2 (for statistical techniques).

Exhibit 4-2. The notes in PARAGRAPH 4.2.1.

Number	Note
Note 1	This note states that documented procedure means that procedures are established (required by management), documented (captured in some retrievable, maintainable form), implemented (put into practice), and maintained (revised to reflect current practice). The note reminds management that the organization not only has to create an initial set of accurate procedural documentation, it also has to commit the resources to revise the documentation as changes occur in technology, products, and the organizational structure. The requirements implied by this note are found in two other paragraphs: • PARAGRAPH 4.2.3 *Control of documents* requires that all documents be updated as necessary • PARAGRAPH 5.4.2 *b*, which requires that top management ensure that the integrity of the quality management system is maintained when changes to the quality management system are planned and implemented.
Note 2	Note 2 answers the question every implementation team asks: How much do I need to write down? Although the note can't answer the question directly, subparagraphs *a*, *b*, and *c* suggest interrelated parameters the implementation team can consider in making its own determination:
Note 2a	Size of organization and type of activities: *How big is the organization?* To operate effectively, bigger, more dispersed organizations typically require more formal communication and more detailed documentation. *What types of activities does the organization perform?* Activities that have significant effect on the organization, for example, that affect health and safety, are typically defined and documented in excruciating detail. Very little, if anything, is left to the discretion of the individuals operating the process. The existence of a step-by-step procedure does not mean that it is consulted at each step of the process—although, like a pilot's preflight checklist, it could be.
Note 2b	Complexity of processes and their interactions: *How complex are the processes and their interactions?* The more complex the processes, the more likely detailed documentation is required to ensure they are executed correctly and completely—no matter how well trained the personnel are. This is especially true when the process requires significant manual intervention. Another dimension, closely related to complexity, is frequency. Processes that are enacted relatively infrequently—like a year-end close in accounting or the release of a new software product to manufacturing—are candidates for detailed procedures.
Note 2c	Competence of personnel: *How competent are the people performing the tasks?* Competence, defined in PARAGRAPH 6.2.1, is a function of professional education, training, skills, and experience. When personnel are already competent in the application of tools and techniques, less-detailed procedures are required. These tools and techniques can range from soldering to accounting, to C++ programming. Although including unnecessary detail might seem benign, it can obscure the few bits of crucial information that are in a procedure.

Exhibit 4-2. (continued)   The notes in PARAGRAPH 4.2.1.

Number	Note
Note 3	Although "documentation" inevitably connotes words on paper (lots of words on lots of paper), this is not intended. For example, documentation can be presented on paper or electronically; it can be literal or graphical. It can be delivered through lines on a hospital floor, signs on a wall, color-coding, laminated checklists, application Wizards, drop-down lists, and context-sensitive, "on-line" Help.
	There is also no restriction on the structure or organization of any particular document or on the set of documents included in the quality management system. One document can be
	• A collection of documents (e.g., a project plan can be a collection of individual plans and procedures; a software development plan can be a document maintained in a word processor and a schedule maintained in a project management tool)
	• Two or more documents can be combined in a single document (e.g., the risk-management plan can be a section in the project plan).
	Documentation is a mechanism for consistent communication across time and space.

Exhibit 4-3 describes the documents required by PARAGRAPHS 4.2.1 *a*, 4.2.1 *b*, 4.2.1 *c*, 4.2.1 *d*, and 4.2.1 *e*. When appropriate, related paragraphs in ISO 9001:2000 are identified.*

ISO 9001:2000 explicitly makes it the responsibility of the organization to determine what additional documents are required. The auditor and the organization assess the organization's success in meeting the requirements of PARAGRAPHS 4.2.1 *c* and 4.2.1 *d* by confirming the existence of the documents identified by the organization in its policies, procedures, and standards. With the exception of the six specified procedures, the decision on whether a "missing" document is an appropriate solution to an operational or a control problem, to a customer requirement, or to a regulation is explicitly the responsibility of the organization.

Under ISO 9001:2000, the focus shifts from specifying an extensive list of required documents to ensuring the effectiveness of activities such as review, inform, identify, monitor, and communicate. By removing references to specific documents, ISO 9001:2000 can be integrated more easily with other standards, such as the Institute of Electrical and Electronics

---

* There is ambiguity in the guidance as to whether all the additional process documentation (policies, procedures, standards, and templates) that the organization determines to be necessary are associated with PARAGRAPH 4.2.1 *c*, with PARAGRAPH 4.2.1 *d*, or are somehow divided between the two. There is no net effect. First, any process documentation is documentation, subject to the requirements of PARAGRAPH 4.2.3 *Control of documents*. Second, as, in varying degrees of detail, process documentation also defines the way in which management intends work to be performed, it is an essential part of the mechanism for the communication associated with establishing, maintaining, and improving effective processes.

Exhibit 4-3. The required documents and records.

Paragraph	Section	Resource
4.2.1 *a*	Quality policy	See PARAGRAPH 5.3 *Quality policy*
	Quality objectives	See PARAGRAPH 5.4.1 *Quality objectives*
4.2.1 *b*	Quality manual	See 4.2.2 *Quality manual*
4.2.1 *c*	Documented procedures required by ISO 9001:2000	PARAGRAPH 4.2.1 c refers to the six paragraphs in ISO 9001:2000 that contain the phrase "a documented procedure shall be established." The six documented procedures explicitly required by ISO 9001:2000 are 4.2.3: For document control 4.2.4: For quality records 8.2.2: For internal audits 8.3: For control of nonconforming product 8.5.2: For corrective action 8.5.3: For preventive action. See these six paragraphs for the specific topics to be addressed by the required procedures. In addition, 4.2.1 c is interpreted to include any additional process-related documentation the organization determines that it needs to provide, including policies, procedures, standards, checklists, and templates.
4.2.1 *d*	Other documents	PARAGRAPH 4.2.1 d contains the general requirement that the organization define any other documents needed by the organization to ensure the effective operation and control of its processes. This category is interpreted to include additional project- and product-related documentation the organization determines it needs to execute and manage its processes. For example, • Project-related documentation includes approved contracts, plans, meeting minutes, team rosters, and assignments • Product-related documentation includes market requirement documents, architecture and design documents, detailed design documents, specifications, test cases, test records, and standards.
4.2.1 *e*	Records required by ISO 9001:2000	4.2.1 e refers to the 18 paragraphs in ISO 9001:2000 that contain the phrase "records of ... shall be maintained (see 4.2.4)." The 18 records explicitly required by ISO 9001:2000 are 5.6.1: Of management reviews 6.2.2: Of education, training, skills, experience 7.2.2: Of the review of product requirements and necessary actions

47

Exhibit 4-3. (continued)   The required documents and records.

Paragraph	Section	Resource
		7.3.2: Of [the review of] inputs relating to product requirements
		7.3.4: Of design and development reviews and necessary actions
		7.3.5: Of design and development verification and necessary actions
		7.3.6: Of design and development validation and necessary actions
		7.3.7: Of the review of design and development changes and necessary actions
		7.4.1: Of the evaluation of suppliers and necessary actions
		7.5.2: Of the validation of production and service processes (as applicable)
		7.5.3: Of the unique identification of product
		7.5.4: Of customer property found to be unsuitable for use
		7.6: Of the calibration and verification of monitoring and measuring devices
		8.2.2: Of internal audits
		8.2.4: Of product conformity with the acceptance criteria and the authority responsible for release of product
		8.3: Of [product] nonconformities and subsequent actions
		8.5.2: Of the results of corrective action
		8.5.3: Of the results of preventive action.
		See these 18 paragraphs for additional information about the content of the specified records.

Engineers standards, Food and Drug Administration Quality System Regulation (from the Code of Federal Regulations), the Capability Maturity Model for Software, the Capability Maturity Model — Integration Models, and ISO 12207, which are intended to capture best practice and define specific documents that have proven to be valuable. Other needed documents typically found in engineering organizations are described throughout this volume.

Some individuals, particularly auditors, express reservations about the disappearance of the list of required procedures and documents from this version of ISO 9001. In the experience of the authors of this volume, that list has proven to be a distraction—focusing auditors and first-time implementers on checklist-driven compliance rather than on the activities and results that build value by securing and enhancing an organization's ability to satisfy its customers.

PARAGRAPH *4.2.2* The Quality Manual

In PARAGRAPH 4.2.2, ISO 9001:2000 repeats the approach taken in earlier versions. It describes the general contents of the quality manual but fails to include any reference to audience or purpose. In some cases, the quality manual is a boring replay of ISO 9001, written for a registrar's or a customer's auditors. In other cases, it is a high-level introduction to the organization—written for new employees in the language of the organization, without explicit reference to ISO 9001. In some cases, the quality manual is written early in the implementation as a high-level design document for the quality management system. In other cases, it is written as an executive summary as the implementation nears completion. In some cases, the quality manual is a single, glossy brochure suitable for potential customers and registrars. In other cases, it is a collection of Web pages and links.

PARAGRAPH 4.2.2 requires that the quality manual address three topics:

1. Scope and exclusions
2. Documented procedures
3. Interactions

Scope and Exclusions. The first topic is the scope of the quality management system. This is the description of the processes that the organization claims comply with ISO 9001. This description can be qualified by location, product line, and organization. For example, one scope might be defined as "for the design and development of the PC-based Tax-Trak home and business federal and state income tax preparation software." The scope captures the determination made by the organization at the very beginning of an ISO 9001 implementation regarding the parts of the organization required to participate in the ISO implementation (e.g., sites, product groups, processes). PARAGRAPH 4.2.2 *a* also raises the issue of exclusions. These are processes for which requirements are identified in ISO 9001, but that are not addressed in the organization's quality management system. For example, ISO 9001 contains requirements for production (e.g., manufacturing) and servicing (e.g., technical support), but a contract software development organization might not have either function. As another example, an organization that develops off-the-shelf software applications might outsource its technical support. As implied in PARAGRAPH 4.2.2, the rules for exclusion are defined in PARAGRAPH 1.2. Unfortunately, applying those rules requires an understanding not only of the contents of PARAGRAPH 7 but also of decisions being made by various organizations, including ISO, involved with the registration process.

To simplify the presentation of this volume, scope and exclusions are discussed in detail in this volume in Appendix B.

Documented Procedures. The second required topic is the documented procedures established for the quality management system, or reference to them. This topic includes not only the documented procedures required by this standard but also any of the other procedural documents that the organization determines that it needs (PARAGRAPH 4.2.1 *c*).

In today's wired, Web-enabled organizations, the quality manual typically describes the architecture of the organization's processes (e.g., the various life cycles that are used by the organization) textually and graphically. Through the quality manual, the reader can go directly to specific policies and procedures or to indexes for sets of policies and procedures.

The highest levels of the organization are responsible for global policies and procedures—such as the quality policy, the quality manual, the procedures required by ISO 9001, and any standard processes that apply across the organization (e.g., monthly management program reviews). The management of each unit of the organization or specialized function determines the need for, creates, and maintains any procedures that apply solely to its members (e.g., engineering, manufacturing, or technical support). Responsibility is clearly assigned (e.g., define, review, approve, and implement) for procedures that span organizational or functional boundaries. This delegation model continues as appropriate, based on the organizations' structure and processes. For example, the engineering group could be aligned by technology (mainframe, client-server, World Wide Web), with each technology group responsible for procedures that are unique to its operation.

It is management's responsibility to ensure that writing procedures does not take on a life of its own. Every process and procedure, every proposed form, report, review, and approval is evaluated against its contribution to the effectiveness and efficiency of the organization in meeting stakeholder objectives.

The only criterion to apply to measure the amount of procedural documentation is the effectiveness of the associated processes in achieving desired results. Too much and too little documentation both result in processes that are not consistently followed and in significant variation in quality. In both cases, the organization operates on folklore and word of mouth; with too little documentation, because there is nothing written down, and with too much documentation, because no one bothers or has the time to read or maintain it. As ISO 9000:2000 warns in PARAGRAPH 2.7.1, "Documentation enables communication of intent and consistency of action. Generation of documentation should not be an end in itself but should be a value-adding activity."

Interactions. The quality manual is also required to describe process interactions: how processes act on or influence each other. ISO 9001:2000 does not require that all interactions be described, and it does not specify the level at which interactions are to be described. When it is built around the top-level representations of the various life cycles (e.g., project, product, or engineering) in use by the organization, the description of the interactions in the quality manual is a framework that glues together the various detailed life cycles and procedures. For example, the quality manual could describe the product life cycle—from concept to retirement—capturing the points at which the various organizations are involved and their responsibilities at those points. The various groups would have more detailed descriptions of how their internal activities support that life cycle. In some cases, those detailed descriptions are also considered life cycles (e.g., software development life cycles, hardware development life cycles, testing life cycles, and customer acquisition life cycles, all of which interact to support a product life cycle).

Another useful technique for describing interactions is to document inputs, sources, outputs, and customers in each detailed procedure; see Appendix D.

Requirements Traceability Applied to ISO 9001:2000. The team responsible for ensuring that the organization achieves ISO compliance typically creates a matrix or table that traces the relationship between the requirements of ISO 9001 and the organization's processes. The matrix is essentially the same response the organization would make to any accepted set of requirements for a project or program.

The document is organized around the requirements; that is, ISO 9001. It lists the processes (e.g., the "product" components) that satisfy each requirement, any associated rationale, and the parts of the organization responsible for defining, implementing, and maintaining those processes (e.g., the allocation). This matrix is the basis for ensuring the initial and continuing accuracy of the organization's claims of compliance. It ensures that all required processes and procedures are implemented—and that no processes, procedures, or bureaucracy are created under the mistaken impression that they are somehow required by ISO 9001. After the implementation is complete and compliance has been achieved, the matrix is an invaluable planning tool for the internal audit team (see Paragraph 8.2.2), which verifies not only that the quality management system is followed but also that it remains in compliance with the requirements of ISO 9001.

Organizations typically do not share the matrix with the registrar's auditors, who independently construct their own matrix based on the quality manual. However, the information in the matrix can be a resource for management to use in disputing a registrar's auditor's interpretation of the standard.

Implementation Considerations. An engineering handbook is an effective form for a software organization's top-level quality manual. It describes

51

how the various functions within engineering interact with each other and with parts of the organization outside engineering—sales, marketing, legal, and so forth. Ideally, the handbook is relatively brief and captures what managers tell prospective new employees about how the organization functions. The handbook supports and is elaborated on in new employee training.

A Suggested Outline and Approach. The following is a suggested outline for an operational handbook written for new employees. The typical implementation makes the various parts of the quality manual available through the organization's ISO portal on the organization's Intranet homepage, with links to various other pages.

- Organizational overview, mission statements for the major organizational units: This material can be contributed by the various groups. It is typically an output from management strategic planning sessions. Depending on the size and nature of the organization, this overview can be difficult to create. It is suggested that this part of the quality manual be started as early as possible and be as brief as possible, as it may require revision each time the organization changes.
- Core procedures—summary, references: These are the required procedures referred to in PARAGRAPH 4.2.1 *c* as well as any of the other procedures that the organization wishes to identify as "core." These "other" procedures can include processes that are outside the scope of ISO 9001 (e.g., travel, human relations), but that are pertinent to all employees. This section contains a brief summary of the purpose of each procedure to ensure that employees are aware of the existence of these procedures. A link enables the employee to access the full procedure when it is needed.
- Top level description or descriptions of life cycles: This section translates the mission statements from the organizational overview in the first section into high-level descriptions of how the organization fulfills its mission. Because these descriptions are for all readers, the level of detail is minimized. The purpose of this section is to provide employees with an appreciation of how the pieces of the organization—the processes—fit together to satisfy customers.
- References to procedure sets: Assuming that responsibility for defining and documenting processes is delegated, this section provides links to the procedures maintained by each group. These are typically links to lower-level home pages, which may provide direct access to some procedures and links to other home pages.
- ISO 9001:2000 traceability matrix: Because of the ongoing value to the organization, it is recommended that this document be maintained as a linked part of the quality manual. Although the audience for this document is relatively limited (i.e., internal auditors, the management representative [see PARAGRAPH 5.5.2], and, possibly, the

registrar's auditors), there is typically no reason to limit access. In addition, open communication about policy, plans, and progress minimizes resistance and supports a successful implementation.

PARAGRAPH *4.2.3* Control of Documents

PARAGRAPH 4.2.3 requires a documented procedure to define the organization's methods for document control. The purpose of these methods is to support "communication of intent and consistency of action."[4] These methods apply to all of the documents identified as part of the quality management system (PARAGRAPH 4.2.1). The documentation includes

- Process documentation: policies, procedures, and templates
- Product and project documentation: development plans, test plans, release plans, specifications, design documents, prototypes, and test scripts.

Implementation Considerations. The organization typically creates a "master" document control procedure that defines the general requirements for document control. The owner of a document is assigned responsibility for ensuring that methods are in place for controlling that document. A single, standard repository may be defined (e.g., project folders on an Intranet), a variety of acceptable methods may be provided (e.g., Intranet or file server), or document control may be left to the discretion of the manager who owns the document. In addition to Intranets, Web portals, and dedicated document management systems, document control may be accomplished through systems identified primarily for configuration management and knowledge management.

If a procedure is associated with the creation of the document, the document control mechanisms can be identified in that procedure.

For each document, the organization defines how the requirements for document control are satisfied.

Because there is no requirement for a single tool for controlling documents, software-engineering organizations typically control internally used documents with the version control or configuration management tool used to control code. When individuals outside the engineering organization do not have (or want) access to the engineering tool, shared documents, such as Requirements Specifications, are controlled through an Intranet-based tool, which provides simplified access to the configuration management repository and that eliminates the potential problems of multiple master copies of documents (one in the configuration management tool, one on a server for the Intranet).

Exhibit 4-4 suggests questions and answers that the implementation team can consider in defining the processes for document control.

Exhibit 4-4. Addressing the requirements for document control.

Requirement	Implementation considerations and questions
a) Approve for adequacy before issue	Who approves the document before it is considered "released?" In some cases, an author can approve his or her own document. In most cases, approval is a management or technical lead responsibility and is based on ensuring that feedback has been solicited from all affected parties and appropriately considered.
b) Review, update, and reapprove	Who reviews the document? How is the document updated? Who updates the document? How are changes requested or submitted? At each phase of the life cycle, who approves change requests—to spend resources on making the change and to absorb the effect of the change (e.g., design changes, additional testing)? Who approves the revised document? Maintaining a document is frequently significantly more challenging than creating the document—and the difficulty can increase depending on where in the life cycle of the project a change is initiated. For example, if the document is a product requirements specification from marketing, the initial review, negotiation, and approval can be relatively straightforward. Early changes and changes that do not affect content, cost, or schedule can be initiated and approved by the project team. Changes that affect schedule and cost may require a higher level of approval. Any content changes late in the project may require an even higher level of approval.
c) Identify changes and identify the current revision status of documents	Is this the latest version of the document? If the document is published electronically on an Intranet, the latest version is, by definition, the one on the Intranet. However, because individuals persist in copying files and printing copies of documents for a number of legitimate reasons, even documents published electronically typically contain version information. What changed? ISO 9001 does not contain any additional requirements for how changes are to be identified. Identifying changes typically serves two purposes. It ensures that readers do not inadvertently overlook small, but significant changes can efficiently review and implement revisions. Typically, individual changes are summarized in a change history section and are marked in the text as the document is undergoing review and revision. If the changes are significant and frequent, it is often more efficient to omit the marking of individual changes, to characterize the global nature of the changes in the change history, and to request that reviewers re-review the whole document or the affected portions.

Exhibit 4-4. (continued)   Addressing the requirements for document control.

Requirement	Implementation considerations and questions
d) Ensure relevant versions are available at points of use	How do individuals who need information access the documents? This paragraph requires that relevant versions be placed in the appropriate location or locations and that intended recipients are able to use the distribution mechanisms employed by the organization. Recipients have the required technology, including access rights, passwords, and so forth. This paragraph is closely related to PARAGRAPH *f*, which requires that individuals be aware of when to access the library. In referring to "relevant versions," ISO 9001 recognizes that, for example, software maintenance and technical support organizations require access not only to the current versions of documents but to earlier versions that correspond to installed or supported versions of the product. Although Intranet Web sites offer a way to accelerate distribution and enhance availability, if there is insufficient planning, administrative resource, and attention, these Web sites can rapidly degenerate into an unwieldy, frustrating tangle of broken links and obsolete and duplicate documents.
e) Ensure documents remain legible and readily identifiable	How does the organization preserve documents for as long as they are needed? Although the language of this requirement is a carryover from paper-based systems, it is typically addressed by systematic versioning (identification) and by regular server backups and off-site storage of back-up media (remain legible). Although it is relatively unusual, if documents are preserved for extended periods of time and if documents come from a number of different sources (both internally generated and externally supplied), satisfying this requirement can entail archiving technology or migrating back-up media—from word processors to tape formats to platforms.
f) Identify and control the distribution of documents of external origin	This paragraph applies to documents like standards, customer requirements specifications, problem reports, and third-party product documentation. The organization does not control the content of these documents, but it does ensure that the correct versions are available to the individuals who need access to perform their jobs. Because most external documents are available electronically, they are typically made available through the same repository mechanism used for internally generated documents.
g) Prevent the unintended use of obsolete documents	How do individuals identify the current version of a document? How do individuals know when a version becomes obsolete?

Exhibit 4-4. (continued)   Addressing the requirements for document control.

Requirement	Implementation considerations and questions
	When documents are made available electronically in a central repository, the challenge is to ensure that all affected individuals know when new versions of documents are available. In many cases, notification is addressed by normal communication among team members. In larger, more dispersed organizations, systematic e-mail notification and automated workflow management are appropriate.

PARAGRAPH *4.2.4* Control of Records

Records are defined as a special class of document, subject to different requirements for control. Similar to those for document control, the control mechanisms for records are documented in one of the few procedures required by ISO 9001:2000. The significant differences between document control and record control are that

- There is no requirement for the review and approval of records
- There is no provision or requirement for updating records
- Retention times and disposition methods are specified for records.

The remaining requirements for control of records—identify, preserve legibility, store, retrieve, and protect—mirror those for the control of documents.

When test records are captured as parts of reports, which are reviewed and approved, the rules for document control and for record control apply.

Implementation Considerations. Although the standard supplies a comprehensive list of categories of required records (see the list in the discussion of PARAGRAPH 4.2.1 *e*), it is the organization's responsibility to determine what specific records to keep in each category—and how long to keep them.

For example, PARAGRAPH 7.3.5 *Design and development verification* requires that the organization maintain records of the results of the verification and of any necessary actions. ISO 9001 does not specify

- How detailed the results need to be (e.g., the record can indicate just that all test cases passed or it can provide specific results for each test case, especially when a certain number of "failures" are anticipated)
- Which verification activities produce records (e.g., unit test, integration test, or system test)

The first step is to deal with specific records that are required by regulatory bodies (e.g., the Food and Drug Administration or the Nuclear Regulatory Commission), by the legal department, and by the customer as part of a contract.

The questions to ask in considering which additional records to keep are: *What purpose does the record serve?* and *For whom is the record intended?* If a record has no business-related purpose or intended audience, it is not worth keeping. The operator of the process accesses records to ensure that all activities are performed (e.g., all tests have been run). Management refers to records to prove that the results of the activities are satisfactory (e.g., to a team leader who has to approve promoting code to an integration library or to a customer's representative).

Preservation and Protection. The selection of storage and handling methods that satisfy requirements for preservation and protection is based on the media in which records are created and the retention times. Each medium has an associated shelf life and storage requirements supplied by the manufacturer.[5]

As more and more records are digitized, the issues of shelf life and retrieval have become increasingly critical. For example, a (relatively) quick scan of the Internet reveals that

- CD-R (Recordable CD) manufacturers report that accelerated life tests and modeling predict 70- to 100-year life expectancies
- Specifications claim 5 to 10 years
- Some users report substantially less based on environmental conditions.

Retrieval. ISO 9001 requires only that records be retrievable. No qualification is provided (e.g., readily), so it is the responsibility of the organization to establish parameters for retrieval that are consistent with any processes that require access to records. These parameters include permissions for access and requests for retrieval and response times for requests. For example, if records are maintained for legal purposes and must be provided by regulation or contract within seven days of an approved request, the process for retrieval should address those requirements.

Experts consistently identify technological obsolescence as the greatest risk to ensuring the ability to retrieve electronic records.[6] Organizations, through painful experience, discover that archiving hardware is a painful necessity to ensure that compatible host environments can be re-created for the retrieval of and access to stored records and other data and documents. This is the same challenge organizations face in ensuring that they can retrieve software products and re-create development environments to meet contractual commitments to support customers using earlier versions of products.

Completing the example of CD-Rs started above, the rapid evolution of hardware and media can only exacerbate the inexplicable and frustrating incompatibilities among currently available media, CD Recorders, and CD-ROM drives.

Retention Time and Tools. Once the set of records is defined, appropriate retention times and disposition methods are determined. Records are kept only as long as they are useful. Although retention time can be a specific time period, it can also be expressed as

- A minimum period (e.g., for at least seven years)
- Permanent
- Until superceded (e.g., results from a round of testing are overwritten when the tests are rerun).

Because no tool is specified by ISO 9001, some records are typically controlled with the same tools used for documents (e.g., records of customer reviews and records of internal audits). Records generated by an automated test tool can be stored in the tool's database—if the database is appropriately backed up.

Disposition. Disposition methods are determined by the contents of the records. For example, signed contracts require secure disposal; printed reports from an automated test tool go in the office-recycling bin.

The Documented Procedure. The organization typically creates a "master" record control procedure that defines the general requirements for record control. The owner of a record is assigned responsibility for ensuring that methods are in place for controlling that record. A single, standard repository may be defined (e.g., project folders on an Intranet), a variety of acceptable methods may be provided (e.g., Intranet, file server, and even file cabinets), or record control may be left to the discretion of the manager who owns the process. If a procedure is associated with the creation of the record, the record control mechanisms can be identified in that procedure. For example, the system test procedure might specify that the report of the results of the final set of tests be placed in the product release directory of the configuration management system and archived with the baseline for the release, which is retained for a minimum of seven years.

Placing the retention times and disposition methods in the associated operational procedures is typically more effective than attempting to maintain a master list of all of the organization's records, retention times, and disposition methods. See the optional records section in Appendix D.

An Audit Trail—Avoid the Pack Rat Trap. For organizations seeking formal ISO 9001 registration, there is no requirement that an audit trail be maintained for the registrar's auditors. Like all forms of records, an audit trail is maintained if it is useful or required from a business and process perspective. If a registrar's auditor asks for a specific record and no examples happen to be available (e.g., because the retention period has elapsed), the auditor can confirm the successful implementation by asking several individuals to describe what has happened in the past and what is supposed to happen regarding the record. A consistent response from multiple individuals is sufficient corroboration of the effective handling of that particular record. (The diligent auditor will note the record as an item to look for in subsequent audits.) The initial registration audit is planned so that a significant number of records are within their retention period so the auditors can have confidence in the completeness and accuracy of their assessment of the organization's quality management system. During periodic surveillance audits, the auditor can expect to see only the records that are supposed to be available.

PARAGRAPH 4—Summary

PARAGRAPH 4 of ISO 9001:2000 provides a framework for the rest of the paragraphs in the standard (in PARAGRAPH 4.1) and specific requirements for the documents that make up the foundation of the quality management system.

References

1. International Organization for Standardization, *ISO 9000:2000 and the Guidance on the Terminology Used in ISO 9001:2000 and ISO 9004:2000*, Document ISO/TC 176/SC 2/N 526R, May 2001, International Organization for Standardization, Geneva, www.iso.ch.
2. Pearsall, Judy, Ed., *The Concise Oxford Dictionary*, 10th ed., Oxford University Press, Oxford, 1999.
3. International Organization for Standardization, Introduction and Support Package — Guidance on ISO 9001:2000 Clause 1.2 'Application,' Document ISO/TC 176/SC 2/N 52412, International Organization for Standardization, Geneva, http://www.iso.ch/iso/en/iso9000-14000/pdf/Guidance_on_ISO_9001.pdf (10 Oct. 03).
4. ISO 9000:2000, PARAGRAPH 2.7.1.
5. Conservation On Line (CoOL), http://palimpsest.stanford.edu/ (9 Mar. 03).
6. The Commission on Preservation and Access, *Preserving Digital Information*, 1996, available at http://lyra.rlg.org/ArchTF/tfadi.index.htm (9 Mar. 03).

Chapter 5
PARAGRAPH 5
Management Responsibility

PARAGRAPH 5 contains requirements for specific activities that management performs in establishing and operating the quality system. The early introduction of management responsibility correctly emphasizes the need for securing and continually renewing management commitment and involvement. Although, regrettably, no sources external to ISO are credited in the standard, the priority placed on management activities reiterates the experience and conclusions of many experts, including Juran,[1] Deming,[2] and Crosby,[3] and is consistent with the many quality programs and models derived from their work. Management works on behalf of the stakeholders to establish and maintain goals and conditions of employment. Management hires, fires, rewards, and corrects. Management plans and oversees the investment of resources and budget. What management pays attention to is what gets done. Joseph Juran aptly sums up the importance of management when he states, simply, that "our quality problems have been planned that way" (p. vii).[1] In relating these quality problems to management's responsibility for an organization's assets, Juran goes on to echo Crosby in identifying the costs of poor quality—resources expended to redo things that went wrong because of poor quality—as 20 to 40 percent of sales.*

Watts Humphrey, in *Managing the Software Process*, identifies six basic principles for process change. The first principle is "senior management leadership is required to launch the change effort and to provide continuing resources and priority."[4]

In 1995, The Standish Group reported frequently quoted results from a survey of the U.S. software industry.[5] These results are summarized in Exhibit 5-1.

---

* Juran, Reference 1, p. 1; Crosby, Reference 3, pp. 18 and 175. It is interesting to note that Watts Humphrey states that the five-level maturity framework on which the Capability Maturity Model for Software "roughly parallels the quality maturity structure defined by Crosby" in *Quality is Free*[3] (p. 4).

Exhibit 5-1. From the standish group.

U.S. information technology application development	$250 billion—175,000 projects
Typical project costs	
Large company	$2.3 million
Small company	$.43 million
Software projects completed on time and within budget	16.2 percent
Software projects cancelled before completion	31.1 percent—Cost: $81 billion
Projects that are completed at 189 percent of their original estimates	52.7 percent—Cost: Additional $59 billion
Projects deployed by the largest American companies	Average 42 percent of the originally proposed content
Projects deployed by small companies	78.4 percent have 74.2 percent of the originally proposed content

The sobering, but not surprising, results of this survey make the terms of W. Edwards Deming's conclusions about the importance of management particularly relevant to the software sector:

> *The basic cause of sickness in American industry and resulting unemployment is failure of top management to manage. … The causes usually cited for failure of a company are costs of start-up, overruns on costs, depreciation of excess inventory, competition—anything but the actual cause, pure and simple bad management.*[2] * *(p. ix)*

In the midst of all of this bad news, every one of these experts also points to top management as an essential part of the solution.

ISO 9001:2000 defines top management responsibility in terms of:

- Public commitment
- Planning
- Assignment of responsibility and authority
- Monitoring and review

The term *top management* is an unsuccessful attempt by the ISO committee responsible for ISO 9001:2000 to address confusion with the term *management with executive responsibility* in ISO 9001:1994. That term, management with executive responsibility, was introduced in ISO 9001:1994 to address confusion about the term management in ISO 9001:1987. Even with the definition in ISO 9000:2000, top management is not clear: top "management … person or group of people who directs and controls an organization at the highest level."

An effective working definition of top management has three parts:

---

* It is interesting to note that Watts Humphrey states (Reference 4, p. 17) that *Out of the Crisis*[2] should be read by "everyone in this field."

1. Actively participates in the management of the organization and is knowledgeable about the activities performed by the organization (e.g., this is not an absentee landlord or a typical member of the board of directors, who has a strategic, business focus; it may not necessarily be a Chief Executive Officer)
2. Is concerned about the continuing health of the organization—not just about a specific customer, release of a product, or project (e.g., this person might cancel a successful project if it made it possible for the organization to pursue a more beneficial course)
3. Has sufficient budgetary and organizational authority to make decisions regarding the organization (e.g., if the organization is part of a larger organization, top management may be a division manager, a vice president, etc.).

Finally, it should be noted that top management could be one or more individuals (e.g., an executive management team, the individuals who report directly to the chief executive officer). If top management is more than one person, it is highly advisable to designate one member of the team as the primary sponsor, a single point of contact for quality management system issues related to top management.

PARAGRAPH 5.1 *Management Commitment*

PARAGRAPH 5.1 requires commitment to the development, implementation, and continual improvement of the quality management system. "Continual improvement" is defined in PARAGRAPH 8.5.1 *Continual improvement*, which contains only references to activities implemented in response to requirements in other paragraphs of ISO 9001:2000. PARAGRAPH 5.1 claims that it contains a list of evidence of management's commitment. Each piece of evidence is related to activities for which requirements are fully developed in subsequent paragraphs. Exhibit 5-2 delineates the paragraphs of ISO 9001:2000 that provide requirements for the activities that produce the evidence of management commitment.

As noted in the second column of Exhibit 5-2, the first four items in the table focus on statements of intent: policies and objectives. These types of statements are necessary, but like all words, are relatively easy to express. The real proof of the commitment is found in the follow-through on the words, in the results of activities, which is the focus of the last two items in the table:

- Reviews, in which top management commits time to the quality management system, asks questions, and acts on the answers (the opposite of the ostrich-style of management, expressed in "don't ask; don't tell")
- Commitment of resources, through which top management demonstrates its belief in the value of a process-based, fact-driven culture

63

Exhibit 5-2. Proving management commitment.

Evidence/requirement	Comments and implementation considerations
1 PARAGRAPH 5.1 *a*, communicate … the importance of meeting customer … requirements"	This communication typically includes a policy statement by the appropriate level of management. As noted in PARAGRAPH 5.2, this policy statement includes language alluding to systematically determining customer requirements and to enhancing customer satisfaction. This policy statement is included as part of the quality policy, required by PARAGRAPH 5.3. The effectiveness of the communication is measured by the care that the organization takes in identifying, confirming, and communicating customer requirements, in monitoring the fulfillment of customer requirements, and in addressing problems in meeting customer requirements. See PARAGRAPH 5.2 *Customer focus*. PARAGRAPH 7.2 *Customer-related processes* describes the elicitation (PARAGRAPH 7.2.1) and review (PARAGRAPH 7.2.2) of requirements related to products.
2 PARAGRAPH 5.1 *a*, communicate … the importance of meeting statutory and regulatory … requirements"	This communication typically includes a policy statement by the appropriate level of management. This policy statement is frequently included as part of the quality policy (addressed in PARAGRAPHS 4.2.1 *a* and 5.3). The effectiveness of the communication is measured by the care that the organization takes in identifying and communicating regulatory and statutory requirements, in monitoring the fulfillment of regulatory and statutory requirements, and in addressing problems in meeting regulatory and statutory requirements. See PARAGRAPH 7.2.1 *Determination of requirements related to the product*.
3 PARAGRAPH 5.1 *b*, "establish the quality policy"	PARAGRAPH 4.2.1 a requires that the quality policy be documented, which serves as the evidence of its existence. This policy is typically a mission, vision, or values statement issued by the appropriate level of management. Establishment is assessed based on organization-wide awareness of the quality policy; consistency of derived policies, objectives, and procedures with the quality policy; measures associated with the derived objectives; results associated with the derived procedures; and actions taken when compliance with the policy fails or is at risk. See PARAGRAPH 5.3 *Quality policy*.

Exhibit 5-2 (continued)   Proving management commitment.

Evidence/requirement	Comments and implementation considerations
4 PARAGRAPH 5.1 *c*, "ensure that quality objectives are established"	PARAGRAPH 4.2.1 *a* requires that the quality objectives be documented, which serves as the evidence of their existence. The quality objectives are typically a network of objectives created at and by management at all levels of the organization, expressed for the business, for groups, for projects and products, and for individuals. Effectiveness of the objectives is assessed based on each individual's awareness of the relevant objectives, measures associated with the objectives (PARAGRAPH 5.4.1 requires that the objectives be measurable), and actions taken when the objectives are not met or are at risk. See PARAGRAPH 5.4.1 *Quality objectives*.
5 PARAGRAPH 5.1 *d*, "conduct management reviews"	The reviews themselves demonstrate top management's commitment of time to the quality management system. The evidence of the reviews is found in the plan for management reviews and in the records of the reviews (see PARAGRAPH 5.6). The effectiveness of the reviews is assessed by the review meeting reports and any resulting changes. See PARAGRAPH 5.6 *Management review*.
6 PARAGRAPH 5.1 *e*, "ensure the availability of resources"	The release of resources—dollars, people, and equipment—to implement and execute the processes defined in the quality management system tends to be the ultimate demonstration of commitment. Management is seen as backing up its words with company dollars. The actual evidence of effectiveness is in staffed and equipped projects and functions and successfully executed processes, plans, and schedules. See PARAGRAPH 6 *Resource management*.

PARAGRAPH 5.2 *Customer Focus*

PARAGRAPH 5.2 expands on PARAGRAPH 5.1 *a*. Not only are customer requirements to be met, they are to be determined and met with the aim of enhancing customer satisfaction. As implied in the references at the end of PARAGRAPH 5.2,

- The process for determining customer requirements is characterized in PARAGRAPH 7.2.1 *Determination of requirements related to the product*.
- The requirement to monitor customer satisfaction is found in PARAGRAPH 8.2.1 *Customer satisfaction*.

Language referring to focusing on the customer and placing a high priority on systematically determining and meeting customer requirements to enhance customer satisfaction is typically included in the mission or vision statements that collectively serve as the quality policy.

Note that the goal of enhancing customer satisfaction is introduced in PARAGRAPH 1.1 *b*.

PARAGRAPH 5.3 *Quality Policy*

In many successful ISO implementations, the quality policy is written by the ISO implementation team leader, signed by the Chief Executive Officer or President, and constructed specifically as the "ISO Quality Policy." Frequently, it is resurrected from a total quality management program. This type of quality policy usually looks something like,

> *It is the policy of Quick Software to deliver commercial software applications that meet or exceed customer requirements. This is accomplished by a companywide dedication to meeting the needs of all of its stakeholders and to continually improving the processes by which Quick Software determines requirements and delivers product functionality.*

This high-level policy takes little effort to construct, says very little, and satisfies the minimal content requirements of PARAGRAPHS 5.3 *a*, 5.3 *b*, and 5.3 *c*. It also

- (PARAGRAPH 5.3 *a*) is appropriate to the purpose of the organization.
- (PARAGRAPH 5.3 *b*) contains the requisite references to customer requirements and improving effectiveness.
- (PARAGRAPH 5.3 *c*) provides a framework for establishing and reviewing quality objectives; in fact, in this example, it is the quality objectives that bring substance to the quality policy.

Posting the policy at strategic locations in the workplace (e.g., conference rooms, lobbies, restrooms, or on the first page of the new employee handbook, linked to the animated ISO GIF on the Intranet homepage) meets the requirement of PARAGRAPH 5.3 *d* that it be communicated. The second requirement in PARAGRAPH 5.3 *d*, that the quality policy be understood, is so vague and unquantifiable that it is typically verified by establishing that individuals are aware of the policy's existence and how to find it.

The final requirement, from PARAGRAPH 5.3 *e*, that the quality policy be reviewed for continuing suitability, is satisfied by including the quality policy in the scope of the internal audits (see PARAGRAPH 8.2.2 *Internal audit*) or as a line item in selected management review agendas (see PARAGRAPH 5.6 *Management review*).

With such a quality policy, implementers and auditors correctly focus on ensuring and verifying that all individuals are aware of the performance criteria and objectives that define quality for their particular jobs (see PARAGRAPH 5.4.1 *Quality objectives*).

Implementation Considerations: Beyond ISO 9001

In establishing the quality policy, management also has the opportunity to explore the benefits of principle-based management, described in ISO 9000:2000 PARAGRAPH 0.2 and in ISO 9004:2000 PARAGRAPH 4.3. The particular principle associated with the quality policy is principle b: "Leadership—leaders establish unity of purpose and direction of an organization."

Depending on the culture and size of the organization, the experts on whose work this principle is based uniformly assert the benefits of a set of stable core values in establishing an enduring and successful organization. Tom Peters places shared values at the center of his McKinsey 7-S framework.[6] Watts Humphrey states simply that "perhaps the most vital single characteristic of the leader is vision."[7] The first point in W. Edwards Deming's theory for management is, "create constancy of purpose toward improvement of product and service" (p. 24).[2] He goes on to state that

> *Innovation, the foundation of the future, can not thrive unless top management have declared unshakeable commitment to quality and productivity. Until this policy can be enthroned as an institution, middle management and everyone else in the company will be skeptical about the effectiveness of their best efforts. (p. 25)[2]*

All of these comments can be addressed by exploiting the quality policy.

More from Dr. Deming. In the interests of full disclosure, Deming takes three additional positions that are relevant to quality policies and to ISO 9001.

- He is vehement about the abolition of slogans, exhortations, posters, and targets (p. 65).[2] He would also probably condemn the use of T-shirts, mugs, and card keys with the quality policy printed on the back.
- He endorses voluntary standards as essential to avoiding waste, duplication, and incompatibility. He specifically states that lack of standards in the computer industry in America is choking the industry and robbing the consumer of more useful products (p. 308).[2] He is equally emphatic in his warnings about most involuntary, government standards, which he characterizes as unnecessary and incorrect limitations, controls, and restrictive procedures that reduce consumer choice (p. 302).[2]
- He stresses that ISO 9001 is not enough. When asked in early 1994 about ISO 9000, he responded:

> *ISO 9000, 9001, and 9002 are conformance specifications—conform to requirements. Of course we must conform to requirements. But that's not enough; that won't do it. One must seek the nominal value of anything, what the best way is, not just pass the course. To meet specifications, do what is required—that is not enough. You have to do better than that. Achieve uniformity about the nominal value, best value. Shrink, shrink, shrink variation about the nominal value. That is where you get your payoff; that is where you get ahead.[8,] **

PARAGRAPH 5.4 *Planning*

PARAGRAPH 5.4 addresses objectives and planning.

PARAGRAPH 5.4.1 Quality Objectives

PARAGRAPH 5.4.1 defines top management's responsibility for ensuring that quality objectives are established. "Quality objective" is defined by weaving together various linked definitions in ISO 9000:2000, starting with PARAGRAPH 3.2.5:

> *Quality objective—something sought, or aimed for, related to the degree to which a set of inherent characteristics (distinguishing features) fulfills requirements (needs or expectations that are stated, generally implied, or obligatory).*

Quality objectives are targets for how well a process, activity, or product is to fulfill its requirements. For example, products have requirements. "No open Priority 1 defects for product installed at customer operational sites" is a measurable objective that defines a target for how well the product is to satisfy its defined requirements.

Earlier, ISO 9001:2000 glibly states that,

> *The quality objectives complement other objectives of the organization such as those related to growth, funding, profitability, the environment and occupational health and safety. The various parts of an organization's management system might be integrated, together with the quality management system, into a single management system using common elements.[9]*

PARAGRAPH 5.4.1 states that quality objectives include those "needed to meet requirements for product."

Key words for implementers and for top management to remember are "ensure" and "measurable." Top management typically defines some quality objectives—for example, business objectives and high-level objectives for products and the organization's product mix. The hierarchy of increasingly detailed objectives spawned to support these high-level objectives and the quality policy are created and implemented by management at relevant functions and levels of the organization.

---

* This represents a significant improvement in his opinion of ISO 9001. A specific comment recorded by the author during a 4-day Deming seminar held in December 1992 was that ISO 9001 is the worst thing to ever happen to quality.

ISO 9001:2000 offers no list of quality objectives, but it does require that the organization's quality objectives be "measurable and consistent with the quality policy." Any objective—quality or other—is not effective if it cannot be determined whether or how well it is satisfied. PARAGRAPH 8.1 *General [measurement]* specifies that the organization implement measurements "needed ... to ensure conformity ... and to continually improve the quality management system." PARAGRAPH 8.2.2 *Internal audit* requires that the internal auditors "determine whether the quality management system ... is effectively implemented and maintained." In these contexts, "effective" can only be assessed by comparing actual performance to management's objectives and expectations. For example, faced with projects that overrun initial cost estimates by 40 percent, management in one organization is ecstatic; in another organization, appalled.

Typically, each objective has an associated performance measurement mechanism. Otherwise, if there is no visibility and no one at any level cares, why bother with the objective?

Although it is implied by "establish," PARAGRAPH 6.2.2 *d* requires that the organization ensure that personnel are aware of how they contribute to the achievement of the quality objectives. In addition, PARAGRAPH 4.2.1 *a* specifies that quality objectives are documented, but not necessarily in one place or in one format.

Two other paragraphs contain requirements that are closely tied to quality objectives. PARAGRAPH 5.5.3 *Internal communication* requires that "communication take place regarding the effectiveness of the quality management system." As noted previously, the effectiveness of the quality management system is measured, in part, by its performance against the quality objectives established by the organization.

PARAGRAPH 5.5.1 *Responsibility and authority* requires that "responsibilities ... are defined and communicated within the organization." Any associated objectives are an essential part of any responsibility—the purpose, goals, or contribution of the assigned area of responsibility (e.g., for people, approval, and activity).

Implementation Considerations. In many organizations, the concept of quality objectives is well understood (probably under some other name), and implementation considerations are insignificant. Sometimes, however, quality objectives can become an unexpected point of contention. In addressing the requirements associated with quality objectives, the implementation team may unexpectedly encounter two significant obstacles.

Because ISO 9001:2000 does not identify any specific quality objectives and because the definition in ISO 9000:2000 is relatively ambiguous, implementation teams can fall into lengthy, frustrating debates about the meaning of "quality objective." For example, at ABC, a procedure states that,

"Any software product released for unrestricted distribution to customers shall have no more than four Priority 2 defects and no Priority 1 defects." Are the limits on open defects a requirement, a quality objective for the product or the product development process, a performance requirement for the development process, or some combination of the three? The answer the team arrived at is that it is all three. As another example, because every objective is required to be measurable and to include any known performance criteria (e.g., how fast, how often, how long, how many defects), the implementation team concluded that every objective was, in part, a quality objective.

- There is no requirement in ISO 9001 that an organization use the term "quality objective" or that it differentiate or segregate its quality objectives from other objectives. In fact, as is discussed in this volume in Chapter 4, there are compelling reasons to avoid the use of the qualifier "quality." Preceding almost any noun by the word "quality, (e.g., quality plan, quality process, quality audit, quality assurance, and quality control) implies that the subject is separate from or an addition to the way the organization conducts business.
- Most organizations do not have any objectives that are labeled "quality" objectives. In fact, they are not interested in adding any more objectives—particularly those that do not add any value to the organization's processes and products. As is implied in this volume in Chapter 4, preceding almost any noun by the word "quality" (e.g., quality objective, quality plan, quality process, quality audit, quality assurance, and quality control) implies that the subject is separate from or an addition to the way the organization conducts business.

A Strategy for Addressing Quality Objectives. An effective and efficient strategy for addressing quality objectives incorporates three activities and avoids any need to define *quality objective*:

- Ensure that there are organizationwide policies and standards for the deployment and content of objectives
- Identify and assess the many objectives that are already in place in most organizations
- Assess current objectives and make recommendations for additions and modifications only when problems are encountered, particularly in respect to satisfying requirements in other paragraphs of ISO 9001.

Policies and Standards for Objectives. A ubiquitous theme in discussions of objectives in the context of either management or instructional design is that they contain at least three parts:

- Activity—a description of what is to be done (e.g., the procedure, tasks, job responsibilities)
- Conditions—prerequisites for beginning the activity and the conditions under which the activity is expected to be performed (e.g., given inputs, available tools)
- Criteria—for successful completion of the activity (e.g., the parameters that are used to assess the successful completion of the activity, expectations).[10]

The purpose of documented objectives is to eliminate surprises and the associated waste: managers who are surprised that someone cannot read their minds, individual contributors who think they are doing good jobs until they submit their work. It is management's responsibility to ensure that the direction provided to the organization in the form of policies, procedures, plans, and standards is clear, complete, and correct. When management fails to meet this responsibility, procedures and plans drift out of alignment with reality and the organization challenges its people to know which procedures and plans are current and which are to be ignored.

Management responsibility for documenting, defining, maintaining, and monitoring performance against objectives within areas of assigned responsibility is typically a fundamental part of the organization's management strategies, administered by human resources, organizational development, and process engineering groups or functions.

Management responsibility for objectives may be established through policies, procedures (e.g., for performance reviews or project definition), plans, project specifications, project and personnel management handbooks, or standard training curricula. The requirements for objectives (measurable, achievable, etc.) are typically part of the same handbook or training.

Identify Current Objectives. The identification of current objectives usually begins by asking about objectives in the gap assessment (discussed with PARAGRAPH 4.1). Assessors ask if there are any objectives you are responsible for meeting or providing. Related questions probe for relevant standards and criteria for:

- Making trade-off decisions
- Approving waivers
- Setting priorities
- Evaluating performance and work products.

Most organizations are already swimming in objectives, so there is no shortage of answers, including:

- Individual performance objectives (e.g., tasks to accomplish at or by specified times, evaluation criteria, stretch objectives)
- Project objectives (e.g., the purpose of the project translated from the justification for the project)
- Design objectives (e.g., "should" statements included in the requirements specification—things that need to be justified if they are not done)
- Product defect-related measures (e.g., defects per thousand lines of code, release criteria, 100 percent of agreed-on product requirements implemented)
- Nominal values and standards (e.g., eight hours without a failure)
- Control limits, calculated or arbitrary (e.g., a value defining significant variation from estimated effort, from estimated memory requirements, or from power requirements)
- Process performance objectives (e.g., standards for response times and effort estimates, lines of text reviewed and defects removed per review meeting, priorities, evaluation criteria)
- Air quality objectives (e.g., quantities of an item per cubic meter and the date by which the listed level is to be achieved)
- Employee handbooks (e.g., workday, absences, etc.)
- Key business or performance indicators
- Business objectives (e.g., grow market share by 25 percent; reduce costs by 25 percent) and goals. There is no consistency in terminology, and battles are fought over the relationship between goals and objectives.

Recommend Additions and Modifications. Each of the objectives uncovered in the gap assessment is compared to the organization's standards for objectives. Any deficiencies that have an effect on the ability of processes to comply with planned arrangements or products to meet requirements are noted (e.g., points of confusion). Corrective action is requested from the manager of the responsible function or group, possibly with support from and facilitation by the ISO implementation team.

The gap assessment confirms that management responsibilities for objectives are understood and implemented. If the gap assessment uncovers quality problems (e.g., defects, missed steps, or unqualified personnel) associated with patterns of ineffective objectives, the problems are referred to the function responsible for that part of the organization's management infrastructure. If such an organization does not exist, the problem is referred to top management for resolution. To motivate the solution (if any motivation is necessary), the problem is examined from two perspectives.

The first perspective describes the observed behavior and its effect on people and the business: waste, rework, lost revenue, frustration, increased risk, involuntary overtime, and so forth.

The second perspective briefly describes the problem through its affect on compliance with ISO 9001:2000. A number of paragraphs may be cited as the basis for the compliance problem. To establish an objective basis for why the observed behavior is a problem, the assessment or implementation team selects the paragraph or paragraphs that most clearly point to a root cause and solution.

For example,

- If objectives are defined, but not communicated, the problem is with PARAGRAPH 6.2.2 (aware of how they contribute to quality objectives).
- If there are no objectives, the problem is with PARAGRAPH 5.4.1 (establish quality objectives).
- If there are no objectives and if responsibility and authority are not defined or communicated, the problem is with PARAGRAPH 5.5.1 (assignment of responsibility and authority).

See Exhibit 5-3.

Finally, eliminating inconsistency between objectives is a significant opportunity for an organization to gain immediate benefits from its ISO 9001 implementation (see Exhibit 5-4).

Some Thoughts about Objectives. There is no necessary conflict between setting objectives and relying on individual contributors' professional experience and judgment. Conflict arises from several sources:

- When errors in professional judgment, for which individual contributors are held accountable, are caused by management failures to communicate known expectations and to follow up to ensure those expectations are understood and implemented.
- When management sets expectations that exceed known process capability and does not listen to feedback from either their own experience or from experienced individual contributors. For example, if a manager sets unachievable objectives for completion of activities and does not listen to the voice of experience, individual contributors typically agree to the unrealistic expectation and then work overtime and skip steps to meet the expectation (causing staff burn out and excessive numbers of defects), or they do the work, which takes as long as it takes, and they let the manager deal with the pain of unmet expectations.

Although objectives are arguably an essential part of the management process, too great a reliance on objectives and associated measures can blind an organization to actual problems and successes. First, no reasonably sized set of objectives can completely define management's expectations—some of which are not and cannot be expressed in measurable terms. In successful organizations, individual contributors are given the

---

Exhibit 5-3. In our experience: patterns of ineffective management.

In an ISO 9001 gap analysis of an established, growing, successful organization, the assessors found problems with the way in which the new role of team leader (e.g., hardware, software, optics) had been implemented. The role was created to support project-engineering managers, who were unable to keep up with either the technology or the number of team members on larger projects. The assessors found no specific responsibilities or authority defined for team leaders. Problems were identified in all projects; the most frequently identified were that:

- Team leaders lack sufficient information to prioritize work, so their plans and assignments to team members frequently require extensive rework.
- Team leaders received no training in technical leadership.
- Engineering project managers continue to go directly to team members. Based on common sense, team leaders provide technical leadership, plan work, and make commitments to the project on behalf of the team; team leaders are frustrated because they are accountable for missed commitments even when team resources are diverted without their knowledge and without any consideration of the effect on the team's plans. Plans are continually being reworked and schedules frequently slip.
- In some projects, the team leaders, who are senior engineers, are frustrated because they spend their time as administrative assistants to the project engineering manager, maintaining project plans and attending meetings; this is not the best use of their time—or of company resources.
- Team leaders are drawn from the ranks of the senior engineers; they are "working" leaders and continue to spend some part of their time as technical contributors, frequently on critical deliverables. When time is short, team leaders correctly focus on their personal deliverables, so leadership is reduced at the time when it is, potentially, most needed.

The assessors selected PARAGRAPHS 5.5.1 *Responsibility and authority*; 7.3.1 *c* (assign responsibilities and authorities for design and development); and 6.2.2 *Competence, awareness, and training*, as the basis for the standard. The issue of training, which would have been the easiest to address (send them to a $795 seminar on technical leadership), was identified as secondary to defining roles and responsibilities.

---

broadest possible objectives, backed by the training, tools, and support they require. Second, to the extent that objectives do become the central focus of an organization's efforts, people will meet (and exceed) those objectives even if the unintended side effects outweigh any benefits to the organization. The authors of this volume have seen numerous examples of the unintended effects of objectives:

- When budget is all that matters, managers meet budget—quality, timely delivery, and customer service become secondary.
- When defect counts are all that matter, testers eventually succumb to the pressure to find fewer defects.

Exhibit 5-4. In our experience: self-inflicted pain.

At ABC, Inc., the new CEO insisted that the technical support group be run as a business unit—with its own profit objective. As a result, support engineers were quick to escalate problems out of technical support to product development. New product and feature development, essential for the company's future, is disrupted and delayed.

In addition, it is now difficult to bring out products with significant new technology. Technical support is reluctant to ramp up before the success of the new product is assured; establishing market confidence in the new product requires that ABC deliver fully capable support.

At XYZ, Inc., marketing identified a critical and urgent need (sometime in the next calendar year) for a Windows version of the company's aging, flagship, UNIX product. Engineering developed and delivered an extremely capable, robust, Web-enabled replacement, written using the latest object-oriented techniques. Two years late. Through three years of planning and reviews, no one succeeded in aligning the mismatched goals.

- When on time delivery is all that matters, products are delivered on time (whether they work or not and whether there is any profit in them are separate issues).
- When customer satisfaction as measured by an industry association's annual survey of customer satisfaction is all that matters, individuals spend time coaching and coaxing customers, time which could be spent on more profitable endeavors.

Deming has several pointed comments to make about managing "by the numbers." Although his observations are not fully supported by research,[11] they do serve as a warning about overindulging in quantitative management:

> *Focus on outcome is not an effective way to improve a process or an activity ... Management by numerical goal is an attempt to manage without knowledge of what to do, and in fact is usually management by fear. (p. 76)*[2]

PARAGRAPH 5.4.2 Quality Management System Planning

Plan in various forms appears 31 times in ISO 9001:2000.* The bulk of the plans are for the delivery of product to customers—for product realization. The majority of the plans appear in PARAGRAPHS 7 and 8 and deal with the operation of the quality management system, with doing work. These operational plans are the mechanisms by which the organization assures all the stakeholders that its commitments are achieved on time; that sufficient, qualified personnel are available and assigned; that any other required

---

* See PARAGRAPHS 5.4.2 (Change), 5.6.1 ([Management] review), 7.1 (Product realization), 7.3.1 (Product design and development), 7.3.4 (Reviews), 7.3.5 (Verification), 7.3.6 (Validation), 7.5.1 (Production and service provision), 8.1 (Monitoring, measurement, analysis, improvement), and 8.2.2 (Internal audits).

resources are provided; and that the proper processes are applied in the proper sequence.

Two sets of plans, for management review and for the internal audits, are associated directly with overseeing the quality management system itself.

In the context of PARAGRAPH 5.4.2 *a*, "plan the quality management system" refers to planning the activities required to establish the quality management system infrastructure. This planning ensures that the defined quality management system (the policies, procedures, standards, resources, people, etc.) address both the needs of the business (the quality objectives) and the requirements of ISO 9001:2000 (as summarized in PARAGRAPH 4.1).

PARAGRAPH 5.4.2 *b* refers to maintaining the integrity of the quality management system when changes to the quality management system are planned and implemented. This paragraph represents a significant challenge, particularly in times when the rate of organizational change is high.

Related Paragraphs. PARAGRAPH 5.5.2 *Management representative* requires that top management appoint a manager who is responsible for ensuring that the plan in PARAGRAPH 5.4.2 *a* is executed and the quality management system is established and implemented. This same management representative is responsible for ensuring that the processes—and the integrity of the quality management system—are maintained.

Implementation Considerations. Systematic project management is the key to the successful implementation of an ISO 9001–compliant quality management system and to meeting the requirements of PARAGRAPH 5.4.2 *a*. The implementation process, discussed in this volume in Chapter 1 and in Appendix F, requires the same level of commitment, planning, and management as the introduction of a new product.

Maintaining the Integrity of the Quality Management System. Although PARAGRAPH 5.4.2 *b* applies to any changes (e.g., the introduction of new methods, new tools), the primary consideration is of organizational changes. Just as it was the key to successful implementation, systematic project management is the key to the successful maintenance of an ISO 9001–compliant quality management system and to meeting the requirements of PARAGRAPH 5.4.2 *b*. These plans typically involve transition plans, succession plans, impact assessments, and mitigation strategies.

The word *integrity* is not defined in ISO 9000:2000, but the meaning as intended by the authors of ISO 9001:2000 is defined in supplementary guidance material[12] from ISO:

- Condition of having no part or element taken away or lacking
- Undivided state
- Completeness

Exhibit 5-5. In our experience: ensuring the integrity of the quality management system.

ABC, Inc. successfully shifted from an internal technical support function to an outsourced function in India. Through careful source selection, planning, frequent face-to-face communication, extensive initial and ongoing training (including commitments to involve the technical support group's trainers in beta tests), the organization was able to ensure that there was no interruption in or degradation of service to customers. They were able to reduce costs, but not as dramatically or as quickly as anticipated.

XYZ, Inc. was able to significantly reduce its engineering headcount and personnel costs by outsourcing the development of part of its product. Two years later, the organization discovered it had:

- Spent more time and money to manage the third party than it had spent previously on in-house development (e.g., more detailed specifications and plans, more formal communication, on-site monitoring, integration problems, and support problems)
- Degraded its ability to innovate and to respond quickly to customer requests, which had been one of its competitive advantages
- Lost the intimate knowledge of one its core technologies, which was readily apparent to customers seeking support and enhancements

Because it is clearly unrealistic to require that a quality management system never shrink (e.g., an organization no longer manufactures or offers proprietary hardware as part of its solutions), the emphasis is on "lacking" and "completeness." From a quality system perspective, PARAGRAPH 5.4.2 *b* requires that top management preserve the internal integrity of the quality management system. Because the parts of the quality management system are interdependent, a change in one part requires that management consider the effect on other parts of the quality management system and make any necessary adjustments. Laying off engineers requires some change to the projects on which they were working—for instance, new schedules, training, content reductions. For example, closing the system test lab to save money (or because it kept holding up product releases) without adjusting the processes that incorporated the closed lab damages the integrity of the quality management system.

The other aspect of ensuring the integrity of the quality management system entails maintaining the organization's ability to meet commitments—or renegotiating the commitments (see Exhibit 5-5).

PARAGRAPH 5.5 *Responsibility, Authority, and Communication*

The first and second subparagraphs of PARAGRAPH 5.5 deal, from a top management perspective, with responsibility and authority; the third, with communication.

PARAGRAPH 5.5.1 Responsibility and Authority

Defining and communicating responsibility encompasses assigning accountability for assets and duties to functions, organizational units, and individuals. ISO 9001 assigns responsibility to top management for ensuring that responsibility is clearly defined and communicated. As part of an effective quality management system, defining responsibility and establishing accountability prevent surprises and inform individuals and units of the organization as to what management requires from them. Responsibility and quality objectives are tightly coupled and typically progress in parallel as processes are defined and evolve.

Authority is the formal decision-making power granted by the organization. All individuals are informed of the extent of their authority, the decisions they are allowed to make and the decisions that belong to another individual or function or to another level of authority. Authority is typically expressed in terms of discretion, latitude, and approval.

Implementation Considerations. ISO 9001 does not specify any specific mechanisms for communicating responsibility and authority, but organizations regularly employ a number of vehicles for communicating responsibility, for communicating who is expected to do what. These vehicles include:

- Organization charts
- Policies (including the quality policy)
- Procedures
- Objectives
- Distribution lists in documentation templates, including approvers
- Plans (project, program, test, development, etc.)
- Approval limits for expenditure

Development plans as a vehicle for communicating responsibility and authority appear in PARAGRAPH 7.3.1 c.

Although it is not required by ISO 9001, the implementation is facilitated by the extent to which individuals participate in defining and agreeing to their own responsibility and authority. The participation of individuals with hands-on experience improves the likelihood that assigned responsibilities and levels of authority are reasonable. This broad participation also allows the implementation team to defuse the fear and resistance that frequently accompanies the transition to more formal definition of responsibility and authority in successful ad hoc organizations. Individuals fear that they will deliberately or accidentally be held accountable for things over which they have no control or authority.

It is also important that individuals be aware not only of their own responsibility and authority, but also of the responsibility and authority of people with whom they interact. This facilitates consistency and reinforces individuals' awareness of their own limits.

Establishing responsibility and authority also frequently collides with organizational cultures in which individuals who see an unanticipated need and step in are rewarded, but:

- What about their regular duties?
- What about the next time it happens?
- What is the implication of rewarding someone (perhaps a manager) for a management or process failure?

The ultimate challenge is to evolve from a culture that recognizes fire-fighting and unusual achievements (e.g., someone staying up 72 consecutive hours to fix the bug) to an organization that recognizes and rewards quiet success (e.g., someone met objectives, or released a new product without a single crisis). The implementation team's responsibility is to encourage and channel initiative, risk-taking, and feelings of ownership without diminishing them.

Overcoming these obstacles is part of management responsibility.

PARAGRAPH 5.5.2 Management Representative

PARAGRAPH 5.5.2 defines the responsibility and authority for a specific role. The management representative appointed by top management is the focal point for managing the quality management system. The management representative ensures that an ISO 9001–compliant quality management system is established, implemented, and maintained. The management representative reports on quality system performance to top management and identifies any needed improvements. As implied in the Note, the management representative also works with external parties (e.g., the ISO 9001 registrar, customers, and regulatory agencies) on matters relating to the quality management system.

Finally, the management representative ensures the promotion of awareness of the importance of customer requirements throughout the organization.

Implementation Considerations. As the manager of a large project working in an unfamiliar domain, process definition, the typical management representative requires project management and facilitation skills and the respect and confidence of both top management and the various line organizations. The management representative requires an understanding of how top management intends the whole organization to work and a general understanding of the work done by each part of the organization.

Although the language of PARAGRAPH 5.5.2 identifies a single person as the management representative, this manager typically facilitates the work of a team whose members represent the various parts of the organization that are involved in the ISO-complaint quality management system. This team is constituted early in the implementation and works with line management and the management representative to ensure that needed processes, procedures, and policies are put in place. Once the initial implementation is complete, the management representative's primary source of input is the audit team (see PARAGRAPH 8.2.2), which, for the first round of internal audits, is frequently made up of members of the implementation team. It is best if they are not told of this added responsibility until after they have worked as the implementation team for some extended period of time.

After the implementation is complete, the implementation team may transition into the role of a process oversight group (e.g., a software engineering process group), supporting the rollout of process into new projects or additional parts of the organization.

Although it is a job that never ends, management representative is not a full-time job, except in the time before, during, and after audits. The management representative is frequently responsible for (nonfinancial) performance metrics, quality (e.g., test and product release), or customer care.

The management representative's reports on progress in the implementation and on the performance of the established quality management system become line items on the management review (see PARAGRAPH 5.6) meeting agendas, which are typically extensions of the normal chain of management meetings that gather, roll-up, and synthesize information at each level of the organization—from the individual contributor to top management.

Recommended tools and techniques for the management representative are described in Appendix F.

The management representative's final responsibility, to ensure the promotion of awareness of the importance of customer requirements, is so vague it can be satisfied by an annual, cheerleading e-mail to all employees stating the obvious message. A homily at employee meetings (videotaped for distribution to remote locations) also satisfies the requirements of this paragraph. These messages start to have teeth when they include examples of successes and the rewards of paying attention to customer requirements. If they are casually constructed, sound "canned," or lack substantive examples, these messages can lead members of the organization to wonder about management's commitment to customer requirements. There is usually little need for horror stories, but what carries incredible weight is when the CEO holds up revenue shipments because they fail to meet customer requirements. This, of course, should not be done too often, and it should never be accompanied by public humiliation or mass firings.

Of far more importance to the organization is the management representative's and audit team's diligent and continuous monitoring of the organization's processes and procedures to ensure that customer requirements are at the forefront of each individual's concerns. This monitoring is justified and supported by:

- Systematic customer communication (see PARAGRAPH 7.2.3 *Customer communication*)
- Mandatory measurement of customer satisfaction (see PARAGRAPH 8.2.1 *Customer satisfaction*)
- The linked requirements that the quality policy include a commitment to comply with customer and other requirements (PARAGRAPH 5.3 *b*) and that the quality objectives conform to the quality policy (PARAGRAPH 5.4.1).

PARAGRAPH *5.5.3* Internal Communication

Communication is a theme that runs throughout ISO 9001. Internal communication is called out explicitly for the importance of requirements (PARAGRAPH 5.1), for the quality policy (PARAGRAPH 5.3), and for responsibility and authority (PARAGRAPH 5.5). The management representative reports on performance of the quality management system to top management (PARAGRAPH 5.5.2). The results of internal audits are reported, presumably to management of the area being audited (PARAGRAPH 8.2.2), and effective communication takes place between "different groups involved in design and development" (PARAGRAPH 7.3.1).

Requirements for external communication — for customer communication (PARAGRAPH 7.2.3) and for communication of requirements to suppliers (PARAGRAPH 7.4.2) — are specified elsewhere.

PARAGRAPH 5.5.3 contains two requirements. First, it requires that top management ensure that appropriate internal communication processes are established. Second, PARAGRAPH 5.5.3 adds a specific topic about which internal communication is required to take place: the effectiveness of the quality management system.

Internal communication is supported by elements of the infrastructure (e.g., telephones, teleconferencing, video conferencing, e-mail, shared repositories, and automated workflow; see PARAGRAPH 6.3 *c*).

Implementation Considerations. Organizations communicate information internally and externally through a number of systematic methods:

- Published documents, including contracts, plans, specifications, designs, procedures, job descriptions, and employee handbooks
- Meetings (virtual or otherwise) and the associated communications, including progress reports and action lists
- Formal training (e.g., self-study programs, instructor-led classes, scripted one-on-one communication)

These activities are typically called out as steps in procedures for the associated processes. For example, at one company, the project management handbook describes when and how to conduct team meetings. One of the activities the project manager is required to perform is to publish a list of action items from the meeting on the team Intranet within 24 hours of the conclusion of the meeting. A format for the report is in the handbook.

PARAGRAPH 5.5.3 does not specify any parameters for communication regarding the effectiveness of the quality management system. In particular, the direction of communication, the amount of information, and the recipients are left to the discretion of top management. This specific requirement is minimally satisfied by the management representative's reports to top management on quality-system performance and need for improvement (PARAGRAPH 5.5.2 b).

Providing broader visibility into performance and systematically soliciting input from all employees offers ways in which top management can go beyond the minimum and reap significant additional benefits.

Provide Broad Visibility. If the culture of the organization permits it, sharing this performance information with all personnel is an effective way to demonstrate management's commitment to establishing and maintaining the quality management system and to build a sense of pride and ownership throughout the organization. Because most people already know what the organization's problems are, there is a sense of relief when management acknowledges them and sets priorities for solving them by improving the organization's processes or infrastructure. Even when problems cannot be resolved, it is not because management is ignoring them. As ISO 9004:2000 PARAGRAPH 5.5.3 points out, there will be successes to communicate.

The risks of broad communication, particularly of recognizing successes, are significant, but so are the benefits.* It is critical that the information be conveyed in terms that are accurate, substantive, and meaningful to the audience—and that do not include the word quality:

- Accurate in that the communication describes what actually occurred (e.g., do not elicit the response, "What planet are they from?"); an important aspect of accurate is that no one person or group feels singled out for blame or missed for recognition
- Substantive in that the audience perceives the results as actually worth commenting on and not contrived (e.g., do not elicit the response, "Are we done yet?")
- Meaningful in that the audience has some degree of control over, influence on, or contribution to the results (e.g., do not trigger despair or depression)

---

* Recognizing success is essential, but the unintended side effects of recognizing success include promoting competition and adversarial behavior, making those whose success was recognized feel uncomfortable and alienating those whose success was not recognized. See References 7, 13, 14, and 15 for more information on the need for and problems with recognition programs and awards.

Typical communication vehicles include periodic employee information meetings and newsletters.

Soliciting Input. As suggested earlier, involving representatives from all functions and levels of the organization provides realistic input to the management representative and the implementation team. Once the quality management system is established, if the organization's culture permits it, the internal audits (PARAGRAPH 8.2.2) can be instituted as a collaborative activity, soliciting input from all levels of the organization, with no secrets, no attribution, and no fear of reprisal.

It is also suggested that any process improvement ideas (both for eliminating problems and improving performance) be a regular agenda item for team and department meetings and communication. If the first-level manager does not have the authority or resources to address the suggestion, it is escalated to the next level of management, and so on. By giving the management representative visibility into improvement activities at all levels of the organization, the value and effectiveness of the quality management system can be more accurately assessed. If the organization is small enough, the management representative or process oversight committee can be copied on the individual reports. For larger organizations, a special roll-up on process improvement may be requested periodically.

PARAGRAPH 5.6 *Management Review*

Management review is top management's most visible ongoing commitment. Management review occurs at planned intervals, and its purpose is to ensure the "continuing suitability, adequacy, and effectiveness." The stated purpose contains three elements:

- Effective is the extent to which planned activities are realized and planned results achieved.[16]
- Suitability is fitness or appropriateness for a purpose, occasion, person's character, and so forth.[12]
- Adequacy is commensurate with fitness; sufficient, satisfactory.[17,*]

Information consistent with the purpose of management review comes in, and decisions necessary to meet the stated purpose come out; records are kept.

PARAGRAPH 5.6.2 defines the inputs, most of which are outputs from activities described in other paragraphs of ISO 9001; PARAGRAPH 5.6.3 describes the outputs. Exhibit 5-6 summarizes the sources of the inputs and the outputs.

---

* Identified in Reference 12 as the standard used by the authors of the ISO standards.

Exhibit 5-6. Management review inputs and outputs.

	5.6.2—Review input	From Paragraphs		5.6.3—Review output
a)	Internal audit results	8.2.2		Decisions and actions
b)	Customer feedback	7.2.3, 8.2.1, and 8.5.2 *a*		related to a) Improving the
c)	Process performance	8.2.3 and 5.5.2 *b*		effectiveness of the quality man-
	Product conformity	8.2.4		agement system
d)	Status of corrective actions	8.5.2		and its processes b) Product improve-
	Status of preventive actions	8.5.3	→	ments related to customer
e)	Follow-up actions from previous management reviews			requirements c) Resource needs
f)	Changes that could affect the quality management system			
g)	Recommendations for improvement	5.5.2 *b*		

Implementation Considerations

In evaluating effectiveness, top management can look at facts supplied by various measurements, audit results, and reports on customer feedback, process performance, product defects, and progress on closing corrective and preventive actions. The questions management considers are: Are we meeting our objectives? Are we following the processes we have established?

When the factual answers to these questions indicate that the outcome of a process is not meeting its objectives, the process and all of its inputs are examined to isolate potential causes of the problem. This examination leads to a number of further questions:

- Are the objectives achievable?
- Are adequate resources provided, including trained personnel?
- Is the process correct and complete?

What is required by ISO 9001:2000 is that management not ignore problems in the hope that they will either go away or escape notice. Management may choose to accept reduced performance, but it will be a fact-based decision.

The management representative, in his or her capacity as the customer care manager, is typically responsible for gathering, synthesizing, and providing the required inputs to top management at each regularly scheduled (e.g., monthly, bimonthly, quarterly) management meeting. The minutes from the meeting capture at least decisions, conclusions, and action items. Open action items (PARAGRAPH 5.6.2 o) from previous meetings are reviewed at the beginning of each meeting until they are resolved. This process prevents management from subscribing to principles such as "Don't ask, don't tell," "What I don't know can't hurt me," and "If I ignore it long enough, it will go away."

PARAGRAPH 5.6.2 *f* relates directly to top management's responsibility to ensure the integrity of the quality management system "when changes to the quality management system are planned and implemented" (PARAGRAPH 5.4.2). In many organizations, top management initiates the changes that have the most significant effect on the quality management system (e.g., reorganizations, facilities changes, mergers, and acquisitions). Because ISO 9001 does not specify that these be future changes, top management's decisions and actions to address the effect of these changes can be made concurrent with the public announcement of the change. As discussed in conjunction with PARAGRAPH 5.4.2, the critical consideration is that top management ensure that the effect of changes is determined and addressed as soon as is appropriate.

Process improvement may be unrelated to corrective or preventive action, and it may originate at lower levels of the organization and be entirely within the span of control of lower level management. For example, a product line manager may have the authority to establish a process under which hardware and software engineers assigned to work on products in the product line participate in joint requirements development meetings with marketing and customers. The motivation could be to shorten a requirements elicitation process that already functions effectively. Although there is no requirement that these changes be reported to top management, visibility into these positive improvements, solicited as part of internal communication (see the discussion of PARAGRAPH 5.5.3), allows top management to determine with greater confidence the continuing suitability and adequacy of the quality management system as reflected in its vitality.

It is also possible for top management to consider whether effective processes are suitable and adequate. Suitability and adequacy are opportunities for top management to look for instances in which the quality management system creates obstacles that people routinely accept and overcome. These obstacles may create inefficiencies or put growth and the organization's future at risk. In considering suitability and adequacy for effective processes, top management brings to bear expert input and its own experience and knowledge of current best practice. This extended consideration is frequently a subject of strategic planning.

ISO 9001:2000 FOR SOFTWARE AND SYSTEMS PROVIDERS

References

1. Juran, Joseph M., *Juran on Planning for Quality*, The Free Press, New York, 1988.
2. Deming, W.E., *Out of the Crisis*, Massachusetts Institute of Technology Center for Advanced Engineering Study, 1986.
3. Crosby, Philip B., *Quality Is Free*, McGraw-Hill, New York, 1979.
4. Humphrey, Watts S., *Managing the Software Process*, Addison-Wesley, New York, 1990, p. 19.
5. The Standish Group, *Chaos*, 1995, www.standishgroup.com.
6. Peters, Thomas J. and Waterman, Robert H., *In Search of Excellence*, Harper & Row, New York, 1982, p. 11.
7. Humphrey, Watts S., *Managing Technical People*, Addison-Wesley, New York, 1997, p. 9.
8. Stevens, Tim, Dr. Deming: 'Management today does not know what its job is', *Industry Week*, 243(2), 20, January 17, 1994.
9. International Organization for Standardization, *ISO 9000:2000, Quality Management Systems—Fundamentals and Vocabulary*, Geneva, 2000, PARAGRAPH 2.11.
10. Mager, Robert F., *Preparing Instructional Objectives*, Fearon-Pittman Publishers, Belmont, CA, 1972, p. 23.
11. Carson, Paula Phillips and Carson, Kerry D., Deming versus traditional management theorists on goal setting: can both be right?, *Business Horizons*, 36(5), 79, September–October 1993.
12. International Organization for Standardization, *Guidance on the Terminology Used in ISO 9001:2000 and ISO 9004:2000*, Document ISO/TC 176/SC 2/N 526R, May 2001, International Organization for Standardization, Geneva, www.iso.ch.
13. Daniels, Aubrey C., *Bringing out the Best in People*, McGraw-Hill, New York, 2000, pp. 150–164.
14. Harrington, H. James, *Business Process Improvement*, McGraw-Hill/ASQ Quality Press, New York, 1991, p. 250.
15. Scholtes, Peter, *The Leader's Handbook*, McGraw-Hill, New York, 1998, pp. 37–39.
16. ISO 9000:2000.
17. Pearsall, Judy, Ed., *The Concise Oxford Dictionary*, 10th ed., Oxford University Press, New York, 1999.

Chapter 6

PARAGRAPH 6

Resource Management

PARAGRAPH 6 is brief. Its four parts provide requirements related to all types of resources (human resources and infrastructure) and to the work environment.

PARAGRAPH 6.1 *Provision of Resources*

PARAGRAPH 6.1 requires the organization determine and provide the resources it needs to satisfy its customers by meeting agreed-on commitments (6.1 *b*) and to implement, maintain, and continually improve the quality management system: the framework of policies, procedures, plans, and standards that defines the way the organization conducts business (6.1 *a*).

The need for resources is determined by the commitments the organization makes and by the methods it chooses to employ in meeting those commitments.

PARAGRAPHS 6.2, 6.3, and 6.4 define requirements related to three categories of resources: people, infrastructure, and work environment.

PARAGRAPH 6.2 *Human Resources*

Because people are part of all organizations, ISO 9001:2000 not only specifies requirements for human resources but also provides detail on steps the organization needs to take in providing human resources.

PARAGRAPH 6.2.1 states that any personnel whose work affects the quality of the organization's products are required to be competent to perform their assigned tasks. Competence, the "demonstrated ability to apply knowledge and skills,"[1] is based on education, training, skills, and experience.

PARAGRAPH 6.2.2 defines five activities the organization carries out to support the provision of competent personnel.

First, the organization determines what competence is necessary for a particular task or responsibility (PARAGRAPH 6.2.2 *a*).

Then, according to PARAGRAPH 6.2.2 *b*, the organization provides training or takes other action to meet these needs. Other action presumably refers to activities like computer-based training, interactive Web-based seminars (Webinars), and mentoring, as alternatives to training delivered in a traditional classroom and instructor format.

Between item (a), determining necessary competencies, and item (b), providing training, the steps required to define these needs are apparently to be inferred. The missing steps are relatively straightforward, and are generally called a training needs analysis:

- Specific individuals are designated to perform specific tasks
- The current competencies of the specified individuals are determined
- Those current competencies are compared with the competencies required by the designated tasks
- Any missing competencies are translated into the needs that are to be satisfied by training or by some other action.

The remaining three paragraphs of PARAGRAPH 6.2.2 describe a variety of requirements:

- PARAGRAPH 6.2.2 *c* requires that the organization evaluate effectiveness of the training or other actions. Although they are closely related, the purpose of this paragraph is to evaluate the effectiveness of knowledge transfer and skills acquisition activities, not the competence of personnel. Determining employee competence is a management function, one of the activities omitted between item (a) and item (b). The internal audits (PARAGRAPH 8.2.2) also follow up on satisfaction and trace problems related to skills deficiencies to determine whether required training was received.
- PARAGRAPH 6.2.2 *d* requires that personnel are aware of the relationships between their activities and the achievement of the appropriate quality objectives. The relationship is defined in terms of relevance and importance. *Relevance* translates into personnel who are aware of which quality objectives apply to their activities, the objectives that are satisfied through their efforts. *Importance* translates into personnel who are aware of the degree of impact their work has on satisfying the relevant objectives. This awareness, which is typically part of the training curriculum, is one outcome of the communication required for quality objectives (PARAGRAPH 5.4.1) and for responsibility and authority (PARAGRAPH 5.5.1).
- PARAGRAPH 6.2.2 *e* requires that the organization maintain appropriate records of education, training, skills, and experience. Records related to education, training, skills, and experience provide evidence that

Exhibit 6-1. Project staffing projections.

	Quarter			
Job Classification	1	2	3	4
3801—Associate engineer			2	2
3802—Engineer			3	7	7
3803—Senior engineer	2	2	3	3
5401—Product architect				
5402—Senior product architect	2	2	.5	.25

identified needs are satisfied. *Appropriate* requires that the organization determine what records are kept (e.g., résumés, test scores, student evaluations, class lists, and copies of certificates and diplomas).

PARAGRAPH *6.2.2 a: Implementation Considerations for Determining Necessary Competence*

It is the responsibility of the organization to define required competency, based on the implemented processes, associated technologies, and any external requirements (e.g., licensing, certification, accreditation, etc.). This responsibility typically belongs to management in the affected area. Organizations determine and document required competency in job descriptions in terms of education and experience (e.g., MS CS and 12 years experience programming) and demonstrated skills (e.g., proven ability to manage complex projects), which are verified through reference checks. Competency requirements can appear in project plans—both in terms of specific skills (e.g., experience in both Assembler and Pascal programming) and in terms of a set of well-defined job classifications, which detail required competencies. For example, Exhibit 6-1 represents a staffing projection from a project plan.

Organizations also define competency requirements in annual performance reviews (typically under the heading "professional development") in terms of objectives to acquire new skills and complete any associated training. In organizations involved in rapidly changing technologies or markets, new skills, associated training needs, and sources of training are frequently determined in real time—often by expert individual contributors who initiate requests through management.

PARAGRAPH *6.2.2 b: Implementation Considerations for Satisfying Needs*

As used by the authors of ISO 9001, training is defined as the act or process of providing or receiving instruction in or for a particular skill, profession, occupation, and so forth.[2] *Training and other actions* goes beyond instruction to encompass any planned activity that systematically transfers

Exhibit 6-2. In our experience: the hidden cost of training.

Management asserted that it only hired professionals so no training was required. During the gap assessment, it was discovered that senior designers spend more than half of their time at the beginning of each project teaching new engineers about the product's architecture, standards, and application domain. As a result, designs are late and development of components frequently starts before the high-level design is complete. The inevitable result is cost overruns, schedule slippages, wasted time, and defective systems.

An investment of resources in a combination of documentation and training resulted in a significant net savings to the organization. How significant the savings were cannot be determined because there is no way to measure business lost because of the organizations' reputation as an innovator that could not deliver.

---

knowledge as part of skills acquisition. Classroom training, seminars, and workshops are all forms of training, whether they are offered on site, at the organization's premises, or through a third party (e.g., a professional society or a university). Self-study and correspondence programs (computer-based or otherwise) are examples of other actions taken to satisfy training needs.

Mentoring is another action that can be taken to satisfy training needs. Mentoring is most successful when a qualified mentor is formally assigned to develop another employee's competence in a specific area: time is set aside and specific skills are identified by management. Although mentoring is one of the most effective methods of providing focused, just-in-time training, a common failure is related to the amount of the mentor's time that is allocated and available. The mentor is typically an experienced senior individual contributor, a top performer, who is also responsible for project deliverables. Unexpected problems or delays put mentoring responsibilities in conflict with the on-time completion of a project. A second cause of failure in mentoring is related to the choice of a mentor. Beyond demonstrated proficiency in the subject matter, a successful mentor also has the communication skills and patience required to work with individuals who are less skilled or knowledgeable.

Mentoring can be facilitated by providing a checklist of topics or skills to be covered. The mentor initials or checks off the items as they are completed to the mentor's satisfaction. The completed checklist becomes the record (PARAGRAPH 6.2.2 e), which is turned over to the manager who files it or disposes of it, as appropriate (see Exhibit 6-2).

By restricting training and other actions to those activities that are planned and that have specific skills and acquisition and knowledge transfer as defined objectives, concerns can be allayed that activities such as brown-bag lunches, design and code reviews, and casual, one-on-one questions will require a record.

If an action is necessary for developing an employee's competence in areas related to work that affects product quality, a record is not only required, it is useful—so management, within the retention period, can confirm that the skills acquisition took place.*

PARAGRAPH 6.2.2 c: Implementation Considerations for Evaluating Effectiveness

ISO 9001 provides no measure for the effectiveness of knowledge transfer and skills acquisition. It is the responsibility of the organization to determine appropriate criteria and methods for evaluating effectiveness based on the nature of the content. In some cases, newly acquired skills may be immediately measurable for each participant. For example, in a course of study on the use of a tool or method the organization can test participants' newly acquired skills with validated instruments[3],** drawn from the organization's experience. In other cases, there may not be an immediate, meaningful way to predict the relationship between the knowledge transferred and the skills employed in assigned tasks. For example, in courses of study addressing subjects like teamwork and creative design, the organization may choose to validate the transfer of knowledge through student evaluations and leave the assessment of the effectiveness of skills acquisition to management.[4]

A number of methods are available for evaluating the effectiveness of the knowledge transfer and skills acquisition activities. These evaluation methods include course-end student evaluations, postcourse follow-up with students and with managers who sent students to determine ongoing satisfaction, and formal evaluation of acquired skills through a graded final exercise or examination. To obtain accurate results, it is recommended that evaluations be performed at different stages of the process (e.g., as described in Kirkpatrick's four levels:[5] reaction—student comment sheets; knowledge—exit test; skills—observation, tests after weeks or months on the job; organizational—after months or years, surveys, financial measures). As the experts note, as time passes and other forces exert their influences, it becomes increasingly difficult to credit results to training.

Because accurate validation requires data, it is recommended that the organization start with simple, qualitative measures like immediate participant and near-term management surveys.

---

* Because failure to provide remedial training or training necessary for advancement can be part of the basis for wrongful termination or discrimination lawsuits, human resources and the legal departments generally specify the retention time for training records.
** Validated instruments are "tests" in any form that have a proven statistical correlation with successful posttraining (e.g., on the job) success. In many industries, rapid changes in technology and content of training and variations in the backgrounds of and expectations for participants make establishing a statistical correlation impractical. For information on creating test instruments see Reference 3.

Maintaining records (PARAGRAPH 6.2.2 e) of evaluations of training effectiveness can provide valuable information for other personnel seeking proven sources of effective training—particularly when outside training sources are under consideration.

PARAGRAPH 6.2.2 d: Implementation Considerations for Awareness of Quality Objectives

To be effective, the knowledge transfer and skills-building activities enable personnel to apply the skills and knowledge to the processes defined in the organization. Linking skills-related knowledge with information about the relationship between activities and quality objectives encourages personnel to apply the skills. Creating this linkage has two positive side effects.* First, it requires that there be a linkage. Constructing training based on objectives sometimes leads the organization to reevaluate the relevance and suitability of the activity. In addition, when personnel are aware of why they are doing something—of management's expectations—they are uniquely positioned to identify and prevent problems through escalation and to suggest process improvements. This is typically effective in collaborative organizations, built on respect. In some cultures, providing personnel with insight into objectives encourages them to ask questions that management is unprepared or unwilling to answer.

PARAGRAPH 6.2.2 e: Implementation Considerations for Training Records

Information about education, training, skills, and experience attained before employment is typically recorded in the employee's employment application, résumé, or curriculum vitae, which is retained in the employee's file.

During employment, skills acquisition is typically from organization-sponsored education and training. It is recommended that the system of records include a provision for records from training completed by employees on their own initiative and at their own expense, especially when the training may be applicable to a future job in a different career.

Because ISO 9001 does not specify a medium or location for these records, they can be electronic forms stored in central, organizationwide repositories, in department files, and in training department databases. A training record can be for a single individual or it can be in the form of class lists. Employees can update their own records directly, or the responsibility can fall to the employee's immediate manager or mentor, with input from the employee. Records for a single employee may be in multiple loca-

---

* The mushroom, which grows well in relative darkness, nourished by waste products, represents the antithesis of the informed, involved employee.

Exhibit 6-3. In our experience: hidden assets.

Management assumed that the training department kept records of all employees' training. During the implementation planning process, team members uncovered a number of interesting details:

- The training department keeps lists of all employees enrolled in courses offered by the training department, whether at the company training center or a remote site, and whether provided by staff or by outside instructors. The lists are checked religiously to ensure that no one attends who is not on the list (or who is not replacing someone on the list). The purpose of checking the lists is to ensure that all departments pay their fair share of course costs. Last-minute no-shows are charged because they keep someone else from filling a seat, so there is no requirement that instructors mark those who are on the list and who are not in attendance.
- Although the training department maintains a large library of self-study courses, which are part of the training programs for new employees and for employees changing jobs, no associated records are kept.
- The company has a program for reimbursing education costs paid by employees. Although the request and reimbursement forms are kept for tax purposes, they also serve as training records.
- No record is kept of courses employees take on their own but that are not eligible for reimbursement because they are not related to the employee's current job.
- No records are kept for mentoring, which is a significant part of the employees first months, or for the many self-study courses that are available through the training department.

tions and formats, depending on the source of information. As noted in Paragraph 4.2.4 *Control of records*, since ISO 9001 does not specify any requirements for how accessible records should be, it is the organization's responsibility to establish storage and retrieval mechanisms for training records that protect privacy and make necessary information available in a manner consistent with any uses defined for those records. Exhibit 6-3 describes some of the ways in which organizations fail to meet requirements for training records.

An organization can leverage the requirement to maintain appropriate records of education, training, skills, and experience as an opportunity to build a skills database. In any but the smallest organizations, such a database can support management's efforts to deploy human resources in an efficient and effective manner. It also allows human resources to match openings with current employees, potentially improving employee retention and protecting the organization's investment in the employee's professional development.

Paragraph 6.3 *Infrastructure*

ISO 9001:2000 Paragraph 6.3 *Infrastructure* requires that the organization determine, provide, and maintain the infrastructure needed to achieve conformity to product requirements. PARAGRAPH 6.3 states that infrastructure includes:

- Buildings, workspace and facilities
- Process equipment, both hardware and software
- Supporting services

The list of categories in PARAGRAPH 6.3 is prefaced by *as applicable*, so there is no requirement that an organization provide the infrastructure listed, unless it does so as part of its business processes. It is the responsibility of the organization to determine the infrastructure it provides and maintains based on the requirements of its defined policies, processes, and procedures.

Implementation Considerations. Buildings, workspace, and facilities can include cubicles and offices, laboratories, and specialized physical environments (e.g., clean rooms) to allow the effective operation of process equipment. A frequently voiced misinterpretation is that if an organization allows or requires employees to work at home, it is required to provide the employees with everything they need, including a home. Although subsidized housing may be part of the commitment an organization makes to employees, it does not fall within the scope of infrastructure needed to achieve product conformity. Support for telecommuting typically includes providing and maintaining a network infrastructure that supports remote access to the extent required by the organization's defined processes.

Process equipment includes all of the hardware and software tools associated with product development. Hardware typically includes computers, simulators, and test beds. The software includes tools for analysis, modeling, prototyping, planning, reporting, design, coding, configuration management, test, creating and publishing documentation and drawings, and bug reporting and tracking.

For providers of systems that include hardware and software, process equipment includes prototype and production hardware product for use in software development and testing. The availability of product becomes a problem when management is required to choose between filling a customer order (revenue) or providing product for development or testing purposes (expense).

Supporting services are varied and may be provided by other parts of the organization (e.g., configuration management, test development, and Intranet or video-conferencing installation and maintenance) or by third parties (e.g., contractors for test or product development and services for facilities maintenance and for off-site storage or escrow of source code).

PARAGRAPH 6.4 *Work Environment*

PARAGRAPH 6.4 *Work environment* contains a single sentence that requires the organization to determine and manage the work environment needed to achieve conformity to product requirements.

The definition of work environment in ISO 9000:2000 states:

> *3.3.4*
> *work environment*
> *set of conditions under which work is performed*
> *NOTE Conditions include physical, social, psychological and environmental factors (such as temperature, recognition schemes, ergonomics and atmospheric composition).*

However, as stated in PARAGRAPH 0.4, ISO 9001

> *does not include requirements specific to other management systems, such as those particular to environmental management, occupational health and safety management, financial management or risk management.*

Appropriate requirements for these aspects of the organization's work environment are supplied by laws, regulations, cultural norms, and other national and international standards, such as ISO 14001:1996, *Environmental Management Systems*, with which it is the responsibility of the organization to identify and comply. It is instructive to follow the evolution of requirements for working environment as ISO 9001:2000 progressed through its various public drafts. This progression is summarized in Exhibit 6-4. These other requirements can be identified as part of the organization's quality management system, monitored by the internal audits and included in management review. They are not areas that registrars' auditors investigate for reasons of specialization and liability.

Implementation Considerations. PARAGRAPH 6.3 requires that the organization determine, provide, and maintain an infrastructure that is consistent with the processes it implements and the objectives it sets for its employees. PARAGRAPH 6.4 requires that the organization determine and manage a work environment in which the trained personnel can effectively use the elements of the infrastructure. For example, in many cases, teams succeed because the individuals are colocated and members have experience working with each other. As the organization grows, management is responsible for ensuring that the work environment and infrastructure continue to be compatible and support the organization's personnel in following the defined procedures to produce product that conforms to requirements.

Exhibit 6-4. The evolution of ISO 9001:2000.

Date	Document	Related content
7/1998	CD1 (Committee Draft 1)	*0.3 Compatibility with other management system disciplines* This International Standard does not address or include requirements for … *6.3.3 Work environment* The organization shall define and implement those human and physical factors of the work environment needed to achieve conformity of product and/or service.
4/1999	CD2 (Committee Draft 2)	*0.3 Compatibility with other management systems* This International Standard does not address or include requirements for … *6.5 Work environment* The organization shall define and implement those human and physical factors of the work environment needed to achieve conformity of product and/or service. This shall include: a) health and safety conditions;b) work methods; c) work ethics;d) ambient working conditions.
12/1999	DIS (Draft International Standard)	*0.4 Compatibility with other management systems* This International Standard does not include requirements specific to … *6.4 Work environment* The organization shall identify and manage the human and physical factors of the work environment needed to achieve conformity of product.
9/2000	FDIS (Final Draft International Standard)	*0.4 Compatibility with other management systems* This International Standard does not include requirements specific to … *6.4 Work environment* The organization shall determine and manage the work environment needed to achieve conformity to product requirements.

References

1. ISO 9000:2000, PARAGRAPH 3.9.12.
2. International Organization for Standardization, *Guidance on the Terminology used in ISO 9001:2000 and ISO 9004:2000*, Document ISO/TC 176/SC 2/N 526R, International Organization for Standardization, Geneva, May 2001, www.iso.ch.
3. Phillips, Jack J., *Handbook of Training Evaluation and Measurement Methods*, 3rd ed., Butterworth-Heinemann, Woburn, 1997.
4. Cronbach, Lee J., *Educational Psychology*, 2nd ed., Harcourt, Brace & World, New York, 1963, chap. 16.
5. Kirkpatrick, Donald L., *Evaluating Training Programs: The Four Levels*, 2nd ed., Berrett-Koehler Publishers, San Francisco, 1998.

Chapter 7
PARAGRAPH 7
Product Realization

The unconventional term "product realization" completes the evolution of ISO 9001 into a framework of requirements that is more accessible to organizations that provide software and services, to organizations that serve exclusively internal customers (e.g., Management Information Systems and Information Technology departments), and to organizations that provide commodity or off-the-shelf products. Product realization encompasses processes that take a product or service from concept and requirements, to design and development, and to manufacturing, delivery, and postinstallation support.

PARAGRAPH 7 is presented in six paragraphs that define requirements for processes that are common to all product and engineering life cycles. Four of the paragraphs address primary processes, which transform concept into delivered product or service:

- 7.1 Planning of product realization
- 7.2 Customer-related processes
- 7.3 Design and development
- 7.5 Production and service provision.

In spite of the title, parts of PARAGRAPH 7.5 apply to design and development as well as to production (manufacturing) and service provision (installation, support, etc.). As portrayed in Exhibit 1-4, the three parts of PARAGRAPH 7.5 that apply to design and development as well as to production and service provision are:

- 7.5.3 Identification and traceability
- 7.5.4 Customer property
- 7.5.5 Preservation of product.

The remaining two paragraphs in PARAGRAPH 7 address activities that support all phases of the product life cycle:

- 7.4 Purchasing
- 7.6 Control of monitoring and measuring devices

Compliance with ISO 9001 does not require that all of the primary and supporting processes be part of an organization's business model or within the scope of an ISO registration. As noted earlier, in conjunction with PARAGRAPH 4.2.2 *Quality manual*, scope and exclusions are recorded in the quality manual and are allowed only for elements of PARAGRAPH 7. Scope and exclusions are discussed in great detail in this volume in Chapter 1 and Appendix B.

With the exception of PARAGRAPH 7.4 *Purchasing*, the paragraphs in PARAGRAPH 7 are discussed below in the order in which they appear in the standard.

PARAGRAPH 7.1 *Planning of Product Realization*

PARAGRAPH 7.1 requires that the organization plan and develop the processes needed for product realization: for customer-related processes (PARAGRAPH 7.2), for design and development (PARAGRAPH 7.3), for purchasing (PARAGRAPH 7.4), for production and service provision (PARAGRAPH 7.5), and for control of monitoring and measuring devices (PARAGRAPH 7.6). *Plan* is used in this context as "the formulation or organized method by which something is to be done." A schedule is only part of a plan.

PARAGRAPH 7.1 goes on to list aspects of planning to which its requirements pertain:

> *In planning product realization, the organization shall determine the following, as appropriate:*
>
> *a) Quality objectives and requirements for the product;*
>
> *b) The need to establish processes, documents, and provide resources specific to the product;*
>
> *c) Required verification, validation, monitoring, inspection and test activities specific to the product and the criteria for product acceptance;*
>
> *d) Records needed to provide evidence that the realization processes and resulting product meet requirements.*

Beyond the first two sentences, the theme of PARAGRAPH 7.1 becomes specific to the product. PARAGRAPH 7.1 requires the organization to determine and implement any changes or additions necessary to tailor the organization's standard processes and quality objectives (as documented in the quality management system) for a specific product, project, or contract (see Exhibit 7-1).

Related Paragraphs

Detailed requirements for planning design and development activities are found in PARAGRAPH 7.3.1 *Design and development planning*.

Requirements for the planning and content of the processes for production and service provision are identified in PARAGRAPH 7.5.1 *Control of*

Exhibit 7-1. Tailoring the organization's standard processes.

production and service provision. Requirements associated with developing the processes for production and service provision are found in PARAGRAPH 7.5.2 *Validation of processes for production and service provision.*

Implementation Considerations

Whether any product-specific change or amendment is required depends on the nature of the product (e.g., how close it is to a "standard" product) and on the nature of the standard processes (e.g., how flexible and comprehensive they are).[1,*]

Requirements for the product-specific elements of planning in PARAGRAPH 7.1 can be addressed in a product development plan by including references or definitions of

- Applicable "standard" procedures, tools, and facilities
- Any new procedures, tools, and facilities to be employed in executing the plan, including any associated skills acquisition (e.g., [re]training or mentoring) that addresses the requirements to plan for changes to the quality system as specified in PARAGRAPH 5.4.2 *b.* Skills acquisition is a cost and, frequently, a risk that can be effectively managed if it is considered in proposals and included in plans.

PARAGRAPH 7.2 *Customer-Related Processes*

PARAGRAPH 7.2 specifies requirements for processes typically identified with requirements engineering:[2,3]

- Determination and review of product-related requirements (PARAGRAPHS 7.2.1 and 7.2.2)
- Management of changes to product-related requirements (PARAGRAPH 7.2.2)
- Conduct of all customer communication, including the provision of feed back on complaints (PARAGRAPH 7.2.3).

---

* Similar to the requirements in the Integrated Software Management Key Process Area of the Capability Maturity Model for Software.[1]

PARAGRAPH *7.2.1* Determination of Requirements Related to the Product

PARAGRAPH 7.2.1 contains requirements for gathering product-related requirements of all types from all sources:

- From the customer
- From prior knowledge
- From related statutes, codes, and regulations
- From the organization

ISO 9000:2000 defines a requirement as a need or expectation that is stated, generally implied, or obligatory.

Implementation Considerations. Requirements engineering typically includes five activities and involves all of the identified stakeholders—internal and external. In the context of requirements engineering:

- A stakeholder is any group that is responsible for supplying or satisfying the set of requirements related to the product (e.g., the customer, technical support, hardware engineering, software engineering, test, publications). For off-the-shelf products, the customer is typically a defined marketplace that can be represented by marketing, sales, an industry or trade association, or an advisory group of customers. In some industries, customers hire and are represented by consultants.
- A product may be a collection of the organization's products. As PARAGRAPH 7.2.2 *a* points out, the product is more than the hardware and software. It includes any requirements for delivery (e.g., schedule and cost) and for postdelivery support (e.g., operational support, maintenance, and repair).
- Delivery potentially includes a host of other activities; for example,
  - Shipping
  - Secure handling
  - Software transmittal
  - Installation, including facilities preparation and conversion of existing data
- Postdelivery activities may include
  - Operational support—help desk or training
  - Product support—maintenance (e.g., updates), problem correction, enhancement requests

Types of Requirements. Because nearly one third of requirements errors are caused by omissions,[4] the organization can prevent or mitigate a significant number of problems with checklists for the types of requirements

Exhibit 7-2. Types of requirements.

Program		Technical	
Process	For example, test for 48 hours under maximum load; monthly meetings to review progress	Functional	By user, by mode of operation
Legal	Regulations, codes, standards	Exception handling	By user, by mode of operation
Schedule	For example, market window	Performance	Quantitative information
Budget		Design constraint	For example, existing environment
		Interface	With user (e.g., Graphical User Interface standards) With existing or proposed external components and other internal components
		Communications System security and access Backup and recovery	Connectivity, access
		Implementation	For example, conversion, installation, hardware acquisition
		Information	Information and examples that may be useful, but that the source does not consider as a requirement

based on previous experience (e.g., PARAGRAPH 7.2.2 *b*'s "prior knowledge"). A typical list might be as listed in Exhibit 7-2.[5,*]

Requirements and Solutions. Whether the organization is considering development of a new product or enhancement of an existing product, the challenge it faces is separating requirements definitions from technical solutions. The requirements engineering process diligently separates requirements from solutions, whether those solutions are unnecessary, counterproductive design constraints inadvertently imposed by the customer, or assumptions made by internal stakeholders based on experience

* This list is based on a number of sources. Note that Reference 5 is a recommended practice and is currently under consideration for revision or reissue as a standard.

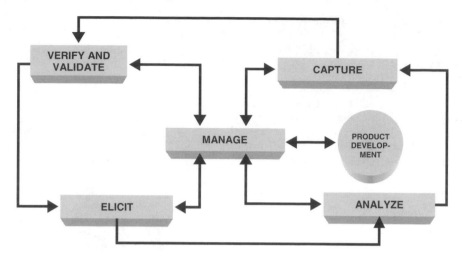

Exhibit 7-3. Requirements engineering.

(e.g., "We've always done it that way."). No information is discarded (it might be the right solution), but the organization maintains a rigid distinction between requirement and solution.

The Five Activities of Requirements Engineering. The five activities of Requirements Engineering are illustrated in Exhibit 7-3.

Elicit begins the cycle. Once the stakeholders are identified, depending on the organization, the industry, and the sophistication of the customer, successful elicitation requires varying degrees of initiation on the part of the organization and includes such techniques as:[6,7,*]

- Receipt of a Request for a Proposal from a customer
- Interviews
- Focus groups
- Questionnaires or surveys
- Qualify function deployment
- Brainstorming sessions
- Role play
- Reviews of incident reports or enhancement requests
- Joint authorship combined with brainstorming
- Benchmark: compare against similar or competing systems
- Prototype to elicit further requirements
  - Throw-away: When critical features or architecture not well understood
  - Evolutionary: To refine and to understand noncritical features.

* In Reference 7, PA 06 and PA 02 are of particular interest.

Analyze is a systematic evaluation of the elicited needs against a set of predefined criteria. The goal of the analysis is to ensure that the internal stakeholders have the information they require to proceed with the next step in the process (e.g., design and development).

Because incorrect facts and ambiguity account for more than half of requirements-related errors,[4] an effective analysis process is based on defined criteria and recognizes that personnel require specialized competency to review, write, and rewrite requirements (PARAGRAPH 6.2.2). The criteria listed in Exhibit 7-4 represent a selection of the evaluation criteria organizations typically apply to elicited needs and requirements.

As noted in Exhibit 7-4 by the ✔s, some criteria apply to individual requirements or needs (e.g., problems reports, change proposals, and enhancement requests), others apply primarily to sets of requirements (e.g., in a Request for a Proposal or proposed for inclusion in a release). The ✔s in parentheses indicate criteria that are primarily intended for a set of requirements but that may apply to an individual requirement.

There is no requirement that elicitation, analysis, and design be separate activities. In following a prototyping life cycle for a Graphical User Interface, the engineers and customers sit side by side and iterate as many times as necessary a process of discovering and analyzing requirements and developing and reviewing a working design.

Capture requires that the organization preserve the inputs and the results of the internal analysis and discussion in forms that can be:

- Verified with the stakeholders who have supplied requirements (e.g., "If the product meets these requirements, will you be satisfied?")
- Used as a basis for managing change
- Communicated to "downstream" processes that receive the requirements as inputs (e.g., design or test)

In some cases, the requirements may be captured in the organization's proposal or a revised Statement of Work produced by the customer. In other cases—for example, when requirements come from a number of sources or when the organization plays a large part in leading the customers to discover their requirements—the requirements may be captured in a tool that can automatically generate a document for customer review and approval and through which approved requirements can be accessed and manipulated by the project.[8,9]

Verify ensures that there is nothing missing and nothing extra. It is typically a series of reviews or inspections with stakeholders to gather feedback on the requirements as captured and to complete the process of determining needs. The result of the verification is a set of requirements that, at a point in time, the stakeholders agree are the requirements. Agreement on

Exhibit 7-4. Evaluation criteria.

Criteria	Individual	Set	Definition
Clear	✔		Stakeholders arrive at a single, consistent interpretation.
Testable, verifiable	✔		Testers and engineers agree they could devise a means to test whether the statement is properly implemented.
Design independent	✔		The requirement describes what, not how. It is stated in terms of a problem, not a solution. It describes function (e.g., provides access to account balance information) and not operation (e.g., the operator presses F7 to view account balance information).
Correct	✔		Accurate and complete as far as all stakeholders are concerned.
Traceable	✔		The requirement can be linked to a specific, legitimate origin.
Complete	✔	✔	All appropriate elements of identification are provided. Internal references are all resolved (e.g., if the requirement is for a printed report, somewhere else there is a requirement for a printer). Identification typically entails the following information. At least the first six items are available at the beginning of the analysis and are refined as the project progresses. The remainder are added at the appropriate time. • Enumeration (a numerical identifier) • Type (see Exhibit 7-2) • Necessity (e.g., essential desirable, optional) • Stability (risk of change, e.g., high, medium, low) • Source (document, paragraph, individual, organization) • Rationale (additional information, purpose, goal) • Allocation (where it will be implemented, e.g., hardware, software) • Parent (if the requirement is developed by decomposing another requirement) • Verification (method, documents) • Changes • Current status (e.g., to be defined, in review, scheduled for implementation, and in test) • Planned release (e.g., date or version)
Consistent	(✔)	✔	All conflicts between requirements have been resolved. There is no duplication or overlap.

Exhibit 7-4 (continued). Evaluation criteria.

Criteria	Individual	Set	Definition
Feasible	(✓)	✓	The implementers agree that it is possible to implement the requirement set within the known capabilities and limitations of the system and its environment—both technically and within costs and schedule constraints. Feasible is based on what is known about the requirements as stated. In some cases the next step in the life cycle may be to gather additional information or to build a prototype to demonstrate the feasibility of a solution.

the content and adequacy of subsets of requirements may be reached at different times, and revisions to requirements progress through essentially the same process. This verification process focuses on the content of the requirements—on ensuring that the requirements are defined. It is not necessarily associated with any delivery commitment on the part of the organization. This verification is also subject to the requirements of PARAGRAPH 7.2.2 *Review of requirements related to the product* for records of results and actions.

Manage serves as the administrator and gatekeeper for the various processes and as the gateway to the product development life cycle. As Van Buren notes,[2] changes in 1 percent to 2 percent of the baselined requirements indicate a healthy project. Too much change prevents progress and ensures start-and-stop waste. Too little change typically means either that communication of change requests has broken down (and will eventually resume with a large backlog of requests) or that no one cares about the product any more.

Scalability. Effective requirements processes are scaleable. The requirements or product change request that initiates a simple bug fix or minor modification early in a project requires significantly less processing than a change request late in the project or a change request that leads to a major enhancement. To be efficient—and to ensure the process is followed—it is critical that the time and effort spent on any one step be commensurate with the nature of the change request.

PARAGRAPH *7.2.2* Review of Requirements Related to the Product

PARAGRAPH 7.2.2 encompasses the review of the requirements from three perspectives, identified in three lettered paragraphs.

The first perspective, from PARAGRAPH 7.2.2 *a*, is addressed by the types of reviews described as verification activities for PARAGRAPH 7.2.1 under *The Five Activities of Requirements Engineering*. The result of these reviews is agreement that the requirements are defined.

The second perspective is in PARAGRAPH 7.2.2 *b*, which addresses the issue of resolving differences between the customer's requirements and the organization's commitments. For example, it is common for both parties to require that a proposal explicitly identify those areas in which the proposed solution does not meet requirements in the customer's request for a proposal (e.g., a compliance matrix). In PARAGRAPH 7.2.2 *b*, resolving the differences means ensuring that any differences are mutually acceptable and are not the result of inadvertent errors (e.g., typographical errors or omissions) or unnoticed changes. The larger the body of requirements listed in the proposed order or statement of work, the more likely it is that significant changes can slip by reviewers, resulting in an enforceable contract and a dissatisfied customer. When organizations deliver standard products, the contract becomes the agreement (e.g., by marketing or sales and engineering) as to the content of the product. In this environment, orders are for units of the standard product.

The third perspective is, perhaps, the most important. PARAGRAPH 7.2.2 *c* addresses the issue of organizational capability. The organization is required to ensure that it has or can develop the ability to meet its commitments. The two primary factors affecting this confidence are technological feasibility and access to adequate, competent resources. Determining technological feasibility may be accomplished by an engineering review, or it may require that the customer or organization fund a separate project that demonstrates feasibility through investigation or construction of a prototype. Determining resources requires that the organization complete some preliminary sizing and high-level planning and have specified resources already in-house or available for acquisition from established sources (e.g., subcontract, buy, or hire).

PARAGRAPH 7.2.2 goes on to provide three additional requirements related to requirements:

- Records are kept of the reviews.
- Where the customer provides no documented statement of requirements, the customer requirements shall be confirmed by the organization before acceptance.
- Requirements changes result in the amendment of relevant documents and the notification of relevant personnel; PARAGRAPH 4.2.3 requires that the organization determine the process for the review, approval, and issue of revised documents.

PARAGRAPH 7.2.2 concludes with a note that the authors of this volume consider absurd and misleading. It says:

In some situations, such as Internet sales, a formal review is impractical for each order. Instead the review can cover relevant product information such as catalogs or advertising material.

PARAGRAPH 4.2.3 already requires that the organization define controls necessary to ensure that this material is reviewed and approved for adequacy before issue (PARAGRAPH 4.2.3). In addition, PARAGRAPH 7.2.3 *Customer communication* requires that the organization determine and implement effective arrangements for communicating with customers in relation to product information. If Internet sales mean automated order processing with no human intervention, many of the current systems demonstrate that there is no reason to consider a review of Web page content as a replacement for reviewing individual orders before acceptance. In these systems, the review is formal; it is also automated. The systems either prevent the customer from ordering items that the organization cannot deliver or they include an automated postsubmission review (e.g., for availability of merchandise), which results in a confirmation or a referral to a customer service agent. The publicized failures of on-line retailers to meet delivery commitments are, in the experience of the authors of this volume, the result of inadequate or overly optimistic capacity planning and process management, not the result of inadequate reviews of orders.

Implementation Considerations. PARAGRAPH 7.2.2 *c*, which requires that the organization ensure it has the ability to meet defined product and process requirements before a commitment is made to the customer, is typically addressed by:

- Participation of all stakeholders (e.g., engineering, support, and manufacturing) in the proposal process
- Cross-functional teams at all stages of the life cycle
- Review and joint authorship (e.g., with marketing) of requirements documents
- Engineering and other internal stakeholder participation in defining product evolution (e.g., product road maps) and in the review and approval of changes to requirements (e.g., through a product management council or a change control committee or board)
- Definitions of the commitments field sales personnel are authorized to make (e.g., for standard products and services) and the conditions under which commitments require review before they are presented to the customer
- Implementation of requirements traceability and any associated tools
- Implementation of an engineering life cycle such as Joint Application Development, in which engineering and customer personnel work together to define and develop a product

In terms of records, each review meeting produces at least a list of action items. To the extent that the business environment requires it, these results may become part of a permanent record, or they may be discarded when all of the changes are made and all the relevant stakeholders agree to the final set of requirements. The record of this final approval may be a meeting report or a signed contract. On the basis of the organization's culture with respect to commitments, some organizations have found it beneficial to have high-level managers sign a paper approval form, visibly committing their organizations to the project.

The text above the note at the end of PARAGRAPH 7.2.2 contains requirements for ensuring that relevant documents are updated and relevant personnel notified when requirements change. The amended requirements documents, in whatever form, are reviewed and approved (PARAGRAPH 4.2.3) and serve as triggers for changes to engineering work products, subject to the requirements of PARAGRAPH 7.3.7 *Control of design and development changes*. Two other paragraphs contain related requirements that ensure that all affected stakeholders are notified:

- PARAGRAPH 7.3.1 requires that the organization ensure effective communication among the different groups involved in design and development (e.g., manufacturing is included as a reviewer and advisor in the design process).
- PARAGRAPH 7.3.3 *b* requires that design and development outputs provide appropriate information for purchasing, production, and service provision.

In the review process, proposed requirements changes are typically analyzed by representatives of all groups participating in the project for effect and feasibility. Approved changes are translated into revised plans and into changes in priorities and content.

Because of the demonstrated ability of requirements changes to overwhelm development resources, procedures and resources for the systematic analysis and incorporation of requirements changes are essential to the success of a project. Providing these resources is particularly challenging when the individuals competent to analyze proposed changes are already fully or overcommitted to executing the current plan.

PARAGRAPH 7.2.3 Customer Communication

PARAGRAPH 7.2.3 requires that the organization determine and implement effective arrangements for communicating with its customers. Three specific subjects are identified as:

- Product information
- Enquiries, contracts, or order handling, including amendments
- Customer feedback, including customer complaints

PARAGRAPH 7.2.3 focuses on communication that:

- Becomes the basis for decisions made by the customer
- Reflects commitments made by the organization

Mechanisms for conveying product information can range from catalogs and Web sites to lengthy, detailed proposals, tailored for a specific customer's needs.

Enquiries, contracts, or order handling refer to how the organization processes such items as:

- Requests for proposals, requests for information, or requests for quotes and telephone queries about catalog items (enquiries; typically a product marketing, sales, or sales support function)
- Contracts, from the point that they are received for approval to the point at which the last commitment is completed (e.g., contract administration and management), including communicating with the customer on progress
- Orders, which are essentially contracts. The organization agrees to provide the ordered products or services as specified in the terms and conditions (e.g., turnaround times).

Customer feedback ranges from reports of product nonconformities to complaints (see section on implementation considerations for PARAGRAPH 8.5.2 for a discussion of how this feedback is handled) to the results of customer-satisfaction surveys (PARAGRAPH 8.2.1).

The goal of effective customer communication is to ensure that the information is as accurate as possible and that customers are satisfied—not just to protect the organization from litigation. Disclaimers not withstanding, policies and processes establish responsibilities, authorities, and the organization's response when incorrect information is discovered by a customer or potential customer.

In all cases, it is recommended that the organization provide a response to each customer communication—even if it is just a postcard or an automated e-mail acknowledging receipt.

When communication is verbal and has the potential to be the basis for a customer's decision, it is critical that the communication be documented (e.g., logged and summarized or documented in a letter or e-mail) and that the communication include an explicit confirmation (PARAGRAPH 7.2.2) that the organization has understood the customer. The more complex the verbal communication, the more important it is that the organization document its understanding and request that the customer confirm the accuracy of the document. Customer communication encompasses situations in which the organization elicits customer requirements and assumes responsibility for documenting those requirements on behalf of the customer (PARAGRAPH 7.2.1

Determination of requirements related to the product and PARAGRAPH 7.2.2 *Review of requirements related to the product*).

PARAGRAPH 7.3 *Design and Development*

PARAGRAPH 7.3 contains the requirements for most of the activities carried out by all types of engineering organizations: systems, hardware, software, process, and so forth. ISO 9000:2000 defines design and development as the:

> *set of processes that transforms requirements into specified characteristics or into the specification of a product, process, or system.*

This definition applies both to hardware life cycles, in which drawings, procedures, bills-of-material, samples, fixtures, documentation, and so forth, are the engineering outputs turned over to manufacturing, and to software life cycles, in which a baseline of the final software product (e.g., source, executables, customer documentation, release notes) is turned over to software production (e.g., manufacturing), and to the design and development of enabling services (e.g., training, field service, and manufacturing), in which capacity planning tools, staffing models, training requirements and tools, documentation, and operational procedures and tools are turned over to the service organization.

PARAGRAPH 7.3.1 Design and Development Planning

ISO 9001:2000 does not specify either a level of detail for design and development planning or a particular format or form for the outputs of planning.

In relation to planning, PARAGRAPH 7.3.1 specifies that the organization ensure that cross-functional interfaces are established to guarantee that the different groups involved in design and development communicate with each other and have a clear understanding of who is responsible for what.

Level of Detail. PARAGRAPH 7.3.1 requires that the level of detail be adequate to allow the organization to control product design and development. A number of other paragraphs converge to supply the information an organization needs to determine whether it has an appropriate level of detail:

- PARAGRAPH 4.2.1 *d* requires that the plans be implemented and that controls be effective.
- PARAGRAPH 7.3.4 requires that the organization monitor progress against the plan propose necessary actions.
- PARAGRAPH 8.2.3 requires that the organization take appropriate corrective action when problems with plan compliance are identified.
- PARAGRAPH 8.5.2 defines the requirements for corrective action, including ensuring that the nonconformities do not reoccur.

Format and Form. PARAGRAPH 7.1 requires that planning output be provided in a form suitable to the organization's method of operation. The last two paragraphs of text in PARAGRAPH 7.3.1 identify criteria that can be used for determining suitability:

- Usability as a vehicle for communicating information and coordinating the activities of different groups. The classic example is the organization that uses a formal project management tool for publishing and maintaining the project schedule; but only the project managers have (expensive) licenses for and access to the tool, so the engineers rely on e-mail and notes from meetings to find out what they should be working on and what else is going on.
- Maintainability in a form that can be sustained with the resources and tools available. In many cases, complex plans evolve into simpler forms as the project progresses and people have to choose between planning and doing the required work.

Content. PARAGRAPH 7.3.1 lists a minimum set of elements that must be determined during planning:

- Stages of design and development
- Appropriate review, verification, and validation activities for each stage (further defined in PARAGRAPHs 7.3.4 [Review], 7.3.5 [Verification], and 7.3.6 [Validation])
- Responsibilities and authorities for design and development activities (implementing PARAGRAPH 5.5.1)

Implementation Considerations. There is no consistency in the way organizations refer to a planned pass through the stages of design and development. This top-level collection of planned activities may be referred to as a program or a project.

ISO 9001 uses "project," but only once, in a note at the end of PARAGRAPH 7.1. "Project" is defined in ISO 9000:2000 as:

> [a] unique process (3.4.1), consisting of a set of coordinated and controlled activities with start and finish dates, undertaken to achieve an objective conforming to specific requirements (3.1.2), including the constraints of time, cost and resources.

The two principle standards[10,11] associated with systems engineering, which set the framework for technical activities, also refer exclusively to projects.

As illustrated in Exhibit 7-5, a well-defined nomenclature facilitates consistent understanding of responsibility and authority and simplifies communication and coordination within and across projects.

The most often overlooked content element is the appropriate review, verification, and validation activities for each stage. Plans never omit the

Exhibit 7-5. In our experience: what's in a name?

At BCC Systems, software engineers are assigned to a release (which is what BCCS calls its top-level projects). Within a release, teams work on features that can be further decomposed into projects. This has been carried forward from the first versions of BCCS' product, which were developed by specialized teams working on discrete functions.

In some cases, however, a feature is developed independent of a release; for example, if the design and development cycle is lengthy or there is a need to investigate feasibility or test market need. This feature development is called a project (sometimes prefaced by "special"). Special projects have a way of suddenly being added to a release (with all the associated integration and testing issues).

In other cases, something (e.g., a utility, protocol handler, or algorithm) is developed that is targeted for multiple releases or for incorporation in multiple features. This type of design and development activity is particularly difficult to coordinate because of the number of conflicting requirements and priorities. The lack of a name for this type of development reflects BCCS' problems in trying to decide how to manage it.

At BCCS, hardware engineers are assigned to products and work on projects. Software engineers are sometimes assigned to work with hardware engineers as part of the project team to ensure that the low-level software remains compatible with the hardware functionality. These software engineers (and the work they are doing) may also be considered part of a feature team.

At BCCS, the product managers (from marketing) and the engineering managers and engineering personnel present the status of their activities at the monthly General Manager Program Review Meeting. Following the proceedings can be quite confusing.

The new General Manager has demanded three changes:

- That product management and engineering management develop and maintain a simple diagram (e.g., a road map) that defines the relationship among all of the things about which she receives monthly reports
- That the managers adopt a single set of descriptive naming conventions—hopefully built around the word project
- That responsibilities be assigned and reports be provided on the top-level projects, subsuming, as appropriate, lower-level projects.

---

major reviews and tests (e.g., reviews with the customer called out in the contract and system test), but the intermediate activities, such as peer reviews of designs and unit tests by software developers, are often assumed to occur without explicit reference in any plan. This is, in theory, not a problem if those activities appear in the associated procedures and are accounted for in a block of effort reserved for "overhead." However, accounting for these reviews and tests in detailed plans ensures that an appropriate amount of effort is allocated and that they are tracked and not arbitrarily or inadvertently omitted to save time.

Plans within Plans. The system-level plan drives—and is built from—lower-level plans that are dependent on the technologies involved, the

nature of the organization, and the architecture of the solution and its associated services. Although ISO 9001:2000 addresses planning for production
and service provision in PARAGRAPH 7.5.1 *Control of production and service
provision*, organizations typically involve representatives of all affected
groups in projects from the beginning of a project—and potentially during
the preparation of a proposal. The integrated product team is the vehicle
for ensuring that the different groups communicate and coordinate their
activities. The level of involvement varies as the project progresses and is
based on the content of the project. For example, a product change might
not require any "design and development" from the technical support organization (e.g., distributing the announcement of the release of the change
is adequate), or it might require that the technical support organization
acquire new skills, develop new scripts, and add resources, from telephone
lines to equipment for a laboratory. Manufacturing may have to implement
special monitoring to minimize scrap, reset minimum stocking levels for
certain items, design new processes, procure new components, add new
fixtures or facilities, and so forth.

Defining *Life Cycle*. *Life cycle* does not appear in ISO 9001:2000, ISO
9000:2000, or the guidance on terminology used by the authors of the ISO
9000 family.[12] Whether a life cycle is a period of time,[13] the evolution with
time of a system,[14] or a series of changes,[15,*] a life cycle is defined in a
model that correlates the stages referenced in PARAGRAPH 7.3.1 *a* with time
and with activities and processes.

For example, a product life cycle might include six stages: (1) concept,
(2) designing and developing, (3) testing, (4) production, (5) maintenance,
and (6) end of life. Each of these stages may be broken down into subordinate life cycles with their own stages. For example, designing and developing
may include its own five stages: (1) analyze requirements, (2) design,
(3) implement, (4) integrate, and (5) validate. These subordinate life cycles
and stages continue to be broken down until they become indistinguishable
from activities and deliverables. A life cycle may be sequential or iterative,
and it can support overlapping or concurrent activities.

The life cycle is selected to support evaluation and decision-making and
to protect the organization's ongoing investment of resources in achieving
customer satisfaction. The stages reflect points at which it is logical—from
the organization's perspective—to review and confirm or revise decisions
and commitments. At the lowest level at which resources are managed,
which may be at the team level, the goal is to subdivide the work into packages that can be completed in a reasonably short time (e.g., in one to two

---

* Reference 15 is identified in *Guidance on the Terminology Used in ISO 9001:2000 and ISO
9004:2000*, Document ISO/TC 176/SC 2/N 526R, as the standard used by the authors of the
standards.

weeks)—short enough that problems can be addressed before they affect the overall success of the project.

The selection or definition of a life cycle model or models that are appropriate for an organization depends on the organization's structure, the size of the project, the scope and nature of the work to be performed, and the technology incorporated into the project both for delivery and to enable project activities.

In many organizations, an industry-standard life cycle, like the Waterfall, V, or Rational Unified Process, is represented in templates and procedures for product and project plans and milestone reviews. These procedures and templates provide a limited number of business rules and an array of building blocks that are assembled into a project plan. The actual plans may indicate that portions of the life cycle are repeated to add or refine functionality as the product is developed. For example:

- In developing the software for a product, the engineering team within a single project develops, integrates, and tests increments of functionality, then repeats the process for new increments.
- A product plan or roadmap balances revenue requirements, market priorities, and engineering capability by defining a sequence of versions of a product, each saleable for a defined market and each adding functionality and value to the previous versions.

Describing Life Cycles. Descriptions of life cycles, stages, and activities tend to be written for the most comprehensive type of project (e.g., for a new system incorporating developed and procured hardware and software). Consistent implementation is achieved when the life cycle descriptions and associated procedures clearly define how the life cycle is applied to all the types and sizes of projects the organization expects to implement. Effective process documentation not only differentiates between discretionary and mandatory activities, it also establishes the criteria and authority required for deciding when a discretionary activity can be omitted. For example, a software-only project is required to follow a different path through the life cycle than a project that involves hardware and software development. A project to make a product change to fix or prevent a problem has yet another path defined. Without such provisions for differences in content, purpose, and scale, the life cycle is destined to be abandoned when personnel feel forced to choose between meeting goals and following the life cycle.

A final provision to include is for circumstances in which the current set of life cycles does not fit. New technology and new methodology appear faster than the organization can modify its documentation. A waiver process can be abused, but it provides a necessary mechanism for a project to request approval to implement a new life cycle or an unanticipated variation on the standard life cycles. The waiver process balances a project's need

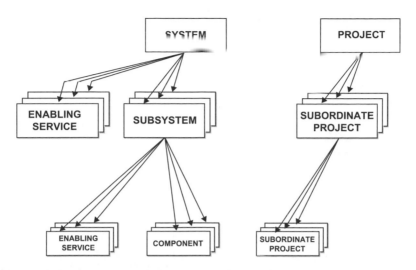

Exhibit 7-6. Example of project and system structures.

for rapid change and an organization's need for stability. Properly and conservatively applied, a waiver process enhances the ability of the organization to satisfy customers.

Responsibility. Success requires that the organization identify at least one individual who is responsible for the timely completion of all aspects of the project. This person (or team) ensures that all of the identified product components, processes, and enabling services required to achieve customer satisfaction are available. Without a focal point, even when responsibilities are clearly assigned and consistently understood, participating groups independently optimize plans and activities—sometimes to the detriment of the overall project.

Exhibit 7-6 is derived from a similar figure in PARAGRAPH 5.5 of *Life Cycle Management—System Life Cycle Processes, ISO/IEC 15288*.[10] This exhibit indicates a structure correlating the project hierarchy and the system structure.

The complementary structures define the roll-up of activity information and the levels of the organization at which resources are planned and managed. The ability to partition technical work effectively is a direct reflection of the foresight of the product architects.

Stages of Design and Development. Organizations typically develop a high-level standard life cycle that all projects follow. The life cycle, which is business or product oriented, provides periodic and event-driven checkpoints at which those responsible for the organization's assets can monitor progress, make appropriate adjustments, and reevaluate their commitment to the project based on any changes in circumstances.

Exhibit 7-7. Life cycle checklist.

May be more than one
Scalable for all sizes of projects
Applicable to all types of projects
Associated waiver process
Clear distinction between optional and mandatory activities.

In parallel with the project life cycle, there are one or more detailed life cycles that are defined in terms of the design and development activities that occur in the various stages of the overall life cycle (see Exhibit 7-7).

The reality of items with long-lead times to purchase or develop and the need to mitigate risks requires that the processes associated with the life cycle provide a mechanism for starting activities before approval to begin the stage in which they "normally" occur is received. For example, before the approval of the set of requirements for a product, it may be prudent for engineering to start designing and developing a high-risk component. Even if subsequent rework is required because of changes in requirements, the head start mitigates some of the schedule risks associated with the project. Defining permissible overlaps and parallel activities is one element of satisfying the requirement to determine the sequence of processes in PARAGRAPH 4.1 *b*.

An effective approach to addressing the inevitable early starts is to describe completion criteria rather than starting criteria. For example, "unit implementation cannot start until the unit design is complete" can be replaced by "unit implementation is not complete until it has been reviewed against an approved unit design." Such a statement relies on the professional judgment of the personnel engaged in the project to ensure that it does not magnify risk by becoming an excuse for deferring verification and validation because of time constraints. Periodic and milestone reviews can prevent the project from unraveling at the last minute if the reviews provide management with visibility into the number and scope of in-progress early starts.

For an example of methods for defining the design and development life cycle, see Appendix E. This case study is in an appendix because of its length; it is recommended that this appendix be read at this point.

The Plan. A plan at any level can be a collection of documents—a collection of individual plans contributed by the participating groups. Organizations typically separate plans into at least two parts:

- The relatively invariant textual descriptions of goals, objectives, purpose, customers, references to other documents, and so forth
- The schedule, which is updated as frequently as is deemed appropriate (e.g., weekly)

PLAN OUTLINE
Objectives
Team structure and
responsibilities
Activities
   •Include verification,
   validation, testing
   •Project management
Stages
Stage inputs and outputs
   •Unambiguous
   requirements
   •Acceptance criteria
Development environment
   •Development methods –
   including reviews,
   verification,
   and validation
   •Standards
   •Resources – people,
   facilities,equipment
   •Tools
Schedule
Risks and mitigation plans
Dependencies
   •Other projects, technology,
   etc.

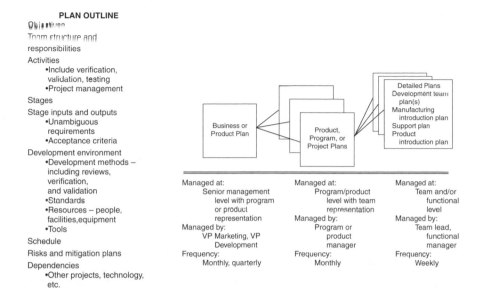

| | Managed at:
Senior management
level with program
or product
representation
Managed by:
VP Marketing, VP
Development
Frequency:
Monthly, quarterly | Managed at:
Program/product
level with team
representation
Managed by:
Program or
product
manager
Frequency:
Monthly | Managed at:
Team and/or
functional
level
Managed by:
Team lead,
functional
manager
Frequency:
Weekly |

Exhibit 7-8. Strategy for planning and project management.

The schedule is maintained in project management and reporting tools. Changes to the rest of the plan are documented in meeting minutes (e.g., considered as amendments). The original planning document is updated only when a significant change requires replanning the development effort, adjusting commitments, and obtaining approvals (e.g., from the customer or from another part of the organization). Exhibit 7-8 represents a typical planning and project management strategy, which eliminates unnecessary documents and facilitates intergroup coordination. The actual scope and number of detailed plans is derived from the system and project architecture, similar to that appearing in Exhibit 7-6.

In interpreting Exhibit 7-8, the outline on the left is carried forward, with appropriate modification, in the product or program plans and in the detailed plans. Each subordinate plan is derived from its predecessor. The intent is that plans refer readers to their predecessors rather than repeating information, with the attendant problems of keeping the duplicated information up to date. The text below the double line describes a project management roll-up strategy.

PARAGRAPH 7.3.2 Design and Development Inputs

The first sentence of PARAGRAPH 7.3.2 states that "inputs relating to product requirements shall be determined and records maintained." The last paragraph answers the obvious question about the source of the records; it

117

specifies that these inputs "be reviewed for adequacy," to verify that they are "complete, unambiguous, and not in conflict with each other." The records of the review are the records referred to in the first sentence of this paragraph.

PARAGRAPH 7.3.2 lists generic categories of requirements inputs:

- Functional and performance requirements
- Regulatory and legal requirements
- Applicable information derived from previous designs
- Any other requirements essential for design and development

PARAGRAPH 7.3.2 parallels the requirements for determining product requirements in PARAGRAPH 7.2.1 and the requirements for review in PARAGRAPH 7.2.2. Specific requirements for reviews are presented in PARAGRAPHS 7.3.4 *Design and development review* and 7.3.5 *Design and development verification*.

Implementation Considerations. Functional and performance requirements and regulatory and legal requirements are typically supplied by the customer in a statement of work or by marketing in a market or product requirements document. Frequently, determining requirements is a collaborative effort, involving engineering, marketing, and, if appropriate, customers. In iterative and incremental life cycles, the requirements for the next iteration or increment can be defined or refined as the previous increment or iteration is completed. In these cases, traceability of requirements from receipt to release as part of the delivered product is essential to ensure that nothing is lost or misinterpreted. Requirements may be received well before the increment or iteration in which they are incorporated into the product, and a requirement planned for one increment or iteration may be deferred to a subsequent increment or iteration. In addition, requirements may change as time passes, as market conditions change, and as new expectations develop.

In PARAGRAPH 7.3.2 *c*, applicable information derived from previous designs can refer to work products suitable for reuse or revision as well as to process and technical experience captured as "lessons learned."

In specifying other essential requirements, PARAGRAPH 7.3.2 *d* includes customer-supplied and internally generated:

- Product technical requirements, such as requirements for platform and technology, upgradeability, and supportability[16]
- Nontechnical requirements, such as budget and schedule
- Process requirements, such as applicable standards and tools for documentation and drawings, configuration management, testing, and coding

These other essential requirements represent inputs that may be received at or may be applicable to any stage within the design and development life cycle.

As noted above, in conjunction with PARAGRAPH 7.3.2, effective life cycles, procedures, and plans recognize that a complete set of requirements is not necessarily available for review at the beginning of a project; requirements can and do arrive in increments, subject to an ongoing review and to change. When requirements change, PARAGRAPH 7.2.2 requires that the organization ensure that relevant documents are amended and that affected personnel are informed.

Documented Requirements. Although ISO 9001 does not specifically state that product requirements are documented, the review, communication, and management of change associated with requirements make it unavoidable. Requirements are the content of one or more of the documents needed by the organization to ensure the effective planning, operation, and control of its processes (PARAGRAPH 4.2.1 *d*), where a document may be, among other things, a database, a working prototype, a drawing, or a textual description.

Conflicting Requirements and the Ability to Meet Defined Requirements. In PARAGRAPH 7.2.2 *Review of requirements related to the product*, requirements are reviewed before any commitments are made to ensure that the organization has the ability to meet them. The ability to satisfy requirements and fulfill commitments is directly related to resolving conflicting requirements. By definition, without some change, it is not possible to fully satisfy two conflicting requirements. Conflicts between product requirements are often the result of inadvertent errors, ambiguity, misinterpretation, and the introduction of unnecessary design constraints. Along with technical capability and feasibility, these types of conflicts are relatively straightforward to identify and resolve systematically.

The greater challenge facing the organization is to find effective methods to determine whether there are conflicts among requirements for system content and capability and requirements for schedule and cost. A standard set of life cycles and activities and historical performance data are prerequisites for developing accurate projections of the organization's productivity and for establishing achievable schedule and cost commitments. Even with accurate historical data, the process for evaluating proposed commitments (e.g., possible future business) can still be ineffective because it inevitably competes with projects that are meeting current commitments (e.g., current business) for technically competent resources.

PARAGRAPH *7.3.3* Design and Development Outputs

PARAGRAPH 7.3.3 requires that design and development outputs be

- Provided in a form and manner that allows verification against the inputs
- Approved before use.

PARAGRAPH 7.3.3 enables verification. PARAGRAPH 7.3.5 requires that, in accordance with planned arrangements, outputs be verified against the inputs.

The first lettered paragraph contains the general requirement that is levied on the activities within design and development that produce design outputs: that the outputs meet, or conform to, the relevant input requirements. Outputs include concept of operations documents, use cases and scenarios, prototypes, functional specifications, design specifications, flow charts, block diagrams, drawings, test scripts and cases, state diagrams, object interaction diagrams, code, and so forth. In incremental life cycles, the outputs from one stage are an input to subsequent stages.

The remaining lettered paragraphs in PARAGRAPH 7.3.3 describe content that must be provided by the set of design outputs (see Exhibit 7-9).

The criteria contained in these paragraphs become the basis for the verification activities for which requirements are identified in PARAGRAPH 7.3.5.

PARAGRAPH *7.3.4* Design and Development Review

PARAGRAPH 7.3.4 describes requirements for conducting systematic reviews of design and development with the participation of representatives of functions concerned with the stage or stages being reviewed. The purpose of design reviews is twofold:

- Evaluate the ability to meet requirements
- Identify any problems and propose necessary actions

Finally, there is a record of the review.

Implementation Considerations. ISO 9000:2000 defines *review* as "activity undertaken to determine the suitability, adequacy, and effectiveness of the subject matter to achieve established objectives." On the basis of this definition, the requirements in PARAGRAPH 7.3.4 apply to two types of reviews: project management reviews and technical reviews.

Project management reviews include stage, readiness, milestone, and periodic reviews of actual progress and completion of activities against the plan. Technical reviews include document review, formal inspection, walkthrough, prototype review, peer review, and brainstorming.

Exhibit 7-9. Design outputs.

Paragraph	Requirements of the design and development outputs	Implementation considerations
7.3.3 *b*	Provide any information specified for specific downstream and supporting activities: manufacturing (operations), service, and purchasing. Requirements for these activities and their information needs are described in PARAGRAPHS 7.4 *Purchasing* and 7.5 *Production and service provision.*	This requires that the downstream organizations and purchasing define their needs. Product teams that integrate all affected functions, coordinated planning, and mutually agreed-on document templates provide real-time communication and ensure that design and development outputs provide downstream organizations—manufacturing, purchasing, customer support, and servicing—with the information those functions require to perform their roles in product and service provision.
7.3.3 *c*	Contain or reference product acceptance criteria. Determining the outputs to which this paragraph applies requires reviewing the definitions of product and process in ISO 9000:2000: • Product is defined as result of a process • Process is defined as set of inter-related or interacting activities which transforms inputs into outputs. On the basis of these definitions and because verification is performed in accordance with planned arrangements (PARAGRAPH 7.3.5), acceptance criteria are required for each intermediate, internal, or deliverable output for which the plan specifies verification (e.g., review, walkthrough, or test). Product acceptance criteria, on which validation is based, are typically design input, included in the product requirements.	In many cases, standard acceptance criteria are documented in policies and procedures. Acceptance criteria can be expressed in terms of threshold values for measures of results (e.g., no outstanding Level A defects) and in terms of process steps completed (e.g., all comments received from manufacturing and support management have been addressed; all identified components have completed unit test and are available for integration.) Component- and project-specific acceptance criteria (e.g., transactions per minute, response time, CPU usage) are typically in plans and specifications.
7.3.3 *d*	Specify any characteristics of the product that are "essential for the [product's] safe and proper use." From ISO 9000:2000, a	Although design teams spend significant effort failure-proofing products, it may not be possible to eliminate all of the aspects of the

Exhibit 7-9 (continued).   Design outputs.

Paragraph	Requirements of the design and development outputs	Implementation considerations
	characteristic is a distinguishing feature; lacking any definition from ISO, essential, safe, and proper default to their standard definitions: • Essential means absolutely necessary • Safe means protected from danger or risk • Proper means correct.	product that provide opportunities for endangering people or property (e.g., the nozzles for leaded gasoline pumps do not fit in the fill-pipes for vehicles that require unleaded gasoline). It is not essential that the product be operated (or installed or maintained) properly if the product handles exceptions and incorrect operation in a way that protects operators and their environment from danger or risk. These characteristics are typically identified in designs and specifications. They are called out in documentation and emphasized in training and frequently result in warning labels affixed to products. They also frequently enter the domains of legal, risk management, and regulatory engineering departments.

Several other paragraphs provide requirements related to design reviews:

- If any problems are identified in reviews, requirements for exercising corrective action, as described in PARAGRAPH 8.5.2 *Corrective action*, are applied.
- Progress reviews are also a mechanism for providing suitable measuring and monitoring of realization processes, as identified in PARAGRAPH 8.2.3 *Monitoring and measurement of processes*.
- Technical reviews of outputs are also verification activities and are subject to the requirements in PARAGRAPH 7.3.5 *Design and development verification*.

Reviews can be conducted through meetings, teleconferences, videoconferences, and e-mail distribution of documents for comment.

The records of reviews at a minimum capture any identified problems, decisions, or assigned actions to ensure that nothing is lost. More extensive records, including detailed minutes (i.e., an official record of the proceedings at a meeting), may be appropriate when the reviews are part of an internal or customer agreement process.

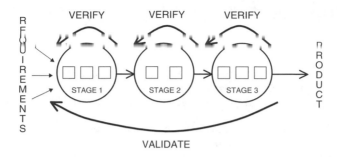

Exhibit 7-10. Verification and validation in a three-stage sequential life cycle.

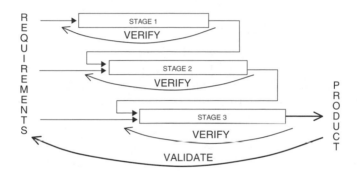

Exhibit 7-11. Verification and validation in a life cycle with overlapping stages.

PARAGRAPH 7.3.5 **Design and Development Verification**

ISO 9000:2000 defines verification as:

> *confirmation, through the provision of objective evidence, that **specified requirements** have been fulfilled [emphasis added]*

This definition is best understood by contrasting it to the definition of validation:

> *confirmation, through the provision of objective evidence, that **requirements for a specific intended use** or application have been fulfilled [emphasis added]*

As illustrated in Exhibits 7-10 and 7-11, verification is conducted stage-to-stage to ensure that design-stage outputs satisfy the requirements of the relevant design-stage inputs. Validation is conducted end-to-end to ensure that product satisfies the customer's requirements.

In Exhibit 7-10, requirements include system or solution-level requirements for functionality, performance, and so forth, as well as all of the other inputs that specify requirements for intermediate inputs. Each verification

123

activity compares the stage outputs with the input requirements that are relevant to that stage. Validation compares the product to the requirements related to the intended use of the product. Because design and development outputs contain or reference acceptance criteria (PARAGRAPH 7.3.3 c), there is no ambiguity about which requirements pertain. There may also be intermediate verification within a stage, where the outputs of an activity are compared with the requirements for that activity.

In Exhibit 7-11, stage 2 and 3 activities start before the activities from the previous stage are done—before all of the inputs against which stage verification will be performed are available. Each verification activity still compares the stage outputs with the input requirements that are relevant to that stage. Validation compares the product with the complete requirements related to the intended use of the product.

PARAGRAPH 7.3.5 requires that the organization

- Plan verification activities and execute the plan
- Select verification activities that ensure that design and development outputs meet design and development input requirements
- Record the results of the verification activities; record any actions determined to be necessary

Related Paragraphs. When, as a result of verification, actions are determined to be necessary to correct or prevent defects, those actions are subject to the requirements of, respectively, PARAGRAPH 8.5.2 *Corrective action* and PARAGRAPH 8.5.3 *Preventive action*. The work product with defects is subject to the requirements of PARAGRAPH 8.3 *Control of nonconforming product*.

Equipment and tools (hardware and software) used in verification are part of the infrastructure (PARAGRAPH 6.3 b) and are subject to the requirements of PARAGRAPH 7.6 *Control of monitoring and measuring devices*.

Verification activities provide the measurement input for monitoring the quality of the product, specified in PARAGRAPH 8.2.4 *Monitoring and measurement of product*. PARAGRAPH 8.2.4 adds content to the records associated with verification activities: "Records shall indicate the person(s) authorizing release of the product."

PARAGRAPH 8.3 *Control of nonconforming product* specifies that when nonconforming product is corrected, it shall be subject to reverification. When test configurations and product evolve during testing (e.g., as new tests are added or existing tests are modified to address defects found in subsequent activities, such as installation and use), effective regression testing of corrected product implies that the record of the test identify the configuration (e.g., the version of the suite of automated tests) as well as the version of the product that was tested. This additional identification prevents the scenario in which a test is run, a problem is found and corrected, and the corrected product is inadvertently retested under a form of the test that would not have found the original problem. The problem may or may not have been fixed. (Requirements to control test software and hardware are found in PARAGRAPH 7.6 *Control of monitoring and measuring devices.*)

Implementation Considerations. In a traditional Waterfall life cycle, an initial design output, for example, a System Requirements Specification, is verified against the requirements for intended use. In subsequent stages of design and development, stage outputs (e.g., a detailed design) are verified against stage inputs (e.g., a detailed design against a high-level design, or a hardware component against a drawing and specifications). Various methods, including technical reviews, inspections, walk-throughs, prototyping, unit testing, integration and integration testing, and regression testing are identified in the plan for specific work products and stages. Reviews can be conducted by holding meetings or by distributing work products and requesting that reviewers submit comments.

PARAGRAPH 7.3.4 *Design and development review* specifies that representatives of concerned function be included in reviews. Whenever a review examines a work product to determine whether it meets input requirements supplied by another part of the organization, including representatives of that other organization, this prevents miscommunication and allows issues to be raised and potentially resolved in real time.

Test plans, procedures, checklists, standards, and work-product specifications identify the characteristics of the work product and the associated requirements that are the bases for verification activities. These characteristics and requirements are frequently supplied to testers in the form of a test case, scenario, or script, with expected results.

With respect to records, any verification activity produces at least a list of exceptions—identified defects or changes. The record may be a hand-annotated version of the work product (e.g., a marked-up drawing or document), or in the case of a formal inspection, it may be a separate list of the identified defects (classified as to type and severity), the agreed-on solutions, the individual responsible, and so forth. As specified in ISO 9001:2000, PARAGRAPH 4.2.4, it is the responsibility of the organization to determine how and for how long each record is preserved and how it is disposed of. As noted earlier, records are kept as long as they are useful. For example:

- If the author marks review comments on a copy of the work product, makes the agreed-on changes, and submits the revised work product for release, there may be no further formal need for the marked-up work product.
- If a test tool produces a "Passed OK" report for a work product, the version of the work product and a copy of the report can be routed

to the release manager to authorize the release of the work product to the next step or phase in the life cycle. The release manager can discard the report once it is reviewed and the decision to release is made.

The usefulness of these records, however, extends beyond the specific project in which they were generated. Verification records are valuable, objective input for lessons-learned reviews conducted at the end of major stages, at the completion of a project, or in periodic comparisons of results across projects. These records refresh vague memories and substantiate assertions in discussions about improving the effectiveness of design and development processes. The retained verification records and the lessons-learned reviews can be a significant part of an organization's implementation of the analysis of data (PARAGRAPH 8.4 *Analysis of data*) as a basis for continual improvement (PARAGRAPH 8.5.1 *Continual improvement*).

PARAGRAPH *7.3.6* Design and Development Validation

The requirements for validation in PARAGRAPH 7.3.5 parallel those for verification in PARAGRAPH 7.3.4, with several important and appropriate additions. Validation, like verification, is planned and conducted to ensure that outputs meet the relevant input requirements. In validation, as discussed above, the relevant input requirements are those that are related to the application or intended use of the product.

PARAGRAPH 7.3.5 adds the requirement that, wherever practicable, validation shall be completed before the delivery or implementation of the product.

Implementation Considerations. The assumption underlying the differentiation between verification and validation is that someone (a customer) commissioned the design and development of a product that is intended to meet some set of requirements (an application) defined and agreed to as part of the commissioning process. To the extent that those requirements describe functionality, end users, and work environments, validation is straightforward to define: it ensures that the product delivers the specified capability to the specified end users in the specified work environment. Validation methods include exercising the product in environments that simulate or reproduce the specified target environments. Testers may follow scripts or user documentation to systematically execute user functions—and inject end-user errors. Representative end users or personnel who deal directly with end users (e.g., field support personnel) may participate as testers.

Wherever Practicable… . The "practicability" of completing validation before delivery or implementation pertains to products that are highly complex and to products that are dependent on a user environment that cannot be completely or cost-effectively simulated or anticipated. For example, in systems that incorporate wireless networking, there is an assumption that, in some cases, unforeseeable characteristics of the user environment will result in postinstallation problems. The supplier and the customer assume the risk that the supplier will be able to address those problems in a timely manner. The more mature and established the technology, the lower the risk. Identifying the right customers—from visionary early adopters to mainstream pragmatists[16]—establishing realistic expectations, and developing implementation and deployment strategies that are appropriate to the degree of risk become keys to ensuring customer satisfaction. When the customer provides a pilot or trial site, validation becomes part of the initial delivery, with appropriate process safeguards, support, and oversight temporarily added.

Typical Implementation Strategies. Nothing in ISO 9001:2000 prevents a design and development activity from being both verification and validation. Likewise, validation may be performed multiple times as different increments or iterations of the product become available. For example, a functional prototype developed early in a project may be validated against the end-user requirements.

Validation typically starts with system testing in a simulated user environment, performed by or on behalf of the organization responsible for the design and development. This validation is frequently misnamed Quality Assurance or Software Quality Assurance testing and is intended to ensure that the product is as ready as the organization can make it. Once the initial validation provides management with an appropriate level of confidence, the product progresses through the rest of the validation life cycle, alpha test, beta test, and software or system acceptance test.

Because there is no requirement to use the terms or distinguish between verification and validation throughout the organization, the requirements for reviews, verification, and validation are addressed by including appropriate activities in the design and development life cycle. Only the implementation team, internal auditors, and management representative need to be aware of how the organization classifies design and development activities as verification and validation.

PARAGRAPH 7.3.7 Control of Design and Development Changes

Design and development changes are any changes in design outputs. These changes may originate within design and development (e.g., a new version of software is released to add a planned function or to correct a problem found in software integration testing), or they may be the result of changes in product requirements that originate outside of the organization (PARAGRAPH 7.2.2).

As a product or project progresses through the design and development life cycle, different, increasingly rigorous change mechanisms are typically invoked for specific work products. Each of the mechanisms is subject to the requirements of PARAGRAPH 7.3.7. The first set of requirements pertains to the changes. Changes are:

- Identified
- Reviewed, verified, and validated, as appropriate: it is the responsibility of the organization to determine what is appropriate for a particular change or work product
- Approved before implementation: In this context, implement is defined as put (a decision or plan) into effect.[12]

Two additional requirements pertain to reviews of changes:

- The reviews shall include evaluation of the effect of the changes on constituent parts and product already delivered. Because constituent means being a part of a whole,[15] "constituent parts" is redundant. The requirement to assess the effect of changes pertains to any part or product that has been delivered. Because a product is the result of a process, delivery pertains to any intermediate (e.g., internal) and final destination and customer.
- Results of the reviews and any necessary actions are recorded.

Related Paragraphs. To the extent that design and development outputs are documents, the requirements in PARAGRAPH 7.3.7 overlap considerably with those in PARAGRAPH 4.2.3 *Control of documents*. To the extent that the changes pertain to product requirements, the requirements in PARAGRAPH 7.3.7 overlap those in PARAGRAPH 7.2.2 for review, record keeping, amendment of relevant documents, and communication to relevant personnel.

PARAGRAPH 7.5.3 *Identification and traceability* and PARAGRAPH 7.5.5 *Preservation of product* contain requirements related to identification (PARAGRAPHS 7.5.3 and 7.5.5) and to handling and protection (PARAGRAPH 7.5.5, which reintroduces constituent parts).

PARAGRAPH 8.2.4 *Monitoring and measurement of product* contains additional requirements for approval and records.

PARAGRAPH 8.3 *Control of nonconforming product* contains additional requirements for the control of product during design and development, before it has been approved for release.

Implementation Considerations. PARAGRAPH 7.3.7 contains the requirements for configuration management from a hardware, a software, and a systems perspective. Together with the other paragraphs identified in related paragraphs, requirements are provided for all four aspects of configuration management, represented in Exhibit 7-12.

A wealth of information about the essentials and best practice of configuration management is captured in numerous standards and technical reports:

Exhibit 7-12. Four aspects of configuration management.

- *Quality Management—Guidelines for Configuration Management,* ISO 10007:1995,[22] International Organization for Standardization
- *National Consensus Standard for Configuration Management,* EIA 649:1998,[23] Electronic Industries Alliance
- *Information Technology—Life Cycle Management—System Life Cycle Processes,* ISO/IEC 15288,[10] International Organization for Standardization
- *Information Technology—Software Life Cycle Processes—Configuration Management for Software,* ISO/IEC TR 15846:1998,[24] International Organization for Standardization
- *Information Technology—Software Life Cycle Processes,* ISO 12207:1995,[25] International Organization for Standardization
- *IEEE Guide to Software Configuration Management,* IEEE 1042,[26] The Institute of Electrical and Electronics Engineers.

All of these standards and reports describe requirements and methods for identifying the current versions of selected work products, for controlling changes to those work products, for reporting the progress of the item through the life cycle, and for ensuring that at a point in the project:

- The versions of all of the work products that are supposed to be available (i.e., as described in the plan) are available (i.e., there is nothing missing).
- No extra work products or changes are found (i.e., there is nothing extra).
- The work products have undergone the specified review, verification, and validation and have achieved the specified results (i.e., the process was followed).*

In the typical implementation, configuration management is a discipline applied throughout the whole organization to all work products—from requirements specifications to delivered product. Proposed changes are submitted to a specified authority. Each proposed change is evaluated for

---

* The first two items—nothing missing and nothing extra—correspond to the Physical Configuration Audit. The third item—process followed—corresponds to the Functional Configuration Audit.

effect by representatives of the groups involved in the project (e.g., engineering, test, publications, and marketing). Records of the review and approval of change proposals are maintained, as are records of the status of the request (e.g., in review, rejected, accepted, planned, implemented, tested, and released). Accepted proposals are planned and implemented by changing affected design outputs (including code and test plans).

The nature of the change (e.g., a change in the functional requirements versus a change to fix a problem), the point in the life cycle (e.g., in design versus in system test), and the effect of the change (e.g., how the change ripples through design, implementation, test, manufacturing operations, and publications) determine who is involved in assessing the change and in approving the change.

Effective configuration management processes apply appropriate levels of control to work products and assign responsibility and authority to appropriate personnel. For example, in one organization, as a work product receives wider and wider distribution and as the effect of changes increases in scope, responsibility for the approval of changes passes from the originator to the feature team leader, to the project engineering manager, to the project manager, and finally to executive management. At each stage of development, the "change control board" is composed of representatives from all the organizations that are affected by the proposed change. The work product is never out of control; the level and nature of control increases in proportion to the potential cost and risk associated with the change.

Modern tools facilitate the institutionalization of configuration management disciplines by automating identification and reporting and by enforcing business rules for notification, distribution, and approval.

It is the responsibility of the organization to develop and implement a configuration management strategy that meets the needs of the organization, that prevents problems, and that does not force personnel to choose between following the rules and satisfying their internal and external customers. If the process for the approval and communication of critical engineering changes to manufacturing is no longer consistent with the needs or capabilities of the organization, personnel will find alternative, faster methods.

Too much control required too soon in the life cycle can cause as many problems as too little control.

Paragraph 7.4 *Purchasing*—A Brief Note

Because the content of Paragraph 7.5 *Production and service provision* is tightly coupled with the content of Paragraph 7.3 *Design and development*, Paragraph 7.4 *Purchasing* is discussed after Paragraph 7.5.

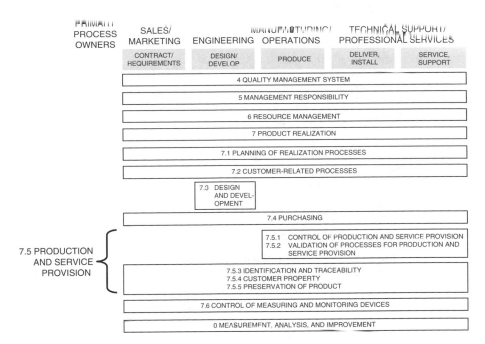

Exhibit 7-13. Scope of application of Paragraph 7.5.

Paragraph 7.5 *Production and Service Provision*

Depending on the nature of the organization and product, production and service provision includes manufacturing, logistics (e.g., warehousing, handling, and storage), delivery, (e.g., packing and shipping), installation, and technical support or professional services (e.g., telephone support, maintenance and repair, and consulting). As introduced above, although the title of this paragraph refers to production and service provision, several of the paragraphs of Paragraph 7.5 contain requirements that explicitly apply to all aspects of product realization, including design and development as well as production and service provision (see Exhibit 7-13).

Although Paragraphs 7.5.1 and 7.5.2 do not apply to product design and development life cycle activities, they may apply to product-related activities and deliverables provided by an engineering organization.

For example, in an organization that produces systems products, parts of the engineering organization may be responsible for production activities, such as:

- Initial production of hardware product
- Documentation and software reproduction
- On-line distribution, including Intranet- and Extranet-based solutions, of documentation, product, patches, bulletins, and so forth

An engineering organization may be responsible for service activities, such as:

- Creation, validation, and distribution of patches and big fixes
- Some level of advanced technical support
- Knowledge transfer (e.g., to support the hand over of responsibility to other organizations)
- Initial sales support (e.g., until a field sales organization is prepared to assume responsibility)
- Initial customer support (e.g., until a Technical Support organization is prepared to assume responsibility)
- Continuation engineering (e.g., software maintenance and sustaining engineering)
- Professional services (e.g., customization, integration with third-party products or existing customer systems)

Defining and planning the interactions between engineering and technical support represents a significant opportunity to improve customer satisfaction through accurate prioritization and timely resolution of problems, through enhanced communication of status, and through the prevention of potential problems.

In some cases, products are delivered directly to the customer following design and development. For example, engineering may deliver operational systems (e.g., hand-built planetarium projectors and software). In the case of software developed under a specific contract, either as a stand-alone product or as part of a system, engineering may make a distribution directly to the customer. In these cases, the requirements for production found in PARAGRAPHS 7.5.1 and 7.5.2 apply to selected engineering activities.

PARAGRAPH 7.5.1 Control of Production and Service Provision

PARAGRAPH 7.5.1 requires that the activities for production and service provision be planned and that they be carried out under controlled conditions. PARAGRAPH 7.5.1 provides specific conditions under which production and service provision are to be carried out—as applicable. Each of the six conditions is discussed individually in the following paragraphs.

PARAGRAPH 7.5.1 *a*: Information about Product Characteristics. The availability of information that describes the characteristics of the product provides the information required in-process verification and final validation of products during production and service provision, for which requirements are described in PARAGRAPH 8.2.4 *Monitoring and measurement of product*.

This information includes product-specific information provided in design and development outputs (PARAGRAPH 7.3.3 *b*) and is closely related to the elements of configuration management as discussed in conjunction with PARAGRAPH 7.3.7 *Control of design and development changes*.

Implementation Considerations. Examples of typical product characteristics include:

- Identification of the individual product and component (e.g., to ensure it is the correct component and version; as described in Paragraph 7.5.3 *Identification and traceability*)
- Status with respect to testing, inspection, and so forth (as described in Paragraph 7.5.3 *Identification and traceability*)
- A list of the expected components (e.g., to ensure the product is complete; a bill of materials)
- Any associated quality objectives (Paragraphs 5.4.1 and 7.1 *a*)

When the product is a service, the characteristics can include process content (the activities that are carried out), performance parameters (response time, turn around time, etc.), as well as specific characteristics of the results (e.g., repaired product returned to full operation).

The processes established by the organization determine the information that is required by personnel performing any particular step. For example, releasing bills of material and assembly instructions to manufacturing typically requires that the approver or approvers have access to product-related information from design and development, including test results. Once the release is approved, personnel may only need a list of part numbers and standard locations (physical or electronic) from which to obtain product components.

If an audit is built into the production process, the audit process may specify that the auditor check against a list of components and correct versions.

When Engineering Produces Product. The requirements for providing comparable information about product characteristics in design and development are addressed in the following paragraphs:

- 7.3.1 *Design and development planning*
- 7.3.7 *Control of design and development changes*
- 8.3 *Control of nonconforming product*

Paragraph 7.5.1 *b*: Work Instructions. Work instructions are examples of documents needed by the organization "to ensure the effective ... operation ... of its processes" (Paragraph 4.2.1 *d*). Work instructions are a method by which an organization ensures "the availability of information necessary to support the operation of ... processes" (Paragraph 4.1 *d*) and by which an organization communicates "responsibilities and authorities throughout the organization" (Paragraph 5.5.1).

Paragraph 7.5.1 *b* also requires that work instructions be available as necessary. Necessity, in this case, is measured by the effective communication of the information that personnel need to do their jobs. The absence of necessary documentation is considered a root cause when there is confusion about responsibility and authority and when processes are not consistently performed as expected by management.

Product-specific process information may be provided in design and development outputs (PARAGRAPH 7.3.3 *b*).

Implementation Considerations. The term "work instruction" is used without definition in ISO 9000:2000 PARAGRAPH 2.7.2 *e* as an example of a type of document that provides information about how to perform processes and activities consistently. In spite of a history of confusing and contradictory guidance,*,** the most effective treatment of work instructions is as procedures. In some cases, organizations find it useful to define work instructions as a class of detailed, step-by-step procedures. The term is most often applied to procedures like manufacturing assembly instructions, to repair procedures, to shipping packing instructions, and to software merge and build procedures.

Frequently, these work instructions serve as a checklist that accompanies the work through final inspection. ISO 9001 has never contained a requirement for making such a distinction or for using the term *work instruction*. No matter how or whether the term is defined, work instructions, like all procedural documentation, are subject to the requirements of PARAGRAPH 4.2.3 *Control of documents*.

When Engineering Produces Product. The term work instruction is not typically used, familiar, or well-received in engineering environments. However, when processes are not automated, detailed, step-by-step procedures may be required for testing (e.g., test scripts) and for building and releasing software product (e.g., build instructions).

PARAGRAPH **7.5.1** *c*: **Use Suitable Equipment.** The requirement that controlled conditions include the availability and use of suitable equipment in production and service provision echoes the requirement in PARAGRAPH 6.3 *Infrastructure* that the organization provide "process equipment (both hardware and software) … needed to achieve conformity to product requirements." Suitability is defined as "fit for or appropriate to a purpose, occasion, person's character, etc."[12]

Suitability, then, is not an absolute, but is determined by the inputs to, activities in, and results expected from the processes and by the characteristics of the personnel assigned to operate the equipment, perform the processes, and achieve the results. Unsuitable equipment is a possible root cause when process performance or results fail to satisfy any associated

---

* Paragraph 7.7 in Reference 27 suggests that the organization give consideration to the distinctions made between policies, procedures, and work instructions.
** Work instruction is also not defined in Reference 12.

objectives. These shortfalls in performance and in the quality of results are discovered through measurement and monitoring of processes (PARAGRAPH 8.2.3) and product (PARAGRAPH 8.2.4) and result in corrective (PARAGRAPH 8.5.2) and preventive (PARAGRAPH 8.5.3) action. The shortfalls are corrected or prevented by adjusting the equipment, the process, the competence of personnel, or the performance objectives (e.g., management's and customers' expectations) until they are compatible.

Additional requirements for the suitability of any equipment that is used for monitoring and measuring are also provided in PARAGRAPH 7.6 *Control of monitoring and measuring devices*. In particular, PARAGRAPH 7.6 specifies that the ability of any software used for monitoring and measurement be confirmed before initial use and reconfirmed as necessary.

Suitable equipment includes any equipment, like wrist straps and grounded workstations, used for safe handling of static-sensitive material.

Implementation Considerations. The brief statement in PARAGRAPH 7.5.1 *c* extends the organization's responsibility to any equipment used in production and service provision, whether or not it is provided by the organization.

By implication, the organization is responsible for determining the suitability of any equipment it provides, specifies (e.g., for equipment it requires others to provide), or allows to be used in production and service provision.

The equipment to use for specific activities is communicated through training and procedural documentation. The requirement to use the specified equipment is established through training, policies, and procedural documentation. Knowledge of the proper use of the equipment is an aspect of the competence of personnel (PARAGRAPH 6.2.2).

Ensuring the availability of equipment in a timely manner is a function of planning (PARAGRAPHS 7.1 and 7.5.1) and of the adequacy of the infrastructure (PARAGRAPH 6.3).

Although PARAGRAPH 6.3 focuses on infrastructure elements needed to achieve conformity to product requirements, there is no reason for an organization to raise unnecessary questions by limiting the use of the word *suitable* to equipment for production and service provision. Because the organization monitors and measures all processes (PARAGRAPH 8.2.3) and takes appropriate corrective action when planned results are not achieved, timely availability and fitness are assured for all equipment.

When Engineering Produces Product. Requirements for infrastructure (PARAGRAPH 6.3), work environment (PARAGRAPH 6.4), and planning (PARAGRAPHS 7.1 and 7.3.1) ensure the adequacy of the work environment and the availability of equipment suitable for design and development activities. PARAGRAPH 7.5.1 *c* requires that the organization ensure that the equipment and work environment provided for design and development is also suitable for production. For example, it may lack capacity (e.g., throughput), accuracy (e.g., a measurement device), or safeguards consistent with production requirements, especially with those related to preserving the conformity of finished product (PARAGRAPH 7.5.5). The organization takes appropriate corrective action when inconsistencies are identified between capability and requirements.

Providing and ensuring the use of equipment specified for the safe handling of static-sensitive material is one of the most common issues that arise when engineering produces product—or when engineering or technical support "borrow" hardware components from manufacturing for testing, evaluation, troubleshooting, and so forth. Problems caused by improper handling are difficult to identify as they are frequently seen as earlier-than-expected component failures in installed product.

PARAGRAPH 7.5.1 *d*: **Use Monitoring and Measuring Devices.** The availability and use of monitoring and measuring devices relates to the requirement in PARAGRAPH 6.3 *Infrastructure*, that the organization provide process equipment (both hardware and software) needed to achieve conformity to product requirements. Requirements for the use of the monitoring and measurement devices are also addressed in PARAGRAPHS 7.6 *Control of monitoring and measuring devices*, 8.2.3 *Monitoring and measurement of processes*, and 8.2.4 *Monitoring and measurement of product*.

Although PARAGRAPH 7.5.1 *d* appears to imply that there is a distinction between devices and equipment, ISO 9000:2000 PARAGRAPH 3.10.4 defines "measuring equipment."

Implementation Considerations. PARAGRAPH 7.5.1 *d* does not add any requirements to those already provided in PARAGRAPH 7.5.1 *c*.

When Engineering Produces Product. Ensure that appropriate (e.g., calibrated) measurement equipment is available when engineering produces product.

PARAGRAPH 7.5.1 *e*: **Implement Monitoring and Measurement.** The implementation of monitoring and measurement refers to the implementation of the associated processes and methods, for which requirements are supplied in PARAGRAPHS 7.6 *Control of monitoring and measuring devices* and 8.2 *Monitoring and measurement*. PARAGRAPH 8.2 includes processes related to:

- Monitoring customer satisfaction (PARAGRAPH 8.2.1)
- Internal audits (PARAGRAPH 8.2.2)
- Monitoring and measuring processes (PARAGRAPH 8.2.3)
- Monitoring and measuring product (PARAGRAPH 8.2.4)

Because PARAGRAPH 4.1 *f* requires that the organization implement actions necessary to achieve planned results, and as PARAGRAPHS 8.2.3 and

8.2.4 require monitoring and measurement of process and product, PARA-
GRAPH 7.5.1 e does not add any requirements to those provided in other
paragraphs.

PARAGRAPH **7.5.1 *f*: Implement Release, Delivery, and Postdelivery Activities.**
Within the context of PARAGRAPH 7.5, release, delivery, and postdelivery
activities refers to activities within the production and servicing processes. Requirements for these activities are specified in a number of other
paragraphs.

Release. As defined in ISO 9000:2000 PARAGRAPH 3.6.13, release refers to
"permission to proceed to the next stage of a process." Within the scope of
production and service provision, requirements for release-related activities are found in PARAGRAPHS:

- 8.2.4 *Monitoring and measurement of product*, which requires that
  records identify the person or persons authorizing release of product and that product not be released until planned arrangements
  have been satisfactorily completed
- 7.1 *Planning of product realization*, which requires that, in planning
  product realization, the organization determine ... as appropriate ...
  (c) required verification, validation, monitoring, inspection, and test
  activities; product realization encompasses production and service
  provision
- 7.4.3 *Verification of purchased product*, which requires that when the
  organization or its customer intends to perform verification at the
  supplier's premises, the organization shall state the "method of ...
  product release in the purchasing information"
- 8.3 *Control of nonconforming product*, which refers to the release
  under concession of nonconforming product

Two other paragraphs contain requirements related to release:

- PARAGRAPH 7.3.3 *Design and development outputs* requires that design
  and development outputs be approved before release
- PARAGRAPH 7.3.6 *Design and development validation* requires that
  "wherever practicable, [design and development] validation ... be
  completed prior to the delivery ... of the product"

Release: Implementation considerations. Just as there are stages within
design and development, there may be stages within production and service
provision. For example, in an organization that builds systems (hardware
and software) to order, production is divided into the following stages:

- Assemble and configure
- Test
- Pack for shipment
- Ship

Each stage in this example concludes with an abbreviated, but well-defined release activity.

The release to test is the responsibility of the associate who assembles and configures the product. The release to test requires that an associate inspect a worksheet to confirm that all activities and serial numbers have been recorded and to initial the bottom of the form. Once the form is initialed, the product is moved to a test staging area.

The release to pack for shipment is the responsibility of the associate who tests the assembled and configured product. The test and report is automated, so the release-to-pack process requires that the associate inspect the test report to ensure that reported results fall within an acceptable range. If the results indicate that the product passes, the associate initials the form and moves the product to a packing staging area.

Product is packed and moved to a shipping staging area. The release to ship packed product is the responsibility of the order administration function and is based on the receipt of an approved purchase order from the customer. The order administrator sends a release notice to shipping. Shipping personnel move the appropriate product from the staging area to the shipping area, prepare the appropriate shipping documents, and dispatch the product to the customer.

Release: When Engineering Produces Product. Well-defined release mechanisms are specified for moving between design and development stages and for moving product to production and service provision (e.g., release to manufacturing or release for general customer availability). An area that frequently requires monitoring is the release of software intended for direct distribution (e.g., by e-mail, Internet, download, or file transfer protocol). As an extension of configuration management, it is the responsibility of the organization to ensure that release processes provide appropriate control for all of the types of product that are made available to customers for download—from full products to upgrades to emergency patches. Experience indicates that an onerous, inflexible release process that prevents personnel from satisfying legitimate customer needs is bypassed. Software finds its way to customers as e-mail attachments or as files placed temporarily on public sites for download. Sometimes, however, dissatisfaction with release processes is one of perception. What appears to be onerous is necessary and appropriate. To prevent problems caused by misperception, ISO 9001:2000 PARAGRAPH 6.2.2 c, which is often overlooked, requires that personnel understand why they are doing things:

> *The organization shall … ensure that its personnel are aware of the relevance and importance of their activities and how they contribute to the achievement of the quality objectives.*

Exhibit 7-14. An example: postdelivery activities

The Electronic Fence Company (EFC) provides a product that keeps nonavian animals within a defined two-dimensional perimeter by causing a box attached to the animal's collar to emit an unpleasant noise. If the animal continues to approach the defined perimeter, the box first emits a natural, non-habit-forming gas that immobilizes the animal and then alerts the system operator, who collects the immobilized, but happy, animal.

The collar boxes come in a variety of sizes and colors and incorporate the latest in Global Positioning System technology and wireless networking to communicate their precise locations to a personal computer that serves as an administrative console. Each collar box is individually addressable. The unpleasant noise (including the owner's voice), gas dosage, and perimeter parameters (including acceptable approach distances and rates of approach) are set for each box or for classes of boxes (e.g., cats, dogs, hamsters, or goats).

Although EFC does not actually deliver fences, it does offer to train customers and to analyze and to set up customers' systems (including the definition of optimal perimeters and parameters). A separate division of EFC provides trained staff to operate systems at customer sites.

EFC marketing is looking into other potential markets and applications for its system.

Delivery. Although the term delivery is undefined, it includes the transfer activities that follow each release (see Exhibit 7-14). These transfers may be between locations or personnel involved in production and service provision and between the organization and its customers. A number of paragraphs provide requirements related to delivery activities:

- Requirements for delivery activities are determined (PARAGRAPH 7.2.1)
- Wherever practicable, design and development validation (e.g., testing against user requirements) is completed before delivery (PARAGRAPH 7.3.6)
- The organization is responsible for preserving "the conformity of product during ... delivery" (PARAGRAPH 7.5.5)
- Product release and service delivery do not proceed until the planned arrangements have been satisfactorily completed, unless otherwise approved (PARAGRAPH 8.2.4)
- Nonconforming product is controlled to prevent unintended delivery (PARAGRAPH 8.3)

Delivery: Implementation Considerations. It is the organization's responsibility to determine how product and product components are moved between internal locations and how product and product components are moved from internal to external locations. There are several considerations:

- The associated release activities ensure that the product is ready to deliver (as required by PARAGRAPHS 7.3.6, 8.2.4, and 8.3)
- The product integrity is maintained throughout the delivery process (PARAGRAPH 7.5.5).

Ensuring that the product is ready to deliver (e.g., permitted to proceed to the next stage of processing) is enabled by appropriate product identification and status reporting, as required by PARAGRAPH 7.5.3 *Identification and traceability*.

Maintaining product integrity encompasses all of the requirements of PARAGRAPH 7.5.5 *Preservation of product* for identification, handling, packaging, storage, and preservation. The organization is responsible for determining the vulnerabilities of its products and product components and for establishing appropriate processes and methods. These processes and methods range from establishing storage environments that provide an appropriate environment (e.g., moisture, humidity, altitude, and temperature) to selecting packaging and shipping methods that protect the product from physical harm caused by handling (e.g., shock, static electricity, and contact) and from exposure to damaging environmental factors (e.g., moisture, humidity, altitude, and temperature).

When a product has a defined shelf life (e.g., a device with an onboard battery), preserving the integrity of product requires that the organization establish methods that both preserve the ability of the organization to fill orders and that ensure that expired product is not shipped (e.g., dates on packaging, periodic inspection of inventory, dates in inventory records for serialized items).

These concepts translate readily to software products as requirements for controlling access to prevent unapproved changes (inadvertent and malicious), for virus protection during reproduction, and for ensuring the integrity of products delivered electronically.

Delivery: When Engineering Delivers Product. Even when the production, handling, and measurement tools and methods discussed above are implemented in engineering, the organization needs to ensure that it has the specialized knowledge required to determine and implement appropriate methods for delivering product:

- How should product be packed to prevent damage?
- What packaging and packing materials are required?
- If specialized materials or devices (e.g., moisture absorption packs, shock sensors, freeze indicators, and tip and tilt indicators) are required, how are they made available?
- What shipping methods are appropriate (e.g., air, sea, truck, camel, courier)?
- What regulations pertain (e.g., for flammables, explosives, or biohazards; export restrictions)?

Postdelivery Activities. There are two classes of postdelivery activities. The first class pertains to activities that are in response to defined requirements, as referenced in PARAGRAPH 7.2.1 *a*. The postdelivery activities in this first class are what are typically thought of as service. They fulfill carefully considered commitments made to external customers (e.g., for on-site support and maintenance, telephone support, warranty repair or upgrade, installation, and consulting). Consulting potentially encompasses a broad range of services and can include site preparation, migration of existing data and integration of existing system components, product configuration, and product customization. These services may be sold as separate products.

The second class of postdelivery activities pertains to activities that occur as a result of the delivery of product to other internal activities within production and service provision. For example, if product is delivered to a test activity (e.g., to a system test function, to beta test, or to acceptance test), it may be determined that rework is required. In the case of software product, development of a new version of the product continues in parallel with the release and maintenance of previous versions.

Because they are part of product realization and the quality management system, the organization is required to provide adequate resources (PARAGRAPH 4.1 *d*) and to plan (PARAGRAPHS 7.1 and 7.5.1), monitor, and measure (PARAGRAPH 8.2.3) all of these postdelivery activities.

Postdelivery Activities: Implementation Considerations. The planning associated with postdelivery activities is frequently found in new product introduction, support, and training plans. When consulting is provided, there may be customer-specific project plans. These activities are the domain of specialized groups that participate in projects to deliver new products and who have ongoing responsibilities for delivered products.

These organizations are typically responsible for ensuring that the requirements of PARAGRAPH 7.5.4 *Customer property* are satisfied. For example, a repair center is responsible for customer property while it is being repaired.

Postdelivery activities frequently put personnel in possession of a customer's intellectual property. For example, a service engineer may have access to proprietary product information as a by-product of diagnosing and correcting a system problem. When a service engineer accesses a remote customer system for whatever, presumably approved, purpose, the account name, passwords, and so forth, are considered the customer's intellectual property and require appropriate care to protect the customer's system from unauthorized access and the service provider from potential embarrassment and liability.

Postdelivery Activities: When Engineering Supports Delivered Product. In the experience of the authors of this volume, engineering is always involved in some postdelivery activities. Early in the life of a new product, engineering may be responsible for postdelivery activities (e.g., sales support, customer support, installation, and consulting) as various other parts of the organization gain the skills and resources necessary to assume their responsibilities. Throughout the life of a product, engineering corrects field-report defects in new versions of the product and designs (or approves) field-installed corrections for delivered product. Engineering also typically provides the final level of customer support, the desk to which field-reported incidents that defy analysis, diagnosis, or duplication are referred.

Planning—ensuring the availability of qualified resources—is the most significant challenge the organization faces. While there is continuing design and development for the product, there are engineers who have the skills and knowledge to provide support. They are, however, probably already assigned to that continuing design and development. Careful planning is required to balance resource requirements and to ensure that project schedules are maintained or adjusted and that support commitments are met.

For legacy products, when design and development are not ongoing, there may not be any engineering personnel who retain the knowledge required to provide support, and if there are, those engineers have presumably moved on to new products, projects, and technologies. In this case, careful planning is required to preserve the organization's ability to meet its support commitments. Not only is capturing knowledge essential, but maintaining the ability to provide support may require archiving the hardware and software associated with the development environment.

It is the responsibility of the organization to ensure that it maintains the resources necessary to meet its customer commitments. This responsibility translates into well-defined policies for product end of life, for withdrawing support, and for migrating customers to current products.

PARAGRAPH 7.5.2 Validation of Processes for Production and Service Provision

PARAGRAPH 7.5.2 contains validation requirements for a unique subset of the processes found in production and service provision. These processes have been previously referred to as *special processes*.* PARAGRAPH 7.5.2

---

* The only remaining use of this term in the ISO 9000 family is in a note in ISO 9000:2000, PARAGRAPH 3.4.1. The note characterizes special processes as processes where the conformity of resulting product cannot be readily or economically verified.

provides two criteria for determining the processes to which it applies The requirements of PARAGRAPH 7.5.2 apply to any process that satisfies one or both selection criteria:

- Resulting output cannot be verified by subsequent monitoring or measurement
- Where deficiencies become apparent only after the product is in use or the service has been delivered

The most common examples of processes to which the requirements of PARAGRAPH 7.5.2 apply are drawn from the chemical industry. General examples include processes for which:

- A characteristic can be measured during processing, but not in the finished product.
- A characteristic of the product changes after the product is delivered.
- The complete characteristics of the product are not known (and, therefore, its postdelivery performance is at risk).
- There is no acceptable method of measuring a product characteristic.[18]

Depending on the definition of product, it would appear that medical procedures and the construction of large, complex structures demonstrate some of these characteristics.

The organization is required to validate processes that fall within the scope of PARAGRAPH 7.5.2. PARAGRAPH 7.5.2 goes on to state that validation shall demonstrate the ability of these processes to achieve planned results and concludes with a mixed list of arrangements that the organization is required to establish for these processes, as applicable. The list combines requirements that pertain both to the process itself (e.g., use of specific methods and procedures and of records) and to the way in which the organization establishes the process (e.g., approval of processes and equipment and qualification of personnel).

Implementation Considerations.　The following implementation considerations are based solely on compliance with the requirements of ISO 9001. They do not take into account any additional requirements imposed by regulations, laws, or standard practices associated with specific processes or industries.

The concept of processes where the resulting output cannot be verified by subsequent monitoring and approval has been part of ISO 9001 since its first version.[19] However, even in the area of processed materials, there is a great deal of variation in expert opinions as to what processes fall within the scope of PARAGRAPH 7.5.2. In addition, for at least three reasons, there does not appear to be any value in distinguishing between processes that fall within the requirements of PARAGRAPH 7.5.2 and those that do not.

- The first reason is that the requirements in Paragraph 7.5.2 are similar to requirements called out in other paragraphs of ISO 9001 for all of the processes in the quality management system.
- The second reason is that the requirements of Paragraph 7.5.2 are satisfied by process development "best practices," which are already implemented in many organizations for all processes.
- The third reason is that in regulated industries (e.g., nuclear, chemical, aerospace, and equipment for military applications), the organization is provided with detailed requirements that specify any applicable validation and arrangements called for in Paragraph 7.5.2. The organization is already required to determine (Paragraph 7.2.1 c) and satisfy these requirements.

The defining criteria and each of the requirements of Paragraph 7.5.2 are analyzed below. Conclusions and comments regarding the selection of processes to which the requirements of Paragraph 7.5.2 apply follow the analysis of the requirements.

Validation. In this context, validation requires the organization to confirm the capability of the process to deliver results that satisfy requirements. Although the term prequalification, with the associated implication that the validation occurs before the process is put into operation, has been used in the past, it is not found in ISO 9001:2000. This reflects the understanding that, because of the inherent nature of the results of these processes, process validation may not be possible until the process has been implemented and product has been delivered. As long as this is known in advance, realistic customer expectations can be established and appropriate follow-up measures can be implemented to mitigate risks.

Process validation supports an organization's efforts to enhance customer satisfaction by determining and implementing processes that are effective in satisfying customer requirements. Process validation, however, is not explicitly called out for processes that fall outside the scope of Paragraph 7.5.2. In the ISO 9001 framework, these "outsider" processes and their results are monitored and controlled (Paragraphs 8.2.3 and 8.2.4). The processes are revised after the fact when planned results are not achieved (Paragraph 8.2.3).

Many organizations already practice process validation. Even when there is not an explicit regulatory, liability, or customer requirement, when a process has a significant effect on the quality of a product, or when the product itself has a significant effect on the customer (e.g., health, safety, legal, and financial products), many organizations plan the implementation like a project. For example, a new process is designed and proven to the extent that is feasible in a nonoperational, laboratory environment. The new process is piloted in one or more operational environments; the results are monitored and validated to the extent that is feasible. The pilot implementations and, perhaps, further initial deployment are controlled and monitored until a reasonable degree of confidence is achieved.

PARAGRAPH 7.5.2 *a*: Defined Criteria for Review and Approval of These Processes. PARAGRAPH 7.5.2 *a* requires that the organization define the criteria used in reviewing and approving these processes. That the organization establishes responsibility and authority for review and approval is required by PARAGRAPH 5.5.1. When processes affect regulatory or other legal compliance, it is the responsibility of the organization to ensure that the appropriate personnel are involved in the review and approval. When the approval of a process is accomplished through the review and approval of a document that describes the process, the requirements for review and for approval for adequacy before use in PARAGRAPH 4.2.3 also apply.

A straightforward strategy that can be implemented for all processes is to designate an organization or individual as the process owner. Depending on the authority (e.g., management position) of the designated individual, the functions that perform activities in the process may be reviewers or reviewers and approvers. Any functions that provide inputs to or receive outputs from the process are also reviewers. When a process affects policies, processes, or commitments owned by another organization (e.g., legal, human relations, export compliance, risk management, regulatory engineering, contract administration, finance, or occupational safety), that organization is also an approver. In some cases, these supporting organizations are automatically added as reviewers for all procedures so they can decide if the process has any implications for their domains.

The defined criteria are that:

- All affected organizations are consulted as reviewers (internal customers, suppliers, and participants).
- All reviewers consider whether the process is adequate for their needs.
- Any proposed changes are negotiated to the satisfaction of all parties before the procedure is approved by the process owner and any other designated approvers.

Once a process is established, the owner, approvers, and reviewers are listed by title or organization in the associated procedural documentation so they can be consulted for any changes.

PARAGRAPH 7.5.2 *b*: Approval of Equipment. PARAGRAPH 6.3 *b* requires that the organization "determines, provides and maintains ... process equipment ... needed to achieve conformity to product requirements." PARAGRAPH 7.5.2 *b* adds the requirement that the equipment be approved. In some cases, this approval is provided by the manufacturer or an external agency (e.g., "approved for use in" or "compatible with"). In other cases, it is the responsibility of the organization to approve the equipment as suitable for use in the associated process (e.g., by a process or manufacturing engineering function). This approval may require proving the capability of the equipment for its intended application.

By designating the equipment in the process documentation and by assigning responsibility for ensuring the capability of equipment, the approval of equipment can be accomplished at the same time the process is approved.

PARAGRAPH **7.5.2** *b*: **Qualification of Personnel.** PARAGRAPH 6.2.2 addresses the competence of personnel. PARAGRAPH 7.5.2 *b* adds the concept of qualification, which, according to PARAGRAPH 3.8.6 in ISO 9000:2000, is "to demonstrate the [person's] ability to fulfill specified requirements." In some cases, qualification is accomplished through certification or licensing by a third party. In other cases, it is the responsibility of the organization to determine how personnel demonstrate their ability. Although in some cases licensing and certification are prerequisites for being assigned to perform a job, PARAGRAPH 7.5.2 *b* does not explicitly require that there be prequalification.

In many cases, ensuring the competence of personnel involves a probationary period, during which tasks of varying difficulty and duration are assigned and during which supplementary support and supervision are provided. Once new personnel develop and demonstrate their ability to perform their assignments (i.e., develop and demonstrate their qualifications), they receive a reduced level of support and supervision. Job families and performance reviews can be used as a similar, but longer-term process for qualification. Job families (e.g., associate engineer, engineer, senior engineer, member of the technical staff) define the levels and areas of competence that are required to be demonstrated to be eligible for promotion. Properly specified, the individual's performance objectives from the previous review and the manager's assessment of actual performance determine whether the individual demonstrates the qualities (i.e., is qualified) to be considered for the advanced position. For example, once an individual's work achieves a specified level of quality as confirmed by tests or inspections, the individual's demonstrated qualification can be recognized and the individual can be rewarded for increased contribution (e.g., less rework, higher productivity, and less required supervision). Qualification and objectives lead inevitably to measurement, which is addressed in conjunction with PARAGRAPH 8.2.3 *Monitoring and measurement of processes.*

PARAGRAPH **7.5.2** *c*: **Use of Specific Methods and Procedures.** PARAGRAPH 4.1 requires that the organization identifies processes and determines criteria and methods. PARAGRAPH 4.2.1, by implication, requires that the organization document any procedures for which such documentation is "needed ... to ensure the effective planning, operation and control of its processes."

Exhibit 7-15. Definitions from ISO 9000:2000

PARAGRAPH in ISO 9000:2000	Term	Definition
3.4.1	Process	Set of interrelated or interacting activities that transforms inputs into outputs
3.4.5	Procedure	Specified way to carry out an activity or a process

Reviewing four definitions, two from ISO 9000:2000, simplifies the analysis of this paragraph. The two from ISO 9000:2000 are in Exhibit 7-15.

In the absence of any specialized definitions,* the following two definitions prevail:[15]

- Method is a particular procedure for accomplishing something.
- Specific is clearly defined or identified, precise and clear, of or relating uniquely to a particular subject.

PARAGRAPH 7.5.2 *c*, then, reduces to use of precise and clear procedures.**

Setting aside clarity, which is an attribute of any communication, it is the organization's responsibility to determine the level of detail with which to direct personnel in carrying out the process. Once an appropriately detailed procedure is defined, training and procedural documentation, including operational checklists, ensure that the precise sequence of steps intended by management is consistently understood and carried out.

PARAGRAPH 7.5.2 *d*: Requirements for Records. The records addressed by PARAGRAPH 7.5.2 *d* are those produced in validating and establishing the process and those produced by the process. It is the responsibility of the organization to specify any records (which are defined as a form of document) associated with its processes (PARAGRAPH 4.2.1 *d* and 4.2.1 *e*). Records produced by validation might be based on customer reports or on extended sampling of delivered product. Records produced in establishing the process might include records of evaluating and approving processes and equipment and copies of the licenses or certificates of personnel. The process itself might produce initialed checklists, intermediate test results, and test reports on inputs.

---

* Method is not defined in either ISO 9001:2000 or in Reference 12.
** This is not intended as an indictment of the intelligence, abilities, or diligence of the authors of the standard. Based on personal experience writing standards, it appears to the authors of this volume that such statements are an inevitable by-product of a process that relies on a large, changing team of volunteers who meet three or four times a year, who represent a variety of user communities with divergent agendas, and who are charged with creating a document that receives the approval of an even larger committee. A relevant story has circulated about the 1987 version of ISO 9001. This version of the standard included inputs from over 5000 individuals. Because the released standard contained about 4800 words, some participants did not get their own word. Many had to be content with an instance of a repeated word. The most unfortunate had to share a word.

These records are subject to the requirements of Paragraph 4.2.4 *Control of records*.

For special processes, contractual commitments, regulations, and potential liability can lead to lengthy retention periods and secure storage for these records.

Paragraph 7.5.2 *e*: Revalidation. The organization can establish periodic or event-driven revalidation. In addition to revalidating the process at fixed intervals (e.g., by sampling delivered product), any major readjustment of equipment, change in personnel, or extended period of inactivity might trigger revalidation.

Conclusions and Comments about the Selection Criteria and Selection. The observations in Exhibit 7-16 are intended to guide implementers in determining whether the organization, in the absence of any law, regulation, customer requirements, or generally accepted practice, has any processes to which the requirements of Paragraph 7.5.2 apply.[12]

Assuming that all externally imposed requirements (customer, regulatory, statutory, etc.) are being satisfied, and if there are no applicable industry standards or common practices that define special processes, it is the recommendation of the authors of this volume that the implementation team declare that the organization has no special processes. The implementation team and internal auditors can use the concepts of Paragraph 7.5.2 to enhance their recommendations and findings based on other paragraphs in ISO 9001:2000, as described above.

For those organizations that are seeking registration (described in this volume in detail in Chapter 1), this is potentially a topic to explore with candidates during registrar selection. It is only potentially a topic because it is not a high-risk item. It is the opinion of the authors of this volume that this is not a high-risk item because:

- If
  - Customer, regulatory, and statutory requirements are being satisfied
  - The organization's processes are implemented
  - The organization states in its quality manual (Paragraph 4.2.2) that it does not have any special processes

- And if
  - The registrar's auditor determines that a process is a special process, based on the registrar's standard interpretation

- Then
  - The auditor's determination results in a minor nonconformity written against the quality manual. The corrective action is to revise the quality manual. The processes remain unchanged.

Exhibit 7-16. Observations regarding the application of Paragraph 7.1?

Number	Observation
1	PARAGRAPH 7.5.2 pertains to production and service provision; design and development activities are outside the scope of PARAGRAPH 7.5.2 (although some activities performed by engineering may fall into the areas of production and service provision).
2	If either one of the criteria—or both—are satisfied by a process, applicable requirements of PARAGRAPH 7.5.2 apply to that process.
3	The second criterion states that deficiencies become apparent only after the product is in use. Two aspects of this criterion deserve examination.
	The first aspect is the use of "deficiency," which is defined as the amount of a shortfall or something lacking, PARAGRAPH 7.5.2 contains the only instance of the word "deficiency" in ISO 9001:2000. In referring to product, the word "nonconforming" is consistently used. The conclusion by the authors of this volume is that deficiency refers to processing as well as product deficiencies.
	The fact that a customer specifies operator certification, environmental conditions, or specific tests and durations does not require that the associated production and service provision processes satisfy the requirements of PARAGRAPH 7.5.2. Compliance with all of these requirements can be monitored.
	The second aspect is the position and use of "only" in the second criterion. In the case of most processes, deficiencies become apparent after the product is in use, but not only after the product is in use. In the absence of any external requirement (e.g., law, regulation, or generally accepted practice), the organization's decision as to whether or not to apply the more stringent requirements of PARAGRAPH 7.2.5 to a process is based on its confidence in its ability to reduce risk to an acceptable level by subsequent monitoring and measurement—by its abilities to detect and correct deficiencies before use.
	The fact that there are field-reported defects does not require that the associated production and service provision processes satisfy the requirements of PARAGRAPH 7.5.2. As a corollary, the fact that a product's performance cannot be tested or predicted in all possible customer environments (e.g., a wireless networking system) does not require that the associated production and service provision processes satisfy the requirements of PARAGRAPH 7.5.2.

If the organization is not satisfying a legitimate customer, regulatory, or statutory requirement, there is a much more immediate and important problem to address than identifying a process and updating the quality manual.

PARAGRAPH *7.5.3* Identification and Traceability

As stated in the first sentence, PARAGRAPH 7.5.3 explicitly applies throughout product realization. The first requirement is prefaced by "where appropriate":

- *Where appropriate*, the organization is required to identify the product by suitable means. It is the responsibility of the organization to determine where in the life cycle identification is appropriate, and what means are suitable, based, typically, on law, regulation, customer requirement, or standard practice. As part of suitability, ISO 9001:2000 leaves it to the organization to determine a level of granularity (e.g., individual unit serialization or lot identification) and a degree of permanence (e.g., encoded, etched, or stamped on the product, or on a throwaway tag that is discarded at a subsequent step in the product realization process). For software products, identification is accomplished through naming conventions enforced by version control tools.

The second requirement is absolute and is independent of whether identification is also implemented:

- The organization is required to establish mechanisms to enable the identification of the status of products or components with respect to monitoring and measurement. Although the method of identifying status varies, the purpose is the same: to ensure that an item does not inadvertently miss any specified monitoring and measurement and, therefore, advance to the next stage of processing with a higher-than-acceptable risk of nonconformity. Status identification is a prerequisite for addressing the requirements in PARAGRAPH 8.3 *Control of nonconforming product*. Although it is not stated explicitly, as with the requirement for identification, PARAGRAPH 7.5.3 requires that the organization determine suitable methods, levels of granularity, and degrees of permanence for the identification of status.

PARAGRAPH 7.5.3 also contains a requirement for creating records related to product identification. In defining this requirement, PARAGRAPH 7.5.3 introduces the concept of traceability, which is the "ability to trace the history, application, or location of that which is under consideration."[20] PARAGRAPH 7.5.3 recognizes, but does not require, bidirectional traceability (e.g., from a point in time back to the beginning of the item's history and from any point in time forward to the current disposition of the item). The organization is responsible for implementing traceability in a manner that is compatible with its processes and that satisfies requirements.

The following is an example of an implementation of complete bi-directional traceability.

EXTREME TRACEABILITY

> *In a company that designs, develops, and manufactures medical devices, regulations and the nature of the application of the product mandate stringent requirements for traceability. The organization is required to serialize and track the locations of individual units (e.g., for recall or maintenance purposes; forward traceability), and the organization is required to maintain the ability to determine the source of any purchased components (e.g., microprocessors, memory chips, lenses, or switches) incorporated into each serialized unit (e.g., in case of a problem with the component; backward traceability). Traceability also extends to identifying the specific personnel and pieces of process equipment associated with the manufacture, test, shipping, or installation of any individual unit.*

PARAGRAPH 7.5.3 requires that the identification of product be in a quality record if traceability is a requirement. The implication is that the method of recording the identification is subject to the requirements in PARAGRAPH 4.2.4 *Control of records*: legible, readily identifiable, and retrievable, stored in a protected manner for a specified period of time and disposed of in a specified manner. The organization establishes a level of granularity that meets or exceeds the requirements for traceability. The organization establishes a retention time that meets or exceeds the period of time for which the organization is required to maintain the ability to trace the history, application, or location of its product or products.

In presenting the requirements for traceability and records, PARAGRAPH 7.5.3 prefaces identification with the word unique. Unique identification at an appropriate level of granularity is a requirement for traceability. Answering either "Where did this come from?" or "Where did this go?" requires that the word "this" be defined. However, once traceability is no longer required to be maintained and the record is disposed of, the identifier may be reused. In some organizations, to avoid any possible problems, identifiers are never reused. In other organizations, to avoid the expense of modifying inflexible tracking systems, part numbers are available for reuse some number of years after the units they refer to are discontinued.

Related Paragraphs. Because a product is, at points in the product realization process, expressed as documents (e.g., requirements specifications, design documents, bills of materials, drawings, or prototypes), traceability may require enhancing mechanisms for document control (PARAGRAPH 4.2.3). Although document control requires that the organization implement identification and revision control of documents, traceability may require adding mechanisms to identify source documents (e.g., Functional Specification version 2 is based on Requirements Specification version 4.2). In addition, when the documents are design and development outputs, the change control mechanisms implemented to meet the requirements of

PARAGRAPH 7.3.7 *Control of design and development changes* may need to be enhanced to support the ability to trace changes through a chain of documents (e.g., Assembly Drawing version 23 addresses the changes introduced in Engineering Specification version 42.3, which incorporates Engineering Change Order 1-004-02).

Implementation Considerations for Software and Systems Providers. As suggested by the note at the end of PARAGRAPH 7.5.3, the requirements of PARAGRAPH 7.5.3 are typically addressed through configuration management practices and tools. These tools and practices ensure that the following are controlled and recorded:

- The identification of product components and product: version control
- Status of identified product and product components with respect to test (e.g., ready for integration test, ready for system test)

Configuration management includes effective control of changes during design and development (e.g., review, impact assessment, approval) and the transfer of accurate information to production and service provision (PARAGRAPHS 7.3.3 *b* and 7.3.7). Basic configuration management enables tracing change requests (including defect reports) forward from submission to implementation in the product (e.g., ensure all approved changes have been implemented; nothing missed) and product changes back to the corresponding approved change request (e.g., only approved changes have been implemented; nothing extra). In many cases, configuration management incorporates or is linked closely to requirements engineering practices* (PARAGRAPHS 7.2.1 and 7.2.2, which address the determination and review of product-related requirements, and PARAGRAPH 7.3.2, which addresses the transfer of requirements to design and development). The close relationship among these paragraphs, including PARAGRAPH 7.5.3, reinforces the concept that the paragraphs and their requirements form a system of interrelated components that cannot be considered or implemented effectively as individual units.

Ineffective or missing configuration management practices are reflected in lost changes (e.g., "What happened to ...?" and "I already did that.") and unexpected changes (e.g., "What's this?"), which translate into rework, the inability to schedule, and organizational stress.

The degree of rigor, the amount of acceptable administrative overhead, and the number of personnel involved in configuration management are functions of the organization's structure and size and the design and complexity of its processes and products. A number of standards provide

---

* Requirements engineering is described in conjunction with PARAGRAPH 7.2.1 *Determination of requirements related to the product.*

Exhibit 7-17. Measure twice, cut once (or invent emptor)

Quotations from the trenches:

- The use of wrist straps and static mats in engineering is time-consuming and unnecessary. Engineers will not use them. They know how to handle $4000 video processor boards without damaging them. And anyway, they put them back in inventory when they're done with them.
- We can respond more quickly to customer needs by having software engineers make minor changes in the release baseline. We try to make sure that the changes get tested in the next release.
- Service people go to local electronics stores if they need standard components they cannot get from the factory in a timely manner. It's better to risk installing a substandard component than it is to have a dissatisfied customer.
- Service people sometimes have to make minor tweaks to the software to get it to run. It happens frequently, so the service people are prepared for it. They try to remember to write down what they did for the next service person.

straightforward descriptions of configuration management best practice.* A wide range of tools, from spreadsheets and word processors to dedicated configuration management systems, is available.

Paragraph 7.5.4 Customer Property

Paragraph 7.5.4 contains requirements for the care of customer property—including hardware, software, and proprietary information—while it is under the control of or in use by the organization. The customer property may be provided either for the organization to build into the product (e.g., shared libraries, interface specifications, components, or data) or for use in the realization of the product (e.g., test data or hardware, operational data and target platforms for compatibility testing, and documentation). Customers' proprietary information, to which personnel may have access during service provision, is also considered customer property subject to the requirements of Paragraph 7.5.4 (see Exhibit 7-17).

The requirements of Paragraph 7.5.4 are specific and require that the organization establish methods to identify, verify, protect, and safeguard customer property, including intellectual property. A quality record (Paragraph 4.2.4) is created and maintained, and the customer is notified if the customer's property is lost, damaged, or otherwise found to be unsuitable for use. Breaches in security potentially constitute damage to confidential information.

Verification is limited to confirming the suitability of the supplied customer property for the organization's intended use and, depending on the

---

* See the list of configuration-management related standards and reports in the implementation considerations for Paragraph 7.3.7.

use of the customer property, may be planned as part of design and development verification (PARAGRAPH 7.3.5), design and development validation (PARAGRAPH 7.3.6), or monitoring and measurement of product during production and service provision (PARAGRAPH 8.2.4).

Protecting and safeguarding is also addressed in the requirements of PARAGRAPH 7.5.5 *Preservation of product.*

Implementation Considerations. Organizations typically develop procedures that track customer property, as appropriate, from receipt to return or other disposition (e.g., destruction or archival). Methods for storage and maintaining security are also established. These procedures may pertain to design and development (e.g., for samples, data, and components for integration), to production (e.g., for materials to be included in the product, test fixtures, and tools), and to service provision (e.g., data, and equipment undergoing repair). In particular, PARAGRAPH 7.5.4 requires that the organization address the proper handling (e.g., to restrict access) of information provided by customers for problem resolution, including information allowing remote access to customers' systems and information gathered while accessing those systems.

A high level of customer cooperation and interaction frequently cause problems with customer property. For example, in response to an urgent need, a customer representative reaches into his briefcase and gives a high-priced small device directly to the engineer who needs it for next week's testing. How does the organization keep track of this item? Who other than the two parties involved knows about it? Or, in a team meeting, the customer representative hands over a CD-ROM with the latest version of software being supplied by the customer. How does the organization ensure that it is the correct version? How does the organization ensure that it is distributed to all those who need access to it?

To support both control and interaction, information about tools, fixtures, and other items used in product realization is frequently recorded in a department or project log by the recipient, who is responsible for the item.

Information about customer property provided for inclusion in the product (e.g., a new version of a software or hardware component) is an input to configuration management (PARAGRAPHS 7.3.7 *Control of design and development changes* and 7.5.3 *Identification and traceability*) and to inventory control (PARAGRAPH 7.5.5 *Preservation of product*).

As a caution, although it shares many attributes in common (e.g., specified and verified), as it remains the customer's property, it is not purchased product (PARAGRAPH 7.4 *Purchasing*). The relationship between purchased product and customer property becomes more complex when the organization purchases components on behalf of the customer. If the customer ιεquiιεε **thαt** η εpεcific piεcε of third-party software or hardware be included in delivered systems and commits to pay for that item, the customer-specified item is both customer property and purchased product, subject to the requirements of PARAGRAPHS 7.5.4 *Customer property* and 7.4 *Purchasing*.

When a customer purchases a number of items for deferred delivery (e.g., ten units a month for the next 12 months), depending on the nature of the product and on when ownership is transferred to the customer, the committed inventory may become customer property. In this case, "protect and safeguard" requires that the organization segregate or reserve the committed inventory to ensure that the committed quantities are available as required.

For software, which has no intrinsic value, escrow accounts for source code and development environments and the hand over of intermediate deliverables during design and development are methods for safeguarding customer property—and for ensuring the ability of the organization to meet any agreed-on requirements for long-term availability and support (PARAGRAPH 7.2.2 *c*).

PARAGRAPH 7.5.5 **Preservation of Product**

PARAGRAPH 7.5.5 contains requirements for "preserving the conformity of product [and product components] during internal processing and delivery." Because preservation is defined as protection,[12] PARAGRAPH 7.5.5 requires that the organization preserve or protect product and product components by implementing suitable methods for identification, handling, packaging, and storage. In this context, preservation and protection pertain to preventing damage or deterioration and to preventing loss.

Although ISO 9004:2000 PARAGRAPH 7.5.4 suggests addressing product preservation throughout the product life cycle, there is no definition of internal processing, especially as it relates to product realization.

Implementation Considerations. It appears that PARAGRAPH 7.5.5 is worded to cover the product during the time after design and development is done and before the product is turned over to the customer (i.e., during production and "early" service provision). The inference is that requirements for product control are supplied for the period of design and development in PARAGRAPH 7.3.7 *Control of design and development changes*. After delivery, PARAGRAPH 7.5.4 *Customer product* pertains.

In practice, because design and development, production, and servicing tend to operate in parallel, organizations find it effective and efficient to apply PARAGRAPH 7.5.5 to product realization. The processes and systems established to identify product and to control changes in design and development (e.g., configuration management, PARAGRAPH 7.3.7) are coordinated with or extended to production and service provision. The processes and infrastructure established in production for handling, storage, and packaging (e.g., for handling static sensitive components or installing software upgrades; PARAGRAPH 7.5.5) are applied as appropriate to design and development and to service provision.

Applying PARAGRAPH 7.5.5 to product realization is consistent with the application of two closely related paragraphs, both of which pertain to product realization: PARAGRAPH 8.3 *Control of nonconforming product* and PARAGRAPH 8.2.4 *Monitoring and measurement of product.*

During design and development, configuration management practices prevent unapproved changes from being introduced into the product and specify related methods for the storage and protection of work products (e.g., for network protection through firewalls and virus checking, for computer backup, and for off-site storage of copies or work products). Configuration management, including or supported by document control, preserves the availability of the current version of the work product. The associated status indicates the level of conformity the work product has achieved. In addition, when configuration management preserves previous versions or histories of changes for work products, the organization is able to revert to any previous version of a product. Handling, storage, and packaging processes that are established in production to address the requirements of PARAGRAPH 7.5.5 apply, with appropriate modification, to design and development. Using common processes (with appropriate modifications to reflect the different work environments) is particularly useful when engineering temporarily "borrows" and "returns" products and components from inventory.

During service provision, once the property belongs to the customer, the requirement to protect customer property in PARAGRAPH 7.5.4 is addressed by the handling and packaging processes that are established in production to address the requirements of PARAGRAPH 7.5.5.

PARAGRAPH 7.4 *Purchasing*

PARAGRAPH 7.4 provides comprehensive requirements for purchased product. Purchased product includes any item or service purchased by the organization for inclusion in the product or for use in any phase of product realization. The following are all purchased products:

- Standard hardware items purchased for inclusion in the product (e.g., components, subassemblies, cables, enclosures, power supplies, modems, printers, and chips)
- Standard software items purchased for inclusion in the product (e.g., drivers, installers, database management tools, and reporting tools and utilities)

- Standard hardware items purchased for use in product realization (e.g., components purchased for evaluation or prototyping, network servers, cables, systems, test tools, measuring devices, and mechanical simulators)
- Standard software purchased for use in product realization (e.g., project management tools, development portals, integrated development environments, test and analysis tools, and compilers)
- Purchased services, including outsourced activities (e.g., customer surveys, product industrial engineering, marketing, hardware design and development, software design and development, software customization, software localization, documentation, software and hardware testing, regulatory and safety certification, manufacturing, software duplication, delivery, installation, and support).

PARAGRAPH 7.4 contains requirements for supplier selection and management (PARAGRAPH 7.4.1), for the specification of items to be purchased (PARAGRAPH 7.4.2), and for verifying that product received from suppliers conforms to the purchase specification (PARAGRAPH 7.4.3).

PARAGRAPH 7.4.1 Purchasing Process

The first step the organization takes to ensure that purchased product meets requirements is to pick a capable source. Suppliers are systematically evaluated, selected, and reevaluated based on criteria the organization establishes. The selection and evaluation activities ensure the supplier's initial and ongoing ability to meet the organization's requirements, as described in the purchase specification (PARAGRAPH 7.4.2).

PARAGRAPH 7.4.1 requires that the organization determine the "effect of the purchased product on subsequent product realization or the final product" and then, based on that determination, establish and apply controls of an appropriate type and extent. Control encompasses the initial selection and assessment as well as any ongoing monitoring, assessment, and communication related to the conformance of purchased product. Control also includes the verification of purchased product, for which requirements are provided in PARAGRAPH 7.4.3 *Verification of purchased product*. As discussed below, this requirement is not as inflexible or prescriptive as it may seem at first reading.

Whether the organization acquires commodity components, implements a comprehensive process for supply chain management, partners with its suppliers, or outsources portions of its product realization process, it is the responsibility of the organization to define and communicate its expectations and requirements and to select suppliers who have the ability to fulfill their responsibilities. Provisions for monitoring and reassessing performance ensure that suppliers maintain their ability to fulfill those responsibilities as the supplier and the organization evolve their businesses independently. When the organization outsources a process, PARAGRAPH 4.1 and the associated guidance are interpreted to require that the organization ensure that the supplier's processes satisfy the relevant requirements of ISO 9001:2000. See the discussion in Chapter 4, under PARAGRAPH 4.1.

Finally, PARAGRAPH 7.4.1 requires that the organization maintain records (PARAGRAPH 4.2.4) related to the evaluations. The precise requirement is stated as, "records of the results of evaluations and any necessary actions arising from the evaluation." Although the layering of prepositional phrases makes two interpretations possible,* the corresponding language in PARAGRAPH 8.5 (for corrective and preventive action) requires that the records associated with PARAGRAPH 7.4.1 document:

- The results of the evaluations
- The results of any actions arising from the evaluation

In some cases, actions and results are indistinguishable (e.g., "approve supplier" or "suspend supplier"). In cases where a chain of actions is initiated to prevent or correct problems, PARAGRAPH 8.5.2 e (for corrective action) and PARAGRAPH 8.5.3 d (for preventive action) require that the organization record the results of action taken.

The controls implemented through the purchasing process address the requirement in PARAGRAPH 4.1 that the organization ensure control over any outsourced processes that affect product conformity to requirements.

Implementation Considerations. Activities related to purchased product are typically coordinated through a purchasing or supplier management function. To meet the requirements defined in PARAGRAPH 7.4, and to minimize the risk associated with purchased product, an effective purchasing process requires collaboration between the purchasing function and other parts of the organization. The purchasing function is typically responsible for establishing and administering the overall legal business relationship with the supplier (e.g., credit and reference checks, specification and enforcement of terms and conditions, monitoring the completion of contractual commitments, and release of funds for payment). The specification of purchased product and the initial and ongoing technical evaluation of supplier's capabilities and of purchased products is the responsibility of subject matter experts from outside the organization or from other parts of the organization. If design and development are outsourced, design engineers assess the processes, resources, and technical competence of candidate suppliers. If manufacturing is outsourced, manufacturing engineers and managers assess the processes, facilities, and resources of candidate suppliers.

---

* The two interpretations, determined by how the prepositional phrases are construed, are, first, records **of** (A) the results of evaluations and (B) any necessary actions arising from the evaluation; second, records **of the results of** (A) evaluations and (B) any necessary actions arising from the evaluation.

Effective purchasing processes require that both the business and technical perspectives be appropriately considered and that neither perspective be arbitrarily dominant.

Successful collaboration begins in the earliest stages of design and development, when decisions are made to make or buy portions of the product. These decisions determine the degree to which the design integrates or isolates the purchased product. The purchasing function supports these decisions with information ranging from the financial viability of a proposed supplier to the price and expected availability of commodity components.

Anticipating cost savings, organizations often underestimate the capabilities required to manage suppliers when core realization processes, such as design and development, manufacturing, and support, are outsourced in whole or in part. Selecting and managing suppliers of outsourced processes requires that the organization retain personnel who have the technical expertise and skills necessary to establish and manage the process being outsourced. For example, outsourcing the design and development of a product component requires sufficient technical knowledge to assess candidates' past successes (i.e., "We've successfully completed a number of similar contracts."), processes, and grasp of technology. As requirements introduce new technology and push the limits of established technology, "supplier" translates into "partner," and selection increasingly incorporates intangible factors, such as trust and the perceived intellectual capabilities and flexibility of candidate suppliers' personnel.

Outsourcing may also strain the capabilities of other organizational processes. In dealing with suppliers, the organization can no longer rely on experience, proximity, professional pride, and common interest to compensate for inadequate or cryptic system requirements or design documentation. For example, when manufacturing is outsourced, the cost of design changes is no longer absorbed into overhead, and project management can no longer be based on frequent or informal communication and on the assumption that commitments can be adjusted in real time as the need arises. In subcontracting software development, the supplier's need to size the work being proposed collides with organizational cultures that mistake varying forms of chaos for legitimate methodologies, like evolutionary and incremental development, prototyping, and initial deployment.

The effect of the purchased product on subsequent product realization or the final product translates into the degree of dependence or risk associated with the purchased product. For example, outsourcing the development of a critical component of its product has a significant effect on the organization's success in delivering the product. In this type of acquisition, appropriate diligence in selecting the supplier can include one or more site visits; monitoring the supplier's performance can be accomplished through frequent, regular meetings and the hand over and evaluation of intermediate work products. In contrast, sourcing a commodity component that is available from multiple, reputable suppliers can entail reference checks and the willingness of the supplier to commit to quantities and schedules. Appropriate monitoring can mean tracking deliveries against commitments and, possibly, inspecting delivered product against requirements, until the supplier's capability is proven. Once confidence in a supplier's capability is established, monitoring can shift to exceptions and periodic evaluation of performance. Exceptions and problems can result in reintroducing higher levels of control.

Partner or Supplier? Based on experience with ISO 9001:1994, the requirements of PARAGRAPH 7.4 *Purchasing* are applied when there is some form of compensation for the delivery of a product or service. This may represent a fine distinction, but development partners, recommended providers, and other entities that are not compensated by the organization are not considered suppliers to the organization from a purchasing perspective and are not subject to the requirements for supplier selection, and so forth. For example, if

- An organization qualifies and recommends third parties to its customers (for complementary, compatible products or for related services, such as installation or maintenance), and if those third parties sell their products directly to the organization's customers, those products are not purchased product.
- Two companies collaborate on the development of a product and both retain rights to manufacture the product, the development activity is not a purchased service for either company.
- A supplier updates its standard product to be compatible with the organization's application, and if the organization buys the updated standard product from the supplier for incorporation into its product, and even if there is a commitment to buy a specified number of units of the updated product, the design change activities are not purchased product, but the updated product is purchased product.

Relationships with partners are similar to and may be as important as those the organization maintains with its suppliers. Partners' capabilities are assessed. Requirements and technical information are clearly communicated. Progress is monitored. Intermediate work products and plans may be exchanged for review or testing.

From an ISO 9001:2000 perspective, the relationship between the organization and its suppliers is derived from any related commitments the organization makes to its customers. Completing the three examples above, if:

- An organization qualifies and recommends third parties that sell their products directly to the organization's customers, the organization's related responsibilities are for any commitments it makes to its customers (e.g., for how the organization qualifies the third parties).
- Two companies collaborate on the development of a product and both retain rights to manufacture the product, the organization's related responsibilities are for the product it provides to its customers, as addressed by the requirements for PARAGRAPH 8.2.4 *Monitoring and measurement of product*. If the companies coordinate their manufacturing, so that each sells part of the product to the other, the part that is purchased is purchased product, subject to the requirements of PARAGRAPH 7.4.3 *Verification of purchased product*.
- A supplier updates its standard product to be compatible with the organization's application, and if the organization buys the updated standard product from the supplier for incorporation into its product, the organization's related responsibilities are for the verification of purchased product as described in PARAGRAPH 8.2.4 *Monitoring and measurement of product*.

Record the Results: The Approved Vendor List. Beyond retaining results of specific evaluations, organizations typically also maintain a list of suppliers, with a current status (e.g., approved, pending approval, suspended, or barred) and, as appropriate, with the products or services to which the status applies. The list, often referred to as an Approved Vendor List, prevents unnecessary proliferation of suppliers and serves as a knowledge base to simplify the job of individuals responsible for sourcing products or services.

PARAGRAPH 7.4.2 Purchasing Information

PARAGRAPH 7.4.2 requires that the organization provide adequate information to its suppliers. In this context, adequacy translates into whether the purchasing information contains the information a qualified supplier requires to deliver a product or service that meets the organization's requirements. Adequate information begins with a description of the product, which, depending on the nature of the purchased product, can be as simple as a manufacturer's part number, quantity, and delivery date, or as complex as a detailed hardware design.

PARAGRAPH 7.4.2 emphasizes the need for the organization to supplement the description of the product or service with any appropriate requirements for the

- Approval of
    - The supplied product (e.g., acceptance tests; further defined in PARAGRAPH 7.4.3 *Verification of purchased product*)
    - The supplier's procedures, processes, and equipment

Exhibit 7-18. In our experience: unstated assumptions about tools.

BCC Systems subcontracted the development of a substantial new series of user's guides to Documentation Inc. (DI). BCC specified that the documents were to be created in FrameMaker so that BCC's publications group could easily take over updating the documents.

The project manager at BCC briefly tried to refuse to accept the final documents (after numerous content and format reviews) when he discovered that the graphics had been created in Adobe Illustrator rather than in FrameMaker's internal drawing utility.

BCC's supplier relations manager intercepted the refusal and pointed out that, as unfortunate as it was, DI had met the requirements of the purchase specification.

- Qualification of the supplier's personnel
- Supplier's quality management system

PARAGRAPH 7.4.2 concludes with the requirement that the organization "ensure the adequacy of specified purchase requirements" before communicating them to the supplier.

Related Paragraphs. PARAGRAPHS 7.2.1 *Determination of requirements related to the product*, 7.2.2 *Review of requirements related to the product*, and 7.3.2 *Design and development inputs* describe the determination of product requirements. PARAGRAPH 7.3.3 *b* requires that the design and development outputs include appropriate information for purchasing. PARAGRAPH 7.4.2 defines the content and mechanism for conveying requirements to suppliers who participate in product realization.

Implementation Considerations. The provisions of PARAGRAPH 7.4.2 are typically addressed through processes for formal requirements specifications. Unstated requirements related to the three areas identified in PARAGRAPH 7.4.2 are frequently the source of problems—even for organizations that convey meticulous payment terms and complete and unambiguous technical requirements for purchased products and services. Careful consideration of these three areas can ensure that both the supplier and the organization realize a satisfactory rate of return on their investment in the relationship (see Exhibit 7-18).

PARAGRAPH 7.4.2 *a*: Requirements for the Approval of Supplied Product. Requirements for the approval of supplied product can be expressed in terms of product and process attributes. For example, the organization can supply specific criteria for form, fit, and function and for the test and measurement processes that are to be applied to determine whether the criteria have been satisfied:

- The device shall process up to 1400 transactions per minute (product performance requirement).
- Before delivery, the supplier shall operate each device continuously for four consecutive hours, achieving the following expected results ... (requirement for testing to be performed by the supplier).

In addition, requirements for the approval of supplied product can be described in terms of tests or inspections the organization intends to perform on supplied product. For example:

- On receipt, 10 percent of the units shall be operated continuously for four consecutive hours, achieving the following expected results ... (requirement for testing to be performed by the organization; verification performed by the organization on purchased product is addressed in PARAGRAPH 7.4.3 *Verification of purchased product*).

These requirements for approval provide a common basis for both the supplier and the organization to apply in determining when the product or service is acceptable. Once confidence in the supplier is established, the requirements for approval can be adjusted to reduce overall cost.

PARAGRAPH 7.4.2 *a*: **Requirements for the Approval of Procedures, Processes, and Equipment.** Requirements for the approval of procedures and processes can include requiring that the supplier:

- Submit procedural documentation for review and approval by the organization
- Implement procedures specified by the organization
- Submit to periodic audits by the organization or by a third party to verify ongoing compliance with approved procedures (see PARAGRAPH 7.4.3 for requirements related to verification performed at the supplier's premises)

Process and procedural requirements express any expectations the organization has for:

- Intermediate work products
- Planning
- Periodic progress reviews and technical interchanges
- Corrective action (including support provided by the organization)
- Change management (e.g., for postrelease maintenance and for enhancement)
- Control of nonconforming product (PARAGRAPH 8.3) and for the release and delivery of conforming product.

Requirements for the approval of equipment can include requiring that the supplier use equipment and tools approved by, specified by, or supplied by the organization. These tools include software tools used for documentation, planning, creating drawings, and configuration management. Requirements for tools are typically imposed to facilitate the exchange of work products, communication between the supplier and the organization, and the coordination of activities.

PARAGRAPH 7.4.2 *b*: **Requirements for the Qualification of Personnel.** Requirements for the qualification of personnel can be expressed in terms of appropriate education, experience, certification, and credentials.

PARAGRAPH 7.4.2 *c*: **Requirements for the Organization Quality Management System.** Requirements for the quality management system can address the degree of management oversight to be exercised by the supplier, which is coordinated with requirements for communication between the supplier and the organization. Additional quality management system requirements can include ISO 9001 compliance, internal audits, and internal processes for corrective and preventive action.

Ensuring the Adequacy of Specified Purchase Requirements. The requirement to ensure the adequacy of purchasing information, which appears in the final paragraph of text in PARAGRAPH 7.4.2, is typically satisfied by internal reviews of the purchasing specification and by the explicit or implicit review of the purchase specification by the supplier before acceptance.

Other mechanisms for ensuring the adequacy of the purchasing information are procedures, templates, and checklists that identify all of the possible topics that should be considered for inclusion in a purchase specification.

PARAGRAPH 7.4.3 Verification of Purchased Product

PARAGRAPH 7.4.3 requires that the organization establishes and implements verification activities (test, inspection, etc.) to ensure that purchased product meets the specified requirements. PARAGRAPH 7.4.3 applies specifically to verification activities undertaken by the organization or by the organization's customer. Because they have the greatest potential to disrupt the supplier's operations, PARAGRAPH 7.4.3 calls specific attention to cases in which the organization or its customer intends to perform verification on the supplier's premises. In these cases, PARAGRAPH 7.4.3 requires that the organization state the intended arrangements and, as the supplied product is still at the supplier's premises, the method of product release as part of the product information.

Although PARAGRAPH 7.4.3 does not specifically refer to records of the verification of purchased product, PARAGRAPH 8.2.4 *Monitoring and measurement of product* does specify that "evidence of conformity shall be maintained," and PARAGRAPH 8.3 *Control of nonconforming product* specifies that "records of the nature of nonconformities and any subsequent actions taken … shall be maintained."

164

Implementation Considerations. The organization's verification activities confirm that the supplied product or service conforms to the purchase specification. These activities can range from receiving inspection (e.g., confirming that the received product conforms to the associated documentation) to successive levels of testing as the supplied product is integrated with other components.

In addition to defining acceptance criteria as part of the purchasing information, ongoing disclosure of the organization's testing methods allows the supplier a greater opportunity to coordinate testing and to identify and correct potential problems before product is handed over. In some cases, factory acceptance tests specified in detail by the organization are performed by some combination of personnel from the supplier, the organization, and, in some cases, the organization's customer. In all cases, disclosure of the planned test is essential for ensuring that the supplier has adequate resources available to support the verification activities and to address problems that, despite everyone's best efforts, only become apparent as additional components are integrated.

If the organization imposes requirements related to the supplier's processes, procedures, equipment, and personnel, the verification activities can include review, inspection, and testing of intermediate work products (e.g., plans, designs, test reports) as well as site visits, audits, and assessments of the supplier.

When the organization intends to perform any verification on the supplier's premises, the purchasing information includes any requirements for facilities, equipment, and personnel to be provided by the supplier.

Supplier Corrective Action and Change Management. One of the key concepts underlying supply chain management is exploiting the opportunity to transform the relationship with key suppliers from supplier to partner to strategic ally.[21] Constant communication and the responsiveness of the supplier and the organization to the other party's needs are critical factors in the success of these relationships.

In defining requirements for responsiveness and communication related to corrective action and the incorporation of changes, purchasing information establishes mutually acceptable processes and responsibilities for addressing

- Problems (e.g., analyzing, determining root causes, and planning corrective action, commensurate with the nature of the problem)
- Changes (e.g., analyzing effect and planning changes, commensurate with the priority of the change request).

In both cases, as the supplier and the organization have finite resources, success requires that responsibilities of both parties be clearly defined— including the process for making the inevitable decisions to balance current commitments and schedules, correcting problems (whatever the cause), and incorporating unanticipated changes.

Typically, the organization responsible for administering the relationship with the supplier (and for authorizing payments) provides detailed procedures for recording the results of verification activities and for making changes that affect contractual commitments between the organization and the supplier.

Receiving Inspection. Receiving inspection is referred to, above, as a possible method for verifying purchased product. When receiving inspection is determined to be part of product verification, the records generated by the receiving inspection are subject to the requirements associated with the monitoring and measuring of product.

There are, however, cases in which the nature of the purchased product limits the receiving inspection function to checking only for a valid addressee, purchase order, and shipping damage. The addressee or the requestor is responsible for verifying that the purchased product is correct, typically as part of installation, product integration, and integration testing. The requester generates any required records.

The challenge faced by the ISO implementation team is to ensure that the organization's procedures and plans clearly delineate responsibilities for verification and that the appropriate records are maintained so that the purchasing function has access to up-to-date information on which to base the supplier's status and on which to authorize milestone-based payments.

PARAGRAPH 7.6 *Control of Monitoring and Measuring Devices*

PARAGRAPH 7.6 contains a compact, complex, challenging set of requirements for monitoring and measurement and for the control of test beds, test fixtures, test software, and measuring devices (e.g., oscilloscopes and voltmeters). Fortunately, the implementation is typically relatively straightforward. Although PARAGRAPH 7.6 does not explicitly state that it applies throughout product realization, PARAGRAPH 8.2.4 *Monitoring and measurement of product*, which describes the use of monitoring and measurement equipment, does apply to activities at appropriate stages of product realization, so it is reasonable to infer that a similar scope applies to PARAGRAPH 7.6.

PARAGRAPH 7.6 starts with a compound requirement. The organization is required to determine:

- The monitoring and measurement to be undertaken to provide evidence that products conform to specified requirements, elicited through the processes characterized in PARAGRAPH 7.2.1 *Determination of requirements related to the product*.
- The devices needed to implement the monitoring and measurement determined to be necessary.

The first requirement, determining what monitoring and measurement to perform, refers to activities for which requirements are provided in numerous paragraphs scattered throughout the standard:

- PARAGRAPH 4.1 *General requirements*, specifically:
  - PARAGRAPH 4.1 *e* "[the organization shall] monitor, measure, and analyze these processes"
- PARAGRAPH 6.3 *Infrastructure*, specifically:
  - PARAGRAPH 6.3 *b*: process equipment (both hardware and software)
- PARAGRAPH 6.4 *Work environment* (e.g., as it affects the ability to monitor and measure)
- PARAGRAPH 7.1 *Planning of product realization*, specifically:
  - PARAGRAPH 7.1 *c*: required ... monitoring activities
- PARAGRAPH 7.3.5 *Design and development verification*
- PARAGRAPH 7.3.6 *Design and development validation*
- PARAGRAPH 7.4.3 *Verification of purchased product*
- PARAGRAPH 7.5.1 *Control of production and service provision*, specifically:
  - PARAGRAPH 7.5.1 *d*: the availability and use of monitoring and measuring devices
  - PARAGRAPH 7.5.1 *e*: the implementation of monitoring and measurement
- PARAGRAPH 8.2.3 *Monitoring and measurement of processes*
- PARAGRAPH 8.2.4 *Monitoring and measurement of product*

PARAGRAPH 7.6 goes on to require that the organization establish processes to ensure that monitoring and measurement can be and are carried out in a manner that is consistent with the monitoring and measuring requirements. Two phrases in this statement require analysis: establishing processes and monitoring and measuring requirements:

- Establishing processes specifies that the organization set [the associated processes] up on a firm or permanent basis.*
- The monitoring and measuring requirements are those determined by the organization as being required to meet:
  - Internal process- and product-related needs
  - Statutory and regulatory requirements
  - Requirements of ISO 9001 in the various paragraphs listed above
  - Contract-related commitments

PARAGRAPH 7.6 provides five detailed sets of requirements, labeled (a) through (e), that pertain to how the established processes ensure that measuring and monitoring can be and are carried out in a manner that produces valid results. These five sets of requirements are applied as appropriate and require that measuring equipment be:

* See the discussion of *establish* in Chapter 4, under PARAGRAPH 4.1.

a. "Calibrated or verified at specified intervals" or before use. The calibration or verification is performed against measurement standards traceable to international or national standards; where no such standards exist, the basis of the calibration or verification is recorded. Note that the next-to-last paragraph of text in PARAGRAPH 7.6 specifies that the organization maintains records of the results of calibration and verification.
b. "Adjusted and readjusted as necessary" (e.g., as determined by the verification, by the usage interval, and by the manufacturer's recommendations).
c. "Identified to enable the calibration status to be determined."
d. Protected "from adjustments that would invalidate the measurement result."
e. "Protected from damage and deterioration" when the equipment is handled, maintained, and stored.

The paragraph of text following the last lettered paragraph contains two independent requirements.

*   The first requirement pertains to what the organization is required to do when measuring equipment is found not to conform to requirements (i.e., the equipment is found to be out of calibration or out of adjustment). Specifically, the organization is required to assess and record the validity of previous measuring results and then take appropriate action on the measuring equipment and any affected product. For example, if it is discovered that a piece of test equipment is not producing accurate results (e.g., because it is out of adjustment or calibration), then the organization determines and records when and where the measuring equipment has been used since it was last known to be producing accurate results, the nature of the inaccuracy, and whether the previous results are still valid* (e.g., the product still passes or fails). On the basis of this information, the organization takes appropriate action on the equipment (e.g., calibrate, adjust, or remove the equipment and revise the process) and the affected products (e.g., no action, recall and retest, notify, extend warranties, and budget for a greater rate of field failures).
*   The second requirement is that the organization maintains records of the results of calibration and verification, both for measuring equipment that conforms to requirements and for measuring equipment that does not conform to requirements.

---

* The degree of error can fall within the precision and accuracy specified for the measurement results. In addition, when the precision and accuracy specified for the measurement results exceed those required to make decisions on the acceptability of product, a degree of error may not invalidate previous results and decisions.

PARAGRAPH 7.6 concludes with the explicit requirement that the ability of software used for monitoring and measuring product conformance to specified requirements be confirmed before use and reconfirmed as necessary. This paragraph is intended for software used in production, assembly lines, and test environments.

Implementation Considerations

Determining what monitoring and measurement is necessary is part of establishing the processes for the quality management system and, in particular, for product realization. In establishing these processes, the organization determines and acquires the appropriate equipment and facilities (e.g., signal generators, ovens, and isolation chambers), including facilities for the storage of equipment. Procedures and training ensure that personnel use and handle the equipment properly.

Because almost all organizations have equipment that is used to monitor and measure product quality, the starting point for implementing the requirements of PARAGRAPH 7.6 is to determine what steps are required to ensure that the equipment produces accurate results. A survey of the equipment used by the organization typically finds some combination of

- Equipment for which there are no user adjustments; training and procedures to ensure proper use are all that are required
- Equipment that requires setup and adjustment by the operator before a specific measurement can be taken; part of that setup may be manual or automatic self-test or self-calibration. Training and procedures to ensure proper setup and adjustment are all that are required, and requirements for records can be eliminated if the established process requires that the operator perform the setup, adjustment, and verification before each use. If there are multiple operators or if the setup is performed periodically, a written log kept with the equipment can be an appropriate record.
- Equipment that requires periodic calibration and adjustment by personnel in organizations that maintain the appropriate accreditation (e.g., laboratories accredited by the National Institute of Standards and Technology under the National Voluntary Laboratory Accreditation Program). When calibration is performed by an accredited organization, a label is placed on the equipment and a certificate is provided by the organization performing the calibration. The label and the certificate state the period of time during which the calibration remains valid. In addition, the organization performing the calibration seals access panels and user accessible adjustment mechanisms that affect calibration to prevent tampering.

The organization's procedures and training determine when calibrated equipment is used for measurements. Before each use, personnel performing measurements using calibrated equipment are directed to check the calibration label to ensure that the calibration is current.

Ensuring that calibration is performed against standards traceable to relevant national and international standards is the responsibility of the organization performing the calibration and is a requirement for maintaining its accreditation. However, even if a piece of measuring equipment can be calibrated, it may not be used in a manner that requires or preserves the calibration. In this case, even though the equipment lacks a current calibration label, to prevent the inadvertent use of the equipment for a purpose that does require calibration, it is recommended that the equipment be clearly labeled as not calibrated.

The documentation provided by the manufacturer of the equipment identifies whether and by whom the equipment can be adjusted or calibrated and the required frequency for the recalibration or adjustment. In addition, statutory and regulatory requirements and contractual commitments may provide relevant requirements.

When Equipment Is Found Not to Conform to Requirements

Assessing the effect of nonconforming measurement equipment requires knowing what equipment was used to perform a particular set of tests. In most cases, test configurations (e.g., type of hardware, type of software, and parameters) are specified in test plans and procedures. The sequence of tests is specified in a test procedure, test plan, or in the software development plan. The test hardware and software actually used are identified in the test report, which is the vehicle for determining what tests and products may be affected by nonconforming measurement equipment.

Because the organization performing the calibration may have the only opportunity to discover that a piece of measuring equipment is out of calibration, it is incumbent on the organization sending the equipment for calibration to request a complete report rather than just an affirmation that the equipment is now calibrated. Obtaining visibility into whether equipment is found to be out of calibration is particularly difficult when the measuring equipment is leased and, as the calibration period expires, the leasing agent replaces the currently installed device with a new, calibrated device.

For Software

For software design and development, PARAGRAPH 7.6 applies to coverage analyzers, tools for measuring complexity, memory-leak detectors, debuggers, and other tools used to determine the quality of the software during development. For all stages of product realization, PARAGRAPH 7.6 applies to test suites, test cases, test scripts, simulators, and other tools used to determine whether software performs as specified.

On the basis of experience with previous versions of ISO 9001, the term calibration is reserved for physical measuring equipment (e.g., gauges, meters, sensors, and oscilloscopes). Although a piece of equipment that contains software (e.g., firmware) can be calibrated, software, by itself, cannot be calibrated. For example, a software test suite can be validated and modified (e.g., to provide more thorough or effective testing), but it is not calibrated. Placing test programs, test data (e.g., input data and expected results), software tools, and test results under configuration management control or in a repository maintained in the test tool satisfies the other applicable requirements for protecting the test software from:

- Changes (e.g., adjustments) that would invalidate the test results and the requirements of PARAGRAPH 7.6 *d*
- Damage or deterioration during handling, maintenance, and storage (PARAGRAPH 7.6 *e*)

The requirement to verify the ability of software test tools to detect defects is satisfied by systematic review of test plans, cases, and scripts and by updating test suites as new types of defects are reported. For third party- and in-house-developed tools, at initial evaluation and as updates are received, the tool is installed in a controlled environment and exercised to ensure that it performs as specified. The records are kept until the tool is rolled out for production.

Establishing a Calibration Program

The following summarizes the steps in creating a basic calibration program that relies on accredited third parties to perform the actual calibration.

Survey the Equipment, Build and Maintain an Inventory. The first step is to survey the equipment in use throughout the organization, identify equipment that requires calibration, and build a list (e.g., in a spreadsheet or database tool) that records serial numbers, models, manufacturers, locations or owners, calibration status (e.g., current or expired), and the dates on which the current calibration expires.

Because calibration can be expensive, it is the owner's responsibility to ensure that calibration is required.

Simultaneously, the organization's process for purchasing or acquiring and receiving measurement equipment is modified so that any new equipment can be added to the list as the equipment is received. When recalibrated measurement equipment is returned from the service provider, the new calibration period is noted in the list.

In creating and maintaining the list, three special cases are sometimes encountered:

- The first case is when the owner determines that a piece of calibratable equipment is not used in a manner that requires calibration. In this case, to prevent inadvertent errors, it is recommended that the organization create and affix a label that identifies the piece of equipment as not calibrated.
- The second case is when new equipment is calibrated by the manufacturer, but no calibration label is applied or provided. To address this case, the organization can create its own calibration label, which is affixed to the new equipment before its first use.
- The third case pertains to calibratable measurement equipment loaned to the organization by the customer for use in product realization. This equipment is subject to the requirements of PARAGRAPH 7.5.4 *Customer property*. The organization may choose to include this equipment in the list or to manage it separately.

Although it may be useful, especially when measurement equipment is shared, there is no need to create a real-time notification mechanism for removing equipment from the calibration program. The equipment can be removed from the active list when it comes due for calibration and the owner reports its new status (e.g., no longer in service and scrapped). The calibration information is retained for as long as any records that refer to the piece of equipment are retained. Although it goes beyond the requirements of ISO 9001:2000, statutory, regulatory, or contractual requirements may make it necessary to retain a complete calibration history to support test records that refer to the piece of equipment.

Find Service Providers

As the equipment is inventoried, based on the manufacturer's requirements and any statutory, regulatory, or contractual requirements, accredited or approved calibration service providers are selected, following the procedures established to meet the requirements of PARAGRAPH 7.4 *Purchasing*. The purchasing information provided to the calibration service provider includes requirements for

- Adjusting the length of the calibration period based on experience with the equipment (e.g., from 12 to 18 months; or from 12 months to 6 months)
- Affixing or providing labels and providing certificates
- Notification if equipment is found to be out of calibration, which typically triggers an ad hoc investigation led by the quality or test manager to determine the effect on product and any appropriate action

On the basis of the input from the service providers, a detailed, nondiscretionary calibration budget is created.

Implement, Monitor, Follow Up

Implementation of the calibration program requires new procedures as well as changes in training and existing procedures, including the following:

- A new procedure assigns responsibility for monitoring the list for equipment requiring calibration, notifying owners, handling non-compliance, and sending the equipment to the service for calibration. Training ensures that owners understand the calibration program and their responsibilities.
- A new procedure requires that personnel check calibration labels before performing any measurement and specifies what to do if equipment is found to be out of calibration (either in use or at recalibration).
- All procedures and plans involving measurement are reviewed and modified as required to specify when calibrated equipment is to be used.
- Test record formats are reviewed and revised as required to ensure that the actual test environment (e.g., versions of test software and serial numbers of test equipment) are recorded.

The internal audit continues to monitor compliance.

PARAGRAPH 7 Conclusions

PARAGRAPH 7 *Product realization* describes requirements for activities that directly relate to delivering products and services to customers—from eliciting requirements to postdelivery support and service. Although it represents the heart of ISO 9001:2000, as illustrated by the frequent references to other paragraphs in the standard in the preceding descriptions, the requirements of PARAGRAPH 7 support and are supported by the other portions of the standard.

References

1. Paulk, M., Weber, C., Garcia, S., Chrissis, M., and Bush, M., *Key Practices of the Capability Maturity Model, Version 1.1*, CMU/SEI-93-TR-025/ADA263432, http://www.sei.cmu.edu/pub/documents/93.reports/pdf/tr25.93.pdf (7 Oct. 03).
2. Van Buren, Jim and Cook, David A., Experiences in the adoption of requirements engineering technologies, *CrossTalk*, December, 1998, http://www.stsc.hill.af.mil/crosstalk/1998/12/cook.asp (7 Oct. 03).
3. Sommerville, Ian and Sawyer, Pete, *Requirements Engineering: A Good Practice Guide*, John Wiley and Sons, New York, 1997.
4. Hooks, Ivy, *Managing Requirements*, http://www.complianceautomation.com/papers/ManagingRequirements.pdf) (07 Oct. 03).
5. IEEE Std 830-1998, *IEEE Recommended Practice for Software Requirements Specifications*, Institute of Electrical and Electronics Engineers, New York, 1998.

6. Davis, Alan M. and Leffingwell, Dean A., *Using Requirements Management to Speed Delivery of Higher Quality Applications*, Rational Software Corporation 1996, http://www.rational.com/products/reqpro/whitepapers.jsp (7 Oct. 03); select paper by title to download 696wp.pdf.

7. Bate, Roger, et al. *A Systems Engineering Capability Maturity Model, Version 1.1,* SE-CMM, SECMM-95-01, CMU/SEI-95-MM-003, Carnegie Mellon University, Software Engineering Institute, November 1995, http://www.sei.cmu.edu/publications/documents/95.reports/95.mm.003.html.

8. Emmerich, Wolfgang, Finkelstein, Anthony, and Stevens, Richard, *The Future of Requirements Management Tools*, 1998, http://www.cs.ucl.ac.uk/staff/W.Emmerich/publications/OeCG/traunpaper.pdf (07 Oct. 03).

9. International Council on Systems Engineering, *Tools Taxonomy: Requirements Management Tools*, 1999, http://www.incose.org/tools/tooltax.html.

10. International Organization for Standardization, *Life Cycle Management—System Life Cycle Processes,* ISO/IEC 15288, CD 2, International Organization for Standardization, Geneva, January 21, 2000.

11. *CMMI for Systems Engineering/Software Engineering/Integrated Product and Process Development, Version 1.01,* CMMI-SE/SW/IPPD, V1.01, Staged Representation, CMU/SEI-2000-TR-030, Software Engineering Institute, Carnegie Mellon University, Pittsburgh, November 2000, http://www.sei.cmu.edu.

12. International Organization for Standardization, *Guidance on the Terminology Used in ISO 9001:2000 and ISO 9004:2000*, Document ISO/TC 176/SC 2/N 526R, May 2001, International Organization for Standardization, Geneva, www.iso.org.

13. Institute of Electrical and Electronics Engineers, *IEEE Standard Glossary of Software Engineering Terminology*, IEEE 610.12, Institute of Electrical and Electronics Engineers, New York.

14. International Organization for Standardization, *Life Cycle Management—System Life Cycle Processes*, ISO/IEC 15288, CD 2, International Organization for Standardization, Geneva, January 21, 2000.

15. Pearsall, Judy, Ed., *The Concise Oxford Dictionary*, 10th ed., Oxford University Press, Oxford, 1999.

16. The Institute of Electrical and Electronics Engineers, PARAGRAPH 6.3.1, in ANSI/IEEE Std 830-1984, *IEEE Guide to Software Requirements Specifications*, The Institute of Electrical and Electronics Engineers, New York, 1984.

17. Moore, Geoffrey A., *Crossing the Chasm*, HarperBusiness, New York, 1991, pp. 29–59.

18. Peach, Robert W., Ed., *The ISO 9000 Handbook*, 3rd ed., Irwin Professional Publishing, Chicago, 1997, pp. 113–116.

19. ISO 9001:1987, PARAGRAPH 4.9.2, Special processes; ISO 9001:1994, clause 4.9, Process control, in the text and note following PARAGRAPH 4.9.2 *g.*

20. ISO 9000:2000.

21. Mabert, Vincent A., *The Design of a Supplier Alliance Program*, *Praxis*, Center for Advanced Purchasing Studies, vol. 1, Tempe, AZ, September 1997, www.capsresearch.org/publications/pdfs-protected/praxis091997.pdf (8 Oct. 03).

22. International Organization for Standardization, *Quality Management—Guidelines for Configuration Management,* ISO 10007, International Organization for Standardization, Geneva, April 15, 1995 (note that a 2003 revision is available).

23. Electronic Industries Alliance, *National Consensus Standard for Configuration Management,* EIA-649, Electronic Industries Alliance, Arlington, Aug. 1998.

24. International Organization for Standardization, *Information Technology—Software Life Cycle Processes—Configuration Management,* ISO/IEC TR 15846, International Organization for Standardization, Geneva, Nov. 1, 1998.

25. International Organization for Standardization, *Information Technology—Software Life Cycle Processes,* ISO/IEC 122076, International Organization for Standardization, Geneva, Aug. 1, 1995.

26. The Institute of Electrical and Electronics Engineers, *IEEE Guide to Software Configuration Management,* IEEE Std 1042-1987 (Reaff 1993), The Institute of Electrical and Electronics Engineers, New York, 1987/1993 (withdrawn standard).
27. International Organization for Standardization, *Guidelines for Developing Quality Manuals,* IJO 10013-1995, International Organization for Standardization, Geneva, 1995.

Chapter 8
PARAGRAPH 8
Measurement, Analysis, and Improvement

ISO 9001:2000 PARAGRAPH 8 *Measurement, analysis, and improvement* contains requirements that pertain to the overall quality system, to processes, and to product.

ISO 9001:2000 PARAGRAPH 8 eliminates the ambiguity of previous versions of ISO 9001 regarding the use of statistical techniques and imposes unequivocal requirements for monitoring and measuring processes and products and for analyzing the data produced by that monitoring and measuring. The graphs, reports, action items, and other results of the monitoring, measuring, and analysis are objective evidence that the processes are implemented.

Exhibit 8-1 summarizes the stated application of each of the paragraphs and paragraphs in ISO 9001:2000 PARAGRAPH 8.

PARAGRAPH 8.1 *General*

PARAGRAPH 8.1 requires that the organization plan and implement the monitoring, measurement, analysis and, improvement processes needed for various purposes (see Exhibit 8-2).

As noted in the table in Exhibit 8-2, the monitoring, measurement, analysis, and improvement processes are found in the remaining paragraphs in PARAGRAPH 8, which, in turn, refer to processes specified in other portions of ISO 9001. Exhibit 8-3 explores the overlapping definitions of monitor and measure.

PARAGRAPH 8.1 concludes with the statement that, as part of the planning and implementation, the organization is required to determine "applicable methods, including statistical techniques, and the extent of their use." The organization is required not only to identify what monitoring, measurement,

177

Exhibit 8-1. Scope of application of requirements of PARAGRAPH 8.

PARAGRAPH	Overall quality system	Processes	Product
8.1 *General*	✔	✔	✔
8.2 *Monitoring and measurement*	(no content)		
8.2.1 *Customer satisfaction*	✔	✔	✔
8.2.2 *Internal audit*	✔		
8.2.3 *Monitoring and measurement of processes*		✔	
8.2.4 *Monitoring and measurement of product*			✔
8.3 *Control of nonconforming product*			✔
8.4 *Analysis of data*	✔	✔	✔
8.5 *Improvement*	(no content)		
8.5.1 *Continual improvement*	✔	✔	✔
8.5.2 *Corrective action*	✔	✔	✔
8.5.3 *Preventive action*	✔	✔	✔

Exhibit 8-2. The requirements of PARAGRAPH 8.1.

Requirement in PARAGRAPH 8.1	Reference criteria	Discussed in PARAGRAPH or PARAGRAPHS
To demonstrate the conformity of product	Specified requirements	8.2.4 Monitoring and measurement of product 8.3 Control of nonconforming product
To ensure conformity of the quality management system	Policies, procedures, contracts, plans, and to ISO 9001	8.2.1 Customer satisfaction 8.2.2 Internal audit 8.2.3 Monitoring and measurement of processes 8.4 Analysis of data
To continually improve the effectiveness of the quality management system	Previous performance	8.5 Improvement

Exhibit 8-3. Monitor or measure?

On the basis of the definitions adopted by the authors of ISO 9001:2000,[2] it is reasonable to conclude that "monitor and measure" collectively covers activities ranging from inspection by eye to fully instrumented measurement:

- Monitor is (1) observe, supervise, keep under review; (2) measure or test at intervals, especially for the purpose of regulation or control
- Measurement is (1) ascertain or determine the spatial magnitude or quantity of (something); (2) ascertain or determine (a spatial magnitude or quantity) by the application of some object of known size or capacity or by comparison with some fixed unit.

and analysis are needed but also to determine the methods by which those activities are carried out. The selected methods can range from determining trends based on inspecting counts and graphs to statistical techniques. In this context, statistical techniques refers to formal methods of gathering and analyzing data (e.g., Design of Experiments and Statistical Process Control).[1]

PARAGRAPH **8.2** *Monitoring and Measurement*

PARAGRAPH 8.2 specifies four areas of required measurement and one required method:

- Customer satisfaction (PARAGRAPH 8.2.1)
- Quality management system (PARAGRAPH 8.2.2)
- Processes (PARAGRAPH 8.2.3)
- Product (PARAGRAPH 8.2.4)

The required method, which applies to the overall quality management system, is:

- Internal audit (PARAGRAPH 8.2.2)

PARAGRAPH 8.2.1 Customer Satisfaction

The organization is required to monitor information relating to customer perception as to whether the organization has met customer requirements.* This data is analyzed (as described in PARAGRAPH 8.4) and the resulting information becomes input for continual improvement (PARAGRAPH 8.5.1), corrective action (PARAGRAPH 8.5.2, through the analysis of customer complaints), and management review (PARAGRAPH 5.6.2, through customer feedback).

The organization is explicitly required to determine the methods for obtaining and using this information. The organization is implicitly required to determine what data it will use. Selecting the data and communicating the results of the analysis (PARAGRAPH 8.4) are typically part of the organization's strategy for meeting the requirements of PARAGRAPH 5, in particular, for ensuring that the organization achieves its "aim of enhancing customer satisfaction" (PARAGRAPH 5.2) and meets requirements for implementing appropriate communication regarding the effectiveness of the quality management system (PARAGRAPH 5.5.3).

To dispel the misconception that no news is good news, ISO 9000:2000 PARAGRAPH 3.1.4 notes that although the presence of customer complaints

---

* ISO 9000:2000 defines customer satisfaction as the customer's perception of the degree to which the customer's requirements have been fulfilled. Reference 2 defines perception as "state of being or process of becoming aware or conscious of a thing, especially through any of the senses."

indicates low customer satisfaction, their absence does not indicate a high level of customer satisfaction. Likewise, high levels of sales or market share can mask both customer frustration and the organization's vulnerability to a competitive challenge.

Organizations exploit a variety of methods to gather data on customer perception.

Direct methods include:

- Surveys—Survey methods range from subscriptions to industrywide surveys conducted by third parties, to questions asked by field personnel on postsale, customer-care follow-up visits, to comment cards included in the backs of documents and with product shipments.
- Focus groups—Typically managed by a third party, representative customers are closely observed as they respond to opportunities to provide the organization with feedback.
- Customer advisory boards—Key customers or potential customers assist in providing direction to the organization's products.

Indirect methods, which provide an indication of customer satisfaction, include:

- Reviews of problem reports and enhancement requests—monitoring and measuring trends in problem reports and enhancement requests (e.g., by product, by market, and by customer)
- Reference sales—the willingness of current customers to publicly endorse a product or service
- Follow-on or repeat sales to existing customers—including service and support contracts and additional units
- Market share

Indirect methods frequently are used to plan and shape direct data-gathering activities.

No matter what methods of analysis are selected (PARAGRAPH 8.4), gaining benefit from the investment in measuring customer satisfaction and achieving improvement (PARAGRAPH 8.5.1) requires that the organization convey relevant information to internal stake-holders, whether or not they are in the formal scope of the ISO 9001–compliant quality management system: from support to engineering, to manufacturing, to human resources, to order fulfillment, to receivables, and to field support (PARAGRAPH 5.5.3).

PARAGRAPH 8.2.2 Internal Audit

PARAGRAPH 8.2.2 characterizes the internal audit process in terms of resources, planning, scope, and follow-up. Audit is defined in ISO 9000:2000 as a "systematic, independent and documented process for obtaining audit evidence and evaluating it objectively to determine the extent to which audit criteria are fulfilled." ISO 9000:2000 goes on to define audit criteria as a "set of policies, procedures, or requirements used as a reference"—the yardstick against which the areas to be audited (e.g., projects, departments, functions, processes) are evaluated.

PARAGRAPH 8.2.2 restates the purpose of the audit in terms of specific audit criteria. The audit determines whether the quality management system:

- Conforms to:
  - The planned arrangements described in PARAGRAPH 7.1 for product-specific activities and, based on the direct reference in PARAGRAPH 7.1, to the general arrangements described in PARAGRAPH 4.1 (e.g., activities are carried out as specified in policies and procedures and planned for projects, processes, and organizational units).
  - The requirements of ISO 9001:2000. The internal audits provide key inputs for the management representative, who is charged with ensuring that the "processes needed for the quality management system are established, implemented, and maintained" (PARAGRAPH 5.5.2) and for management review (PARAGRAPH 5.5.2 *a*).
  - Any other quality management system requirements established by the organization (e.g., customer commitments, quality objectives).
- Is effectively implemented and maintained (e.g., is deployed throughout the organization and reflects current practice).

PARAGRAPH 8.2.2 requires that the audits occur at planned intervals, according to an audit program that is based on the "status and importance areas to be audited and on the results of previous audits" (e.g., previous problems). As part of the program, the audit criteria, scope, frequency, and methods are defined. "Audit program" and "scope" are defined in ISO 19011.[3] "Audit program" is defined in PARAGRAPH 3.11 as a set of one or more audits planned for a specific time frame and directed toward a specific purpose and "audit scope" is defined in PARAGRAPH 3.13 as the "extent and boundaries of an audit." Examples supporting the definition are physical locations, organizational units, activities, and processes.

To fulfill the requirement for independence, ISO 9001 PARAGRAPH 8.2.2 requires that the organization select auditors and conduct audits in a manner that ensures that the findings are objective and impartial. Specifically, auditors do not audit their own work.

PARAGRAPH 8.2.2 assigns to the "management responsible for the area being audited" responsibility for ensuring that corrective action (PARAGRAPH 8.5.2) is taken in a timely manner. To complete the corrective action, the audit process is required to include follow-up—including "verification of the actions taken and the reporting of the results" (e.g., that the problem has been addressed).

The organization is required to establish and support an audit process with a documented procedure that addresses responsibilities and requirements for planning audits, conducting audits, reporting results, and maintaining records.

Efficiency and the Internal Audits. Although "efficiency" is defined and used frequently in ISO 9000:2000, it is used only in ISO 9004:2000, which provides guidance that goes beyond the requirements stated in ISO 9001:2000. Nothing prevents an organization from establishing efficiency-related objectives for the processes that form the quality management system and from monitoring them through the internal audit process. Even when an organization does not establish efficiency-related objectives, processes have a tendency to evolve as personnel skip steps that do not seem to have any value and find new, more efficient (e.g., easier) ways of doing their jobs. Although this type of initiative is something management wants to encourage, it also requires control. What does not seem to have value may be critical for another part of the process. What makes one part of a process easier may increase risk or problems for another part of the process.

A well-defined process for submitting, evaluating, and implementing improvements is essential to prevent processes from drifting out of control and to ensure that the quality management system is systematically maintained. Although the internal audits ensure that the quality management system is implemented and maintained, they can also serve as a vehicle for identifying and capturing improvement ideas, including those related to efficiency.

Implementation Considerations. The implementation team is faced with decisions in three closely related areas:

- Auditor selection and qualification
- Achieving independence
- Selecting strategies and methods.

ISO offers comprehensive guidance for auditing in *ISO 19011 Guidelines for Quality and/or Environmental Management Systems Auditing*,[3] which replaces the guidance for auditing quality management systems (ISO 10011) and for auditing environmental management systems (ISO 14010:1996, ISO 14011:1996, ISO 14012:1996). In addition to ISO guidance, two texts are recommended for serious auditors.[4,5]

Auditor Selection and Qualification. The audit criteria define the collective knowledge that the audit team is required to possess:

182

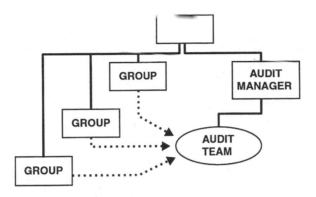

Exhibit 8-4. A suggested structure for the audit team.

- What is supposed to happen—knowledge about the organization's processes and any product-specific (e.g., project) variations. Although the auditors do not have to be expert practitioners, they do have to be able to understand the processes, technologies, and work products found in the area being audited. Without this level of knowledge, it is easy to miss all but the most obvious points (of which everyone is already aware) and to be deliberately or inadvertently misled.
- When it is supposed to happen and who is supposed to do it—knowledge about the organization's plans and schedules. This knowledge allows the auditors to translate their understanding of process and work products into a list of artifacts and questions that are appropriate for the area being audited.
- What is required by the standard. To monitor ongoing compliance, the auditors require detailed knowledge of the relationship between the organization's processes and the requirements of ISO 9001:2000.

Exhibit 8-4 portrays a strategy in which groups (departments, functions, projects) contribute. During the audit, auditors report to the audit manager, maintaining "dotted-line" relationships with their groups.

As is discussed below, verifying effective implementation and maintenance requires that the audit go beyond examining documents and other artifacts to include interviews with selected individuals from all levels of the organization (managers and individual contributors). Effective implementation is confirmed by a consistent understanding throughout the organization. Effective maintenance means that

- The quality management system—the policies, procedures, and standards—reflects current practice
- Personnel are aware of their responsibility to follow procedures and to request changes; there is a method for requesting changes
- Process changes are understood, communicated, planned, and appropriately introduced.

The audit methods define attributes of successful auditors: the ability to read and analyze documents and other artifacts, the ability to interview individuals or small groups to gather information, and the ability to present findings to small groups.

By pairing auditors with complementary knowledge and analytical and interpersonal skills, the organization can reduce the specific skills and amount of knowledge a single auditor requires, preserve independence, and significantly improve the quality of the results.

Achieving Independence. ISO 9001:2000 requires that auditors not audit their own work. Because this would not be an issue for a separate, permanent audit organization, the correct inference is that auditors can be drawn from the areas being audited on some type of temporary or part-time basis, as illustrated in Exhibit 8-4. The value of involving these subject-matter experts far outweighs the additional training costs and the administrative time that is spent ensuring that auditors do not directly audit their own work. Membership on the audit team can be for a fixed period, one or two years, with selected second-year auditors mentoring new auditors, leading teams of auditors, and bringing continuity to the audit process.

Another benefit of rotating individuals through the audit team is that they go back to their jobs with an increased understanding of how the organization conducts business and with an ingrained habit of looking for ways to improve the effectiveness—and the efficiency—of the processes they perform.

To reduce pressure, organizations try to assign auditors so that they do not audit work that is within the span of control of the auditor's immediate manager.

Independence is, however, more a matter of organizational culture than it is a result of clever planning. Even in organizations that have a separate reporting structure for auditors, when the audit is not a valued and valuable part of the organization's processes, findings are ignored or auditors are diverted into politically acceptable channels. In other organizations, engineers line up to become auditors because it is viewed as a way to gain the career advantage of a greater understanding of the business while contributing to the health of the organization.

Part of the implementation team's responsibility is to establish and reinforce a culture that views the audits as not only necessary, but also valuable. Managers are responsible for supporting the audits by providing an occasional auditor, by supplying requested information and personnel for scheduled audits, and by responding to identified problems in a timely manner. The extreme opposite of this environment is one in which the auditors are viewed as policemen, problems are concealed, people are late for interviews, and problems uncovered in audits result in black marks, blame, and increased resolve to do a better job of concealing problems in the next audit.

Selecting Strategies and Methods. Although ISO 9001:2000 does not specify methods, a number of best practices, some of which can be traced at least as far back as 1911 in the work of F. W. Taylor,[6,*] continue to be rediscovered, reinvented, and renamed.

Successful audits require:

- A systematic, disciplined approach; the audit process includes:
  - Published plans for auditors, interviews, and presentation of results to build confidence
  - Thorough training and standard templates for results to ensure consistency
  - Regular reports that provide management with visibility into audit schedules and follow up corrective action plans to provide motivation.
- An approach that verifies compliance and identifies opportunities for improvement; the purpose of the quality management system and the audit process is not to prevent creativity and stifle improvement
- Examination of documents and records, and interviews with individuals at all levels of the organization
- Thorough checklists used in preparation and retained for future audits; reduced to a top five- or six-item punch list that is carried into the interviews
- Well-written findings that document problems in as much detail as is necessary to communicate the problem to the person responsible for solving the problem and to auditors conducting follow-up or subsequent audits; for example:
  - Where the auditor found the problem (e.g., department, project, location)
  - What the auditor found
  - Why it is a problem (what requirement is not being satisfied; the standard or procedure that is being violated)
  - When appropriate, suggestions about how to address the problem
- Complete corrective action plans furnished by the manager or managers responsible for correcting the problem; "complete" can include analysis of the problem, process and procedure changes, equipment changes, and training and communication

---

* Although Taylor does not directly reference audits, a constant theme in his work is objective observation, measurement, and recording and analyzing observations.

Exhibit 8-5. In our experience: who to interview?

Registrars' auditors seek to talk to or observe approximately 15 percent to 20 percent of the personnel in an organization as a representative sample. When there are large numbers of people doing identical jobs, the percentage is adjusted downward accordingly. This represents a reasonable minimum for internal audits. In many cases, higher coverage rates are established for internal audits.

For example, at management's request, one organization targets 100 percent coverage to ensure that all personnel felt fully engaged in process improvement. The organization comprises 280 software and hardware engineers, marketing personnel, and managers supporting four product lines.

In this organization, a team of 14 auditors, divided into subteams of six or eight auditors, conducts interviews in pairs twice a year.

Each auditor commits four weeks per year: three full weeks of preparation, auditing, and report writing (one and a half weeks per audit) and one week of time spent in weekly meetings between audits. Each of the seven pairs of auditors interviews approximately 20 individuals (five to six one-hour interviews per day for three and a half days) to achieve 100 percent coverage of the organization each year.

- Appropriate follow up (e.g., check in the next internal audit, reaudit the particular activity, review a revised procedure)
- A simple mechanism (e.g., database and spreadsheet) for tracking, analyzing, and reporting the disposition of audit findings

The implementation team also establishes a strategy for defining the scope and frequency for audits.

Scope depends on the nature of the organization. As suggested by ISO 19011, scope can be expressed in terms of combinations of physical locations, organizational units, activities, and processes. Audits can go across locations (e.g., when two locations share common processes or perform coordinated activities, such as developing components of a common product) and organizational boundaries (e.g., when product requirements move between marketing, engineering, test, and customer support). See Exhibit 8-5 for suggestions about how many individuals to interview.

The findings that offer the greatest benefit are typically those that cross boundaries—between locations, functions, or organizational units. The ability of an audit process to uncover these types of problems and opportunities is contingent on a high level of coordination and consistency—so that problems identified in one audit can be traced to activities found in another audit and assigned for resolution to the appropriate organization or organizations. Close coordination and consistency in the audit process allow the organization to leverage experience in one part of the organization to solve or prevent problems in another part of the organization.

In terms of a scheduling strategy, based on the rates of change encountered in today's organizations and technologies, it is reasonable to schedule audits so that all parts of the organization are seen at least once a year. Based on unusual rates of change and past histories of problems, some may be seen more frequently. Scheduling strategies, based on the size of the pool of auditors, range from small audits conducted monthly to one- or two-week-long audits twice a year. A semiannual or quarterly strategy seems to offer the best balance among administration and planning effort, maintaining focus on the audits (e.g., minimize rescheduling and maximize responsiveness) and avoiding conflicts with job-related priorities.

An Editorial Postscript. Internal audits conducted as peer reviews and as a temporary assignment offer significant benefits to an organization—both in the improvements and changes resulting directly from the audit findings and in the indirect cultural changes that occur, increasing numbers of individuals who have developed an auditor's perspective toward their work disperse throughout the organization.

Paragraph 8.2.3 Monitoring and Measurement of Processes

Paragraph 8.2.3 requires that the organization applies suitable methods for monitoring and, where applicable, measurement of processes. Monitoring is a "shall"; measurement is a "shall, where applicable." Exhibit 8-3 explores the difference between monitor and measure.

The purpose of monitoring and measuring is to demonstrate the "ability of the processes to achieve planned results." Suitability, then, is based on the ability of the methods to achieve the stated purpose of the monitoring and measuring.

When planned results are not achieved, appropriate corrective action (Paragraph 8.5.2) is invoked to ensure product conformity. Because corrective action requires that the organization evaluate the need for action to prevent the reoccurrence of nonconformities (Paragraph 8.5.2 c) and then determine and implement the action needed (Paragraph 8.5.2 d), failure to achieve planned results may not result in process changes. Even repeated instances of process failures might not be sufficient to trigger process changes, as preventive action (Paragraph 8.5.3) contains the same requirements to evaluate the need for action to prevent the future occurrence of nonconformities (Exhibit 5-5).* It is the responsibility of the organization to determine when there is a need for action.*

---

* "Masochism" is defined in Reference 7 as "the tendency to derive ... gratification from one's own pain." Organizational masochism does not yet have wide currency in the literature of organizational behavior. It is briefly characterized in Reference 8 and is referenced obliquely in Reference 9. See also Exhibit 5-5.

Implementation Considerations. The requirements for monitoring and measuring "to demonstrate the ability of processes to achieve planned results" is typically addressed at the project or product level through a hierarchy of progress reviews (see PARAGRAPH 7.3.4) and reports that allow management to take appropriate corrective (see PARAGRAPH 8.5.2) and preventive action (see PARAGRAPH 8.5.3). Typical measures that support monitoring are on-time completion of milestones, schedule slippages, accuracy of estimates of effort and time, scrap percentages, rework percentages, requirements changes, requirements completed (e.g., content delivered), requirements decommitted (e.g., content removed), and resource availability.

Project- and product-focused monitoring and measurement are supplemented by the internal audits, management review, and preventive action, which examine performance across iterations of processes (e.g., across projects or releases) to ensure that the quality system continues to be effective.

In many cases, the project management, requirements management, configuration management, bug tracking, and call-handling tools automate the collection, synthesis, and presentation of data on process performance. Automated reports, which highlight exceptions, are inspected or analyzed by management to determine when action is necessary.

PARAGRAPH 8.2.4 Monitoring and Measurement of Product

PARAGRAPH 8.2.4 requires that the organization "monitors and measures the characteristics of product." There is none of the equivocation (e.g., suitable and where applicable) associated with process measurement. The purpose of monitoring and measuring product is to "verify* that product requirements have been met."

The monitoring and measurement is planned (as required by PARAGRAPH 7.1 *d*) and occurs at appropriate stages of product realization.

Because monitoring and measurement of product is an activity intended to ensure product requirements are satisfied, when it occurs in the design and development phase of product realization, it is also subject to the requirements of PARAGRAPH 7.3.5 *Design verification* and PARAGRAPH 7.3.6 *Design validation*.

In defining the requirements for records, PARAGRAPH 8.2.4 specifies two attributes:

- Evidence of conformity with acceptance criteria ... be maintained.
- Records shall indicate the person(s) authorizing release of product.

---

* "Verify" is apparently used in a generic sense in PARAGRAPH 8.2.4, although verification and validation have very specific meanings. This is consistent with the fact that ISO 9000:2000 contains definitions for verification and validation but not for verify.

Paragraph 8.2.4 concludes with the requirement that product release "shall not proceed until the planned arrangements have been satisfactorily completed, unless otherwise approved by a relevant authority." As noted, approval may also involve the customer.

Although it is left unstated, when product monitoring and measurement uncover nonconformities, the product is subject to the requirements of Paragraph 8.3 *Control of nonconforming product*, and appropriate corrective action (Paragraph 8.5.2) is invoked.

Implementation Considerations. Paragraph 8.2.4 contains requirements that affect a number of processes: verification and validation in design and development (i.e., monitoring and measurement) and configuration management (i.e., release approval) throughout product realization.

Verification and validation are discussed earlier under Paragraphs 7.3.5 *Design and development verification* and 7.3.6 *Design and development validation*. Configuration management is discussed under Paragraph 7.3.7 *Design and development changes*.

In implementing configuration management processes that satisfy the requirements of Paragraph 8.2.4, the words "unless otherwise approval" are critical. Products routinely advance through their life cycles with known defects, some of which are remediated in parallel with subsequent work, installation, or delivery; other defects may remain for the life of the product. Although some criteria can be specified (e.g., "no class A defects," or "no safety-critical defects"), the focus of Paragraph 8.2.4 is on designating individuals who have the authority to grant a waiver, to approve the release of product for which planned arrangements have not been satisfactorily completed. Note that planned arrangements and waivers cover both product defects (e.g., all agreed-on product characteristics not met) and process defects (e.g., all agreed-on testing not completed).

Approval and Configuration Management. The level of approval required typically increases as the product progresses through the development life cycle (see Exhibit 8-6). For example, Exhibit 8-6 describes the approval process for software units product in an organization that develops hardware and software that it combines into systems products. Projects designate managers for software development and hardware development. The company has system test, customer support, and manufacturing managers who work across all projects and products. Within a project, the project software development manager is responsible for several teams of programmers, each headed by a team leader. Exhibit 8-6 describes the criteria, roles, responsibilities, and processes for approving the release of code in each stage of design and development.

Exhibit 8-6. Approval criteria and processes for the release of code.

Phase	Approval criteria and processes
Unit	The author of the code performs unit tests and determines when it is ready to check in to the team's software baseline. During the phase The criterion used by programmers to determine when to check new or modified code into the team baseline is: no defects that prevent the team baseline from being built nightly. Phase exit criteria: The criteria used by programmers to determine when the code is ready for team-level integration testing are: (1) unit tests completed, (2) code review completed, (3) no defects that prevent the team baseline from being built nightly, (4) component detailed design draft approved, and (4) known defects are documented in the programmers notes.
Team software integration	Once team-level software integration begins, the team leader approves all changes before they are checked in to the team baseline. Team-level integration activities are planned based on dependencies and interactions among the team's software components. Phase entry criterion: The entry criterion for team-level integration testing is that all components specified in the plan satisfy the Unit Phase exit criteria During the phase: Criteria for making changes to the team baseline during team-level integration are: (1) unit tests completed and (2) only planned changes (e.g., staged increments of functionality) or fixes to defects identified in team-level integration testing are permitted Phase exit criteria: Criteria for completion of team-level integration tests are: (a) approval by the team leader, (b) component detailed design approved, and (c) known defects are documented in the programmer's notes.
Project software integration	Once software project-level integration begins, the project software development manager (who manages several teams) approves changes before they are checked in to the project software baseline. Software project-level integration activities are planned based on dependencies and interactions among the teams' software components. It is interesting to note that integration and integration test are distinct steps; problems identified in either step are tracked, resolved, and result in changes to the project software baseline. Phase entry criteria: The entry criteria for software project-level integration testing are: (a) all components specified in the plan satisfy the team software integration phase exit criteria, and (b) draft software high-level design is approved.

Exhibit 8-6 (continued). Approval criteria and processes for the release of code.

Phase	Approval criteria and processes
	During the phase:
	The criteria for making changes to the project software baseline during project-level integration are: (a) team software integration phase exit criteria are satisfied and (b) only planned changes (e.g., staged increments of functionality) or fixes to defects identified in project-level integration testing are permitted.
	Phase exit criteria:
	The criteria for completion of project-level integration tests are: (a) approval by the project manager, with the concurrence of the project software development manager, the project hardware development manager, and the system test manager; (b) software high-level design is approved; and (c) known defects are documented in the defect tracking database.
System integration	Once system integration begins, a board chaired by the product manager and composed of the project software development manager, the project hardware development manager, and the system test manager approve changes before they are checked in to the system baseline. System integration activities are planned based on dependencies and interactions among the product hardware and software components.
	Phase entry criteria:
	The entry criteria for system integration testing are: (a) all components specified in the plan satisfy the project software integration phase exit criteria, and (b) draft system design is approved.
	During the phase:
	Criteria for making changes to the project baseline during system integration are: (a) all project-software integration tests are completed, (b) only planned changes (e.g., staged increments of functionality) or fixes to defects identified in system integration testing are permitted.
	Phase exit criteria:
	The criteria for completion of system integration are: (a) approval by the product manager and the system test manager, (b) system design approved, (c) draft acceptance test plan approved, and (d) known defects are documented in the defect tracking database.
Acceptance	Once acceptance testing (e.g., beta testing) begins, changes to the acceptance baseline are approved by a board chaired by the product manager and composed of the project software development manager, the project hardware development manager, the system test manager, and the manufacturing manager. Acceptance testing activities are planned based on dependencies and interactions among user functions.

Exhibit 8-6 (continued). Approval criteria and processes for the release of code.

Phase	Approval criteria and processes
	Phase entry criteria: Entry criteria for acceptance testing are: (a) product has completed system integration testing with no Class A (Major) defects affecting identified acceptance test sites and no more than four Class B (Minor) defects, and (b) acceptance test partner agreements signed.
	During the phase: Criteria for making changes to the product baseline during system integration are: (a) all system integration tests completed, (b) only planned changes (e.g., staged increments of functionality) or fixes to defects identified in acceptance testing are permitted.
	Phase exit criteria: Criteria for completion of acceptance testing are: (a) approval by the product manager, the hardware development manager, the software development manager, the support manager, and the manufacturing manager; (b) new product introduction plan approved; and (c) known defects are documented in the defect tracking database.

With respect to records of product monitoring and measuring:

- Because there is no requirement in ISO 9001:2000 for the level of detail, the evidence can be a complete test report, showing the results of each test, or a one-line statement in a change control board meeting report that says "all tests in test plan v22 passed." Likewise, retention times for test records can range from brief (e.g., until the approver sees it) to lengthy (e.g., for seven years after the product is last sold). In some cases, legal, regulatory, risk management, or customer requirements specify a level of detail and a period of retention. As always with records, retention time is determined by the useful life of the record from a business perspective, not out of concern for maintaining an audit trail for an ISO auditor. See the end of Chapter 4 for additional comments on audit trails.
- The method of indicating the person or persons responsible for approval is not specified, so examples of valid indicators in the record are:
  - A name or title in the record
  - A report from the change control board, showing attendees, identifying that the release is authorized. In this case, the report becomes part of a record, and so it must have designated retention times, retrieval methods, and so forth, as specified in PARA-GRAPH 4.2.4.
  - Clear assignment and indication of responsibility is particularly important in the case of geographically distributed development teams.

PARAGRAPH 8.3 Control of Nonconforming Product

PARAGRAPH 8.3 requires a documented procedure that defines the controls, responsibilities, and authorities implemented by the organization to ensure that "product that does not conform to product requirements is identified and controlled to prevent its unintended use or delivery." Although it is not explicitly stated, the requirements of PARAGRAPH 8.3 apply to work products in any stage of product realization.

PARAGRAPH 8.3 then goes on to require that the organization deal with nonconforming product in one or more of three ways:

- Correct the problem: Corrected product is required to be reverified that, as corrected, it does conform to requirements
- Use it anyway, under a concession (or waiver) approved by the relevant authority (which may include the customer)
- Take action to preclude its original intended use or application.

In all cases, the organization is required to maintain records of nonconformities and of any subsequent actions, including any concessions or waivers that are obtained.

These requirements amplify the requirements for corrective action found in PARAGRAPH 8.5.2 *Corrective action*.

PARAGRAPH 8.4 concludes with the statement that the organization is required to take action on nonconforming product "detected after delivery or use has started." The action is required to be "appropriate to the effects or potential effects of the nonconformity." This duplicates requirements in PARAGRAPH 8.5.2 (effects) and PARAGRAPH 8.5.3 (potential effects).

Implementation Considerations. The requirements of PARAGRAPH 8.3 are typically addressed through two dependent mechanisms: problem reporting and configuration management.

During development and after release, problem reporting and tracking procedures and tools ensure that specific problems are identified and corrected. Once a work product is made available to individuals other than the author, a mechanism needs to be provided to ensure that identified defects are communicated to the author and that others who have access to the work product are informed of changes, known defects, and resolutions. The degree of structure incorporated into the bug-tracking mechanism depends on the frequency of contact between engineers (e.g., within a collocated project team or within a distributed team that maintains close contact through a development portal with automated action item tracking) and on the purpose for which the work product has been made available (e.g., for advance notice, review, integration testing, or incorporation into a related work product).

Customer technical support mechanisms typically define how defects in delivered product are reported, evaluated, escalated as appropriate, and tracked to closure.

Requirements for regression testing product after nonconformity has been corrected are defined in PARAGRAPH 7.3.7, which states that, "changes shall be verified and validated, as appropriate." Retesting also addresses the requirements of PARAGRAPHs 8.5.2 *f* and 8.5.3 *e*, which require that corrective and preventive actions be reviewed (for effectiveness).

Configuration management tools and practices ensure that product that does not conform to requirements (e.g., incomplete or untested product) is not *inadvertently* promoted or released. This satisfies PARAGRAPH 8.3's requirement that the organization prevent *unintended* use. As is evident from the three ways PARAGRAPH 8.3 states that an organization addresses nonconforming product, deliberately releasing nonconforming product for use under appropriate circumstances is permitted. The practice of deliberately releasing nonconforming product during design and development is discussed under "Implementation considerations" for PARAGRAPH 8.2.4 *Monitoring and measurement of product*.

Finally, to implement the option of taking action to preclude its original intended use or application, the organization could:

- Destroy the defective product
- Reduce or disable functionality to eliminate the nonconformity
- Offer the defective product for a different use or application (e.g., for home use, for veterinary use only, or "do not immerse") for which it is suited
- Change the brochure

PARAGRAPH 8.4 *Analysis of Data*

The requirements of PARAGRAPH 8.4 are explicitly defined as applying to activities associated with demonstrating "the suitability and effectiveness of the quality management system and to evaluate where continual improvement of the quality management system can be made." In this context, *analysis* is the "resolution or breaking up of something complex into its various simple elements; the exact determination of the elements or components of something complex."[2] Analysis is independent of any specific method.

The analysis described in PARAGRAPH 8.4 considers outputs from monitoring and measurement of processes (PARAGRAPH 8.2.3) and product (PARAGRAPH 8.2.4), along with data related to customer satisfaction and suppliers. This is represented in Exhibit 8-7.

As an enabler of improvement, systematic analysis of data represents a source of significant benefit to organizations.

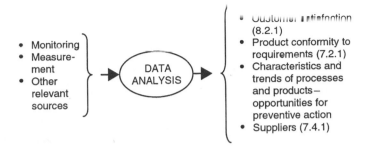

Exhibit 8-7. Analysis of data.

Performing the analysis and reporting the results is one of the responsibilities of the management representative (PARAGRAPH 5.5.2 *b*). The results of the analysis are an input to management review (PARAGRAPH 5.6.2 *c*), corrective action (PARAGRAPH 8.5.2), preventive action (PARAGRAPH 8.5.3), and planning internal audits (PARAGRAPH 8.2.2) as indicators of current status—and risk.

Implementation Considerations. Analysis, whether it employs statistical techniques (e.g., to determine whether events are related or independent, and to determine whether one event causes or predicts another) or inspection (e.g., this shows improvement), converts data into conclusions. Analysis is a step in the chain that links goals and measurements to management decisions and action.

Although there is no requirement to employ any particular method or analyze any particular data, the implementation team's priority is to identify the key performance indicators associated with product and process (quality objectives, PARAGRAPH 5.4.1), ensure that associated monitoring and measurement is implemented (PARAGRAPHS 8.2.1 *Customer satisfaction*, 8.2.3 *Monitoring and measurement of processes*, and 8.2.4 *Monitoring and measurement of product*), and then ensure that the monitoring and measuring data related to the key performance indicators is analyzed to serve as the basis for decisions related to continual improvement (PARAGRAPH 8.5). One technique that is applied in software development is the Goal-Question-Metric.[10,*]

The key to successful measurement programs is establishing a reasonable number of measurements that can be readily performed and that provide data that can be analyzed to guide management decisions regarding the improvement of processes and products. At first, spreadsheets, pie charts, and graphs should be sufficient for analyzing data. Once a measurement program establishes its value and builds a performance baseline, the scope and sophistication can be increased.

* The Goal-Question-Metric is a relatively popular method. The application of the Goal-Question-Metric to software is typically attributed to Victor Basili. See Reference 10.

An initial set of measurements can include:

- Performance against schedules and plans: How accurate are schedules and budgets? How accurate are projected schedules and budgets at each stage of the life cycle? How accurate are schedules in predicting when each major milestone will be achieved?
- Failures and defects:
  - Field failures: What types (severity, priority) of product defects are reported? What customers? What products or components are involved? What are the sources of the problems? How do these reports compare to projections? How long does it take to respond?
  - Specific in-process failures: What levels of scrap (e.g., content that is deleted after partial completion) and rework (e.g., pre-ventable changes) are found? What processes fail repeatedly? What is the cost of these failures? What percentage of a project's effort is wasted? What are the sources of the process failures?
  - Customer complaints: What nonspecific or global complaints (e.g., above and beyond product failures) do customers make?
- Corrective and preventive action: How many problems are fixed? What is the cost of correcting or preventing the problems? What is the recovered cost (e.g., the savings)? What is the time frame for response (e.g., aging)?
- Internal audit results, follow-up performance: What types of problems and opportunities are found? What is the response time and support for corrective action plans? What is the performance against those plans?

PARAGRAPH 8.5 *Improvement*

"Improvement" comprises three topics:

- Continual improvement (PARAGRAPH 8.5.1)
- Corrective action (PARAGRAPH 8.5.2)
- Preventive action (PARAGRAPH 8.5.3).

Each is discussed in its own paragraph.

PARAGRAPH 8.5.1 Continual Improvement

ISO 9000:2000 defines continual improvement as recurring activity to increase the ability to fulfill requirements. PARAGRAPH 8.5.1 finally establishes requirements for this fundamental concept. Continual improvement is implemented through the quality policy (PARAGRAPH 5.3), quality objectives (PARAGRAPH 5.4.1), audit results (PARAGRAPH 8.2.2), analysis of data (PARAGRAPH 8.4), corrective (PARAGRAPH 8.5.2) and preventive (PARAGRAPH 8.5.3) actions, and management review (PARAGRAPH 5.6). Continual improvement, then, is a by-product of processes implemented to address the requirements of other paragraphs of ISO 9001:2000.* Continual improvement knits the various sections of ISO 9001:2000 into a system that has the capacity to learn from its experience and evolve more rapidly than its competitors.[11]

Implementation Considerations. As suggested above, under PARAGRAPH 8.4 *Analysis of data*, the organization defines key performance indicators as part of the quality objectives. Associated with these objectives are methods to collect and analyze performance and to interpret the meaning of observed changes.

Once a performance baseline is established and it is determined that the overall process is relatively predictable, goals for improvement can be established and appropriate methods of control can be implemented to achieve the objective. A stable, well-defined process and an accurate performance baseline are required to prevent the failures well illustrated by Deming's "red beads" experiment.[12] The seven steps in process improvement are relatively straightforward, but not simple:

- Define a process and provide training, tools, and performance targets.
- Implement and refine the process in a pilot.
- Implement the process in all appropriate locations.
- Measure key aspects of the process including the quality of its outputs.
- Analyze the measurement data to establish a performance baseline and eliminate special causes (e.g., an untrained project manager, an improperly configured tool, a misunderstood process).
- Solicit and identify opportunities for improvement—changes in performance that would be of value to the organization.
- Solicit and identify ways in which the process can be effectively modified to achieve the desired improvements (accepting that there may not be any cost-effective solutions). Return to Step 1 once a candidate process improvement is identified.

Related Paragraphs. Exhibit 8-8 depicts some of the relatively complex relationships among the various activities that are listed as components of Continuous Improvement.

In Exhibit 8-8, the dotted lines indicate three categories of inputs to management review that can be provided directly, as illustrated by the dotted path, or that can be reported as part of the reports of the results of analysis. The curved arrow from audits depicts audits as one of the mechanisms for monitoring and measuring process.

---

* Continual improvement is a concept that underwent significant change as ISO 9001:2000 progressed through its various drafts. For those who followed the evolution of continual improvement through the various drafts of the standard, references to efficiency (e.g., improving processes that work) and the incorporation of the Total Quality Management concept of continual improvement **do not** appear in the released version of ISO 9001:2000.

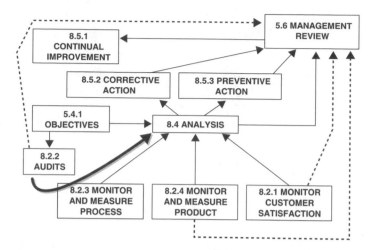

Exhibit 8-8. Relationship among the components of continuous improvement.

Ensuring that all of the requirements of ISO 9001:2000 are addressed becomes more challenging when top management receives some management review input from participation in regular program and project progress reviews. The simplest solution is to include a report from the management representative in selected progress reviews (e.g., once a quarter or monthly).

PARAGRAPH 8.5.2 Corrective Action

PARAGRAPH 8.5.2 contains familiar requirements that are invoked as a reaction whenever a process or product defect or problem is identified.

The corrective action process is described in a documented procedure, which establishes requirements for six specific areas of activity:

- Review nonconformities, including customer complaints.
- Determine causes.
- Evaluate the need for action to prevent reoccurrence.
- Determine and implement the needed action.
- Record the results of the action.
- Review the corrective action taken; the criteria for the review of corrective action are those listed in ISO 9000:2000's definition of review: suitability, adequacy, and effectiveness.

When the corrective action pertains to product, the requirements of PARAGRAPH 8.3 *Control of nonconforming product* also apply, especially as they relate to records and the types of actions that can be taken (see Exhibit 8-9).

Exhibit 8-9. About customer complaints

"Customer complaints" has appeared in every version of ISO 9001, but it has never been well defined. Any customer calling with a problem is theoretically complaining about something not working as expected (whether the problem is in the product or the expectation).

Based on experience with previous versions of ISO 9001, an effective definition of a customer complaint is any report of dissatisfaction that does not readily fall under a defined resolution process (e.g., it is not a product problem). An extreme example of a customer complaint is a telephone call or letter from the CEO of a major customer to the organization's General Manager stating that the customer is considering replacing the organization's product with a competitor's.

Since this type of customer complaint is relatively rare, many organizations assign responsibility for managing the organization's response to a Quality Manager, to Customer Care or Customer Relations Manager, or to the Management Representative.

The person to whom responsibility is assigned ensures that the steps of corrective action are appropriately applied to ensure that all aspects of the complaint are addressed.

Implementation Considerations. The documented procedure referred to in PARAGRAPH 8.5.2 typically addresses general responsibilities for reporting and managing any problems or opportunities for improvement. The procedure typically refers to other detailed processes and procedures for reporting specific types of problems (e.g., product and documentation) and frequently contains a simple procedure available to all management personnel for reporting problems and opportunities that fall outside any established procedures and responsibilities.

The process for addressing reported nonconformity mirrors the process for requirements engineering described in "Implementation considerations" for PARAGRAPH 7.2.1 *Determination of requirements related to the product.* This is particularly appropriate because the person reporting a valid problem cannot always be relied on to determine whether a product or process requires correction (e.g., it is not meeting a requirement that is supposed to be satisfied) or enhancement (e.g., the person has uncovered a new requirement). From the user's perspective, there is a problem with the results, whether or not the system is operating as designed. To avoid premature reaction, reports are referred to as incidents until they can be classified as problems or enhancement requests.[13],* Because corrective

---

* In Reference 13, Philip Crosby describes a five-step process for eliminating nonconformance: "Step 1—Define the situation (1A Clearly describe the problem, 1B Plan the solution); Step 2—Fix the problem [temporarily] (e.g., buy time); Step 3—Identify the root causes; Step 4—Take corrective action (4A Generate possible actions, 4B Select an alternative action to implement, 4C Plan and communicate the implementation, 4D Implement the selected action); Step 5—Follow up (to ensure the corrective action stays in place and does not have unintended side effects)."

action for product problems is typically part of product realization (e.g., as either a design and development change [PARAGRAPH 7.3.7] or part of service provision [PARAGRAPH 7.5]). PARAGRAPH 7.1 *Planning of product realization* requires that these activities, particularly the implementation activities, be planned in an appropriate level of detail.

Although it is unstated, to ensure that problems or opportunities are systematically addressed, each reported problem or opportunity for improvement is identified and recorded so that it can be communicated to personnel who have the expertise to process the report and so that the progress of the resolution can be traced from report to implemented change (PARAGRAPH 7.5.3).

Throughout the corrective action process, as defined in the documented procedure, clear responsibility and authority is defined for all of the steps in the corrective action process (e.g., prioritizing, planning, assigning resources, determining disposition, and monitoring and reporting on progress).

Review the Nonconformities. The first step in each process that addresses corrective action is to review the nonconformity to determine whether the report is correctly constructed (e.g., does it provide the required information) and to determine an appropriate disposition; for example:

- Rejected
- Combined with another report as a duplicate or an amendment
- Suspended pending the receipt of additional information
- Approved for analysis as a problem
- Approved for analysis as an enhancement request.

In all cases, it is essential to notify the submitter of the disposition and, when appropriate, keep the submitter apprised of progress. Notification and progress reports keep lines of communication open, ensure a continuing flow of real-time information about product and process performance, allow the organization to take credit for the work it is doing, and build loyalty. Unless a report results in instantaneous, obvious change (e.g., the arrival of the fire department), which most do not, submitters tend to infer that the report was not even read and are less willing to expend any additional effort to make subsequent reports. The attitude is expressed as, "Why bother? They don't listen anyway." Unfortunately, this negative attitude develops not only when a report is rejected but also when a report results in a change that will not be available for some weeks or months. When the change finally arrives, the submitter assumes it is just coincidence or that it is the result of someone else's priority. The negative attitude remains.

Determine the Causes, Evaluate the Need for Action, and Determine the Action Needed. These three activities are typically interleaved.

For problems information on causes provides the organization with an initial indication of the difficulty of solving the problem and with a list of individuals who need to be consulted in evaluating the impact of the problem. The need for action is assessed independently, based on the impact, benefit, or risk associated with the problem or opportunity. Candidate solutions and associated costs and schedules are evaluated to determine the action needed.

In some cases, "determine the action needed" encompasses trial periods for one or more actions, to ensure that the action taken prevents the problem from reoccurring within a reasonable period of time.

Implement the Action Needed. The action occurs in at least two stages. The first stage addresses the immediate operational problem. The initial response can range from issuing a recall or a warning (e.g., a technical advisory), to a work-around, to a quick fix to the product (e.g., a software patch or a field repair). The second stage addresses the action intended to prevent the problem from reoccurring or to ensure that the improvement remains in place. This second-stage response can range from building the first stage response into the product or process to making significant product and process changes and making training and documentation changes.

In planning the stages of response (which may exceed two), there is a potential trade-off between resources needed for the initial, temporary response and those needed to create a lasting, permanent response; applying more resources to deliver a rapid initial response can delay the delivery of a permanent solution.

Record the Results of the Action. ISO 9001:2000 and the associated guidance documents do not provide any guidance into what results need to be recorded or the associated level of detail. Under a literal interpretation, the result of action taken to correct a problem could be recorded as "problem corrected." On the basis of experience with previous versions of ISO 9001 and experience with implementing successful corrective actions systems, it is recommended that the organization record the actions taken (e.g., the plan) and the results of the review of the corrective action (Paragraph 8.5.2 *f*) or of the reverification of the corrected nonconforming product (Paragraph 8.3).

The following example describes the way in which one organization addressed a problem with records of corrective action.

BACKGROUND

> *An organization plans to resolve a security problem in its e-mail product by the release of a self-installing change that fixes the problem in currently installed systems, but that reduces performance. The change will be available for download within two weeks. The process for releasing such*

201

changes specifies the abbreviated testing that takes place before the change is made available to customers.

In the longer term, the organization plans a more extensive and efficient change to address the reported problem. This change is targeted for the next release of the product (three months away) and will be fully tested as specified in the product development life cycle. As part of the corrective action and release process, tests based on the corrected problem are added to the standard suite of tests.

Finally, for the future, the organization starts considering whether to establish a security roundtable, to keep abreast of trends in security and in ways unscrupulous individuals break through security. The decision as to whether to proceed with the security roundtable should be made sometime in the next six months, unless it is delayed.

THE QUANDARY

The management representative is responsible for reporting on the timely completion of corrective actions to provide senior management with an accurate view of the health of the organization's products and quality management system.

THE SOLUTION

The organization's corrective action process provides an elegant mechanism for classifying the problem as closed without losing sight of the longer-term or more speculative actions that may also arise from the initial problem report. The specific problem report in this example will be closed as resolved when:

- *The self-installing change is released and the test results from the change process are reviewed by the sustaining engineering manager and are discarded once the change is approved for release to customers.*
- *A product change request has been submitted for the next release of the product and the product change request includes a reference to the problem report.*
- *A process change request has been submitted for the security roundtable and the process change request includes a reference to the problem report.*

The record for the initial problem report shows the date on which each of the three identified actions is accomplished as the results of the action. Further information on each can be found in the configuration management system (for the release of the change), the requirements engineering system (for the product change request), and in the process engineering system (for the process change request).

The corrective action procedure specifies that a problem report is closed and resolved when the immediate action is successfully implemented, the proximate cause of the problem is confirmed to be eliminated, and any derived, longer-term actions directed at more removed root causes have been initiated. When the second-stage action occurs almost immediately, the problem report may be kept open until the second-stage action is completed. For example, if a system ships without a power cable, the immediate response is to ship the missing power cable. If it is discovered that the power cable is missing from the bill of materials for the system, the problem report can be kept open until the bill of materials is corrected.

The data on customer satisfaction is accurate and none of the longer-term actions are lost.

A factor in determining appropriate content and detail for records of corrective action is that they are a form of organizational memory. These records assist organizations in avoiding the waste of reintroducing problems previously solved and of reinventing solutions to problems previously solved, and they assist organizations in discovering patterns* that can lead to solutions that address a class of problems or opportunities for improvement.

Review the Corrective Action Taken.   As noted above, the criteria for the review of corrective action are listed in the ISO 9000:2000's definition of review: for suitability, adequacy, and effectiveness. The review is typically an examination of the completed corrective action to ensure that it was completed as planned and that no problem is solved.

Corrective action incorporates a number of intermediate reviews (e.g., the nonconformity report is reviewed; the plan is reviewed; any resulting design changes are reviewed, verified, and validated; and pilot implementation results are reviewed before roll-out). The most significant review takes place when the corrective action is closed—to ensure that all of the planned steps (including any appropriate pilot implementations, verification, and validation) have taken place. The record of this review is implicit in the approval to close the corrective action. The requirements for review can also be satisfied by specifying that each internal audit examine a sample of closed actions to ensure that they were correctly executed and that the problem remains solved or the improvement remains in place.

Corrective Action for Product Problems.   For product problems, the requirements of PARAGRAPH 8.5.2 are typically addressed through problem reporting and tracking processes. For third-party-developed product, a supplier corrective action process may also be invoked (PARAGRAPH 7.4). Questions about suitability, adequacy, and effectiveness are determined in the planning process.

---

* See Reference 11, p. 350, for a capsule discussion of the types of learning and of the distinction between pragmatic and theoretical approaches to improvement and problem solving, with references to the implications of Frederick Taylor's approach to scientific management, as it divides an organization into "thinkers" and "doers."

Effectiveness is evaluated in any verification and validation of the modified product, including regression testing (Paragraph 8.3).

Records of results are in the problem tracking and product configuration management systems. Information about changes is communicated to affected parties as required by Paragraphs 7.2.2 ("where product requirements are changed"), 7.3.3 b, and 7.3.7.

Corrective Action for Process Problems. When process problems are identified as a result of reported product problems, the resolution is tracked in the problem-tracking tool. For example, if a customer reports the receipt of a system with incorrect or missing components, the initial response is to deliver the missing components to the customer (and, if appropriate, request the return of the incorrect components). The second-stage response, based on investigation, is to correct any problems in the bill of materials for the system. The immediate response is recorded in the problem tracking system, as is the process change request initiating the second-stage response.

Process change requests can be handled through the same system that supports product change requests (e.g., tracked as a type of change request and assigned to the appropriate department or process owner). In many cases, however, organizations establish a process change request system, with e-mail submissions to an administrator (who frequently works for the quality manager or management representative), who is responsible for forwarding the request to the appropriate parties, requesting a plan, and monitoring progress (following a process similar to or based on the process associated with internal audit findings [Paragraph 8.2.2]).

In addition to process changes initiated through change requests, nonconformities and changes are also identified in real time by a combination of management communication and feedback from in-process verification. For example, progress reviews and test results give appropriate levels of management visibility into an engineer's or manager's need for additional training (e.g., unfamiliarity with writing a design document) and into processes that may be causing the problems (e.g., an engineer cannot check in code in a timely manner because the configuration management tool is not as capable as advertised or because the number of licenses is inadequate). In this case, if it is within the manager's span of control, the corrective action or improvement may be implemented at the unit level. What adds value is ensuring that changes and improvements that may have value for other parts of the organization are noted in management reports and given general visibility through the corrective action system.

When organizational units (e.g., software engineering, manufacturing, and field service) establish process groups that serve as a focal point for process improvement and changes within their organizations, these activities are

EXHIBIT 8-10. Comparing corrective and preventive action.

8.5.2	Corrective action	8.5.3	Preventive action
a	Review nonconformities, including customer complaints	a	Determine potential nonconformities and…
b	Determine causes		[Determine] their causes
c	Evaluate the need for action to prevent reoccurrence	b	Evaluate the need for action to prevent occurrence
d	Determine and implement the needed action	c	Determine and implement the action needed
e	Record the results of the action taken	d	Record the results of the action taken
f	Review the corrective action taken	e	Review the preventive action taken

described in the quality manual and are referenced in the procedure for corrective action.

PARAGRAPH 8.5.3 Preventive Action

PARAGRAPH 8.5.3 contains requirements that are invoked whenever a *potential* process or product defect or problem is identified. Preventive action is proactive. Its stated purpose is to prevent the occurrence of nonconformities. Adjusting for an irritating editorial inconsistency in the construction of PARAGRAPH 8.5.3 *a Preventive action* exactly parallels corrective action. Both are governed by established documented procedures that define requirements for six activities (see Exhibit 8-10).

Implementation Consideration. Once a candidate for preventive action is identified, it typically falls under the same process that is used to process actual nonconformities. Because these opportunities deal with future events, the focus in preventive action is in identifying opportunities. This typically entails ensuring that systems are in place to capture any reports of potential nonconformities and that some effort is invested in trying to generate those reports systematically.

Some examples of common, systematic methods for generating candidates for preventive action are:

- Risk management processes
- Project "lessons learned" reviews
- Periodic process reviews
- Surveys
- Focus groups
- Engineering Councils and Software Engineering Process Groups
- User groups
- Internal audits results that identify opportunities for improvement
- Review of metrics for trends (PARAGRAPHS 8.2.3 and 8.2.4).

What is most often missed is ensuring that the results of preventive action are communicated and incorporated into future activities, projects, and products.

References

1. Internatinoal Organization for Standardization, ISO/TR 10017:1999 *Guidance on Statistical Techniques for ISO 9001:2000*, International Organization for Standardization, Geneva, 2003.
2. International Organization for Standardization, *Guidance on the Terminology Used in ISO 9001:2000 and ISO 9004:2000,* Document ISO/TC 176/SC 2/N 526R, May 2001, International Organization for Standardization, Geneva, www.iso.ch.
3. International Organization for Standardization, *ISO 19011 Guidelines for Quality and/or Environmental Management Systems Auditing,* International Organization for Standardization, Geneva, 2002.
4. Sayle, Allan J., *Management Audits,* 2nd ed., Allan J. Sayle, 1988.
5. Mills, Charles A., *The Quality Audit,* McGraw-Hill, New York, 1989.
6. Taylor, Frederick Winslow, *The Principles of Scientific Management,* W. W. Norton Company, New York, 1911 (reprinted, 1967).
7. Pearsall, Judy, Ed., *The Concise Oxford Dictionary,* 10th ed., Oxford University Press, New York, 1999.
8. Adams, Dory, *Time Out—Why, When Things Get Busy, We Should Work Less,* Independent School, National Association of Independent Schools, Spring 2001, http://www.nais.org/pubs/ismag.cfm?file_id=558&ismag_id=18.
9. Markel, Scott, OMG/LSR Overview, paper presented at the Second International Meeting on Microarray Data Standards, Annotations, Ontologies and Databases, May 25–27, 2000, Heidelberg, http://www.mged.org/Meetings/m2/mged25052000-agenda.html.
10. Basili, V.R. and Weiss, D.M. A method for collecting valid software engineering data, *IEEE Transactions on Software Engineering,* SE-10(6), 728–738, November 1984.
11. Senge, Peter M., *The Fifth Discipline,* Doubleday, New York, 1990, pp. 106–113.
12. Deming, W.E., *Out of the Crisis,* Massachusetts Institute of Technology Center for Advanced Engineering Study, 1986, p. 110.
13. Crosby, Philip, *Quality Education System for the Individual,* Philip Crosby Associates, Winter Park Florida, 1988, pp. 93–126.

Section III
The
Appendices

The following appendices are included in this section:

- A. A Brief History of ISO 9001 from 1987 to 2000
- B. Rules for Claiming Conformity under ISO 9001:2000
- C. Achieving Compliance with PARAGRAPH 4.1
- D. A Template for Procedures
- E. A Case Study: One Approach to Life Cycles
- F. Implementation as a Managed Process
- G. Mapping the Standard to Core Competencies
- H. A Sample Questionnaire for Registrar Selection

Appendix A
A Brief History of ISO 9001 from 1987 to 2000

The origins of ISO 9001 are summarized by Donald W. Marquardt in an early version of *The ISO 9000 Handbook*.[1] In 1959, the Department of Defense published the MIL-Q-9858 quality management program. This program was adopted in principal in 1968 by the North Atlantic Treaty Organization and published as the AQAP1, AQAP4, and AQAP9 series of standards. In 1979, the British Standards Institution released commercial versions of these standards as BS 5750 Parts 1,[2] 2, and 3.

These three British documents significantly influenced the efforts of the International Organization for Standardization in creating a single set of standards for the European Community. In 1987, when ISO released ISO 9001, ISO 9002, and ISO 9003, BSI adopted the text of the ISO standards new versions of BS 5750. In the foreword of BS 5750:Part 1:**1987**, BSI notes that the requirements of ISO 9001 are very similar to those of BS 5750:Part 1:**1979**, but that a small number of quality system elements have been included, and other elements enhanced.

The titles of the three 1987 ISO standards provide insight into their content:

- ISO 9001:1987 Quality systems—Model for quality assurance in design/development, production, installation, and servicing[4]
- ISO 9002:1987 Quality systems—Model for quality assurance in production and installation[5]
- ISO 9003:1987 Quality systems—Model for quality assurance in final inspection and test.[6]

Although the three standards were intended to address increasingly narrow scopes, there were minor, unnecessary inconsistencies in the wording in comparable clauses.

The 1994 revisions of the three standards eliminated the inconsistencies. The only differences between ISO 9002 and ISO 9003 and ISO 9001 were in clauses that are identified as "not applicable" (e.g., clause 4.4,

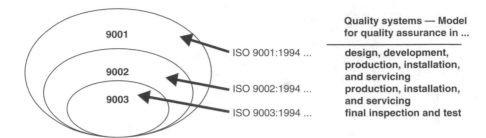

Exhibit A-1. The relationships among the three standards.

Design and development, is identified as "not applicable" in ISO 9002). Exhibit A-1 represents the relationships among the three standards.

About ISO 9000-3

In 1991, ISO published ISO 9000-3 Guidelines for the Application of ISO 9001[:1987] to the Development, Supply and Maintenance of Software.[7] This version of the software guidance remained current (even though it referred to an obsolete version of ISO 9001) until it was superceded in 1997 by ISO 9000-3 Guidelines for the Application of ISO 9001:1994 to the Development, Supply, Installation and Maintenance of Computer Software.[8]

The three-year lag, from 1994 to 1997, in the availability of an updated ISO 9000-3 correctly suggests a lack of market pressure for a revision to ISO 9000-3:1991. Although it could be construed that the nature of the 1994 revision to ISO 9001 allowed the continued use of ISO 9000-3:1991, a more likely reason for the apparent lack of priority is identified in a 1996 study by Stelzer, Mellis, and Herzwurm.[3] Based on a study of 36 European software houses that had achieved ISO 9001 registration, the authors concluded that,

> *ISO 9000-3[:1991] is not of great help for software houses. Quality managers only read it when they begin to study the ISO 9000 family. When they realize that ISO 9000-3 is as difficult to read as all other parts of ISO 9000, they ignore it and use ISO 9001 instead. (p. 10)*

Although ISO 9001:1987 and ISO 9001:1994 are cited as hard to read, Stelzer, Mellis, and Herzwurm also report, with some qualification, that

> *Nearly 100% of the company representatives [from companies included in the survey] would decide in favor of implementing an ISO 9000 quality system once again. They are convinced that the benefits of installing a quality system exceed the costs. (p. 10)*

A revision of ISO 9000-3 is underway, targeted for completion with the December 2003 expiration of ISO 9001:1994. The content is aligned with ISO 9001:2000. It is, however, not clear whether it will be any more useful than its predecessors. In spite of comments to the contrary, there has been little or no perceptible industry pressure for an update to ISO 9000-3. Some have pointed out that the new format of ISO 9001:2000, intended to make the standard more readily usable, should be given a chance. In fact, the lagging rate of transition to ISO 9001:2000 points to a general lack of interest in ISO 9001. In any event, ISO 9000-3 has been, is, and will be guidance. It has not, does not, and will not specify requirements.

Rules for Claiming Conformity under ISO 9001:1987 and ISO 9001:1994

In the 1987 and 1994 versions of the ISO 9000 family of standards, there are no explicit criteria defining the conditions under which an organization can claim conformity. ISO 9001:1994 states in the *Introduction* that, "It is intended that these International Standards will be adopted in their present form, but on occasions they may need to be tailored by adding or deleting certain quality-system requirements for specific contractual situations."

ISO 9002:1994 and ISO 9003:1994, as subsets of the requirements in 9001, provide two straightforward mechanisms for identifying to customers when and which requirements are excluded.

Even the three, nested standards are, however, inadequate for addressing the variety of ways in which suppliers and customers adopt the standards. In some cases, driven by regulatory requirements, by market requirements, or by business needs, only part of an organization seeks to conform to the requirements of the standard (e.g., manufacturing, but not product engineering). In some cases, organizations choose to stage the implementation of compliant processes based on the relative stability of the organization—for example, starting in manufacturing and then, subsequently, extending conformity to engineering and technical support. In other cases, the standards are applied to organizations or parts of organizations offering a specialized service (e.g., contract manufacturing, no product engineering or service; or field service, no manufacturing or product engineering).

Registrars—operating until 1996 without explicit direction from the International Organization for Standardization—apply an effective, commonsense benchmark for determining when activities or functions and the related requirements can be excluded and conformity still claimed. The benchmark is expressed as the ability to write a scope statement that clearly and unambiguously represents to potential customers what activities have been assessed by the registrar and found to meet the requirements of the standard.

Registration-certificate scope statements incorporate one or more of three dimensions: activity, product, and location. The registrar audits only those portions of the organization whose activities fall within the defined scope. For example, XYZ Corporation develops client-server and mainframe software in its Sunnyvale, CA, Software Design Center. Proof of compliance with ISO 9001 is not sought for mainframe software design and development, as it is being phased out. In granting registration for the design and development of client-server software, the registrar ignores XYZ's mainframe-software design and development processes. The scope statement on the registration certificate states that the certificate is for "The design and development of client-server software at XYZ Corporation's Sunnyvale, CA, Software Design Center." The limitation to client-server software development is clearly expressed in the scope statement. The exclusion of mainframe-software development is clear from the absence of any reference to it in the scope statement. The ethical dilemma created if XYZ sells products that incorporate both technologies is left to the discretion of the registrar to resolve or to ignore.

In defining permissible exclusions based on organization, geography, and product, by convention, registrars do not permit the requirements of common infrastructure paragraphs of ISO 9001:1994 to be excluded. Paragraphs like 4.1 *Management responsibility*, 4.5 *Document and data control*, 4.6 *Purchasing*, 4.14 *Corrective and preventive action*, 4.17 *Internal quality audits*, and 4.18 *Training* cannot be excluded, although the associated policies and procedures may be provided by a separate, central organization (e.g., corporate purchasing). Paragraphs that address product delivery, such as 4.4 *Design control* and 4.19 *Servicing*, can be excluded, whether or not the functions are present. Paragraphs such as 4.3 *Contract review*, 4.10 *Inspection and testing*, and 4.13 *Control of nonconforming product* apply to those product delivery activities (e.g., design and development, manufacturing, servicing) that are not excluded.

References

1. Marquardt, Donald, Background and development of ISO 9000, *The ISO 9000 Handbook*, edited by R. Peach, CEEM Information Services, Fairfax, VA, 1992, pp. 1–17.
2. British Standards Institution, *Quality Systems, Part 1. Specification For Design/Development, Production, Installation and Servicing*, BS 5750:Part 1:1987, British Standards Institution, London, May 1987.
3. Stelzer, Dirk, Mellis, Werner, and Herzwurm, Georg, Software process improvement via iso 9000?, *Proceedings of the 29th Hawaii International Conference on System Sciences*, January 3–6, 1996, Wailea, Hawaii, http://www.computer.org/proceedings/hicss/7324/73240703ahsihtm (for purchase) (08 Oct. 03).
4. International Organization for Standardization, *Quality Systems—Model for Quality Assurance in Design/Development, Production, Installation, and Servicing*, ISO 9001:1987, International Organization for Standardization, Geneva, 1987.
5. International Organization for Standardization, *Quality Systems—Model for Quality Assurance in Production and Installation*, ISO 9002:1987, International Organization for Standardization, Geneva, 1987.
6. International Organization for Standardization, *Quality Systems—Model for Quality Assurance in Final Inspection and Test*, ISO 9003:1987, International Organization for Standardization, Geneva, 1987.

7. International Organization for Standardization, *Quality Management and Quality Assurance Standards—Guidelines for the Application of ISO 9001 to the Development, Supply, and Maintenance of Software,* ISO 900-3:1991, International Organization for Standardization, Geneva, 1991.

8. International Organization for Standardization, *Quality Management and Quality Assurance Standards—Part 3: Guidelines for the Application of ISO 9001:1994 to the Development, Supply, Installation and Maintenance of Computer Software,* ISO 900-3:1991, International Organization for Standardization, Geneva, 1997.

Appendix B
Rules for Claiming Conformity under ISO 9001:2000

This appendix assumes the reader is familiar with the information in Appendix A.

To support the elimination of ISO 9002 and ISO 9003, ISO 9001:2000 PARA-GRAPH 1.2 defines the conditions under which an organization may claim conformity to ISO 9001. The definition of these conditions allows organizations to plan valid exclusions based on information in the standard rather than on anecdotal information garnered from extended negotiation with a registrar. Consistent definitions of conformity and of permissible exclusions are essential if registration and claims of conformity are to be valuable for supplier evaluation and selection.

In PARAGRAPH 1.2, ISO 9001:2000 institutionalizes the conventions that have evolved since 1987. The rules for excluding requirements are clear and incorporate two criteria:

- The first criterion overrides the second and states that the exclusion can "neither affect the organization's ability, nor absolve it from its responsibility, to provide product that meets customer and applicable regulatory requirements."
- The second criterion is that exclusion applies only to requirements found in ISO 9001:2000 PARAGRAPH 7 *Product realization*.

PARAGRAPH 1.2 goes on to state that exclusions

may be due to the following:

a) the nature of the organization's product;
b) customer requirements;
c) the applicable regulatory requirements.

A Problem: Organization or Company?

It does not appear to be difficult to determine the original intentions of the authors of ISO 9001:2000 with respect to exclusions. In PARAGRAPH 3.3.1, ISO 9000:2000 defines organization and provides examples:

organization—group of people and facilities with an arrangement of responsibilities, authorities and relationships

EXAMPLE Company, corporation, firm, enterprise, institution, charity, sole trader, association, or parts or combination thereof

In addition, ISO's stated requirement for the revision was that it not significantly affect organizations that already comply with the standard (e.g., that are already registered).[1]

On the basis of these two pieces of information, it appears logical to assume that any portion of a company could seek registration if a clear scope statement could be constructed. For example, a company that has ISO 9002:1994 registration for manufacturing could continue to claim conformity in manufacturing even if the company also has product engineering and customer service functions. This interpretation is consistent with current usage (e.g., service departments registered when neither engineering nor manufacturing are registered), and it allows many more "organizations" to adopt ISO 9001:2000 conformity (with or without registration) as a public demonstration of commitment to customer satisfaction.

However, at the time this volume is being written, registrars and accreditation bodies, including the Registrar Accreditation Board, claim that under the new rules for exclusion of requirements, if a company includes product engineering and manufacturing functions, they must both be included in the scope of the registration. In the opinion of the authors of this volume, ISO guidance[2] (p. 3) adds unnecessarily to the confusion with ambiguous statements and contrived examples.

The apparent discrepancy between registrars' interpretation and the ISO definitions is significant because the integrity of the standard requires that all claims of conformity (whether supported by registration or not) be based on the same rules. It is reasonable to expect that a company that legitimately self-certifies that its processes satisfy the requirements of ISO 9001:2000 should be able to corroborate its claims by undergoing a registration audit.

Implications for Software

Because the internal product design and development processes of software engineering organizations are subject to ISO 9001, the determination of permissible exclusions pertains to the relationship between software engineering and the rest of the organization. The key issue associated with exclusion is whether a software engineering organization can claim conformity—with or without seeking registration—unless other organizations in the company, such as manufacturing, technical support, hardware engineering, marketing, and sales, also achieve conformity.

A similar question might be whether the manufacturing division of a commodity home appliance company could be registered if the engineering group were not. Registering manufacturing would seem reasonable and useful, especially since product safety certification (e.g., Underwriters Laboratories [UL]) is based on manufactured samples. The current answer from registrars would appear to be that this would not be allowed.

If exclusion is an issue, the only sources of information continue to be the organization's registrar (or candidate registrars) and the guidance provided by ISO.[2]

Reference

1. International Organization for Standardization, *1. Introduction to the Revision of the ISO 9000 Standards, ISO/CD1 9001:2000 and ISO/CD1 9004:2000*, N415, International Organization for Standardization, Technical Committee 176, Subcommittee 2, Geneva, 30 July 1998, p. 5.
2. International Organization for Standardization, *Guidance on ISO 9001:2000 clause 1.2 'Application'*, ISO/TC 176/SC 2, N524R3, International Organization for Standardization, February 2002, http://www.iso.ch/iso/en/iso9000-14000/pdf/Guidance_on_ISC_9000.

Appendix C
Achieving Compliance with PARAGRAPH 4.1

PARAGRAPH 4.1 is an excellent example of types of problems with requirements.

- There are compound sentences, which make it difficult to determine what phrases apply to what antecedents. For example, in lettered PARAGRAPH (b), it is clear that "of these processes" pertains to both sequence and interaction. In lettered PARAGRAPH (g), "achieve planned results ... of these processes" does not make sense, so it appears that "of these processes" applies only to "continual improvement."
- There is no consistent identification of requirements and relationships among requirements within PARAGRAPH 4.1. Some requirements are in lettered paragraphs. Some are not. Those in lettered paragraphs address, without distinction, both infrastructure (a through d) and implementation (e and f). The first sentence states that "the organization shall ... continually improve its [the QMS'] effectiveness." Lettered PARAGRAPH (f) requires that "the organization shall implement actions necessary to achieve ... continual improvement of these processes." There is either too subtle a distinction or repetition.
- In addition to duplication within PARAGRAPH 4.1, many of the requirements in PARAGRAPH 4.1 are decomposed into or restate requirements in subsequent paragraphs, but there is no explicit traceability. Exhibit C-1 traces the overlap, duplication, and hierarchy. It also exposes the few requirements that are unique to PARAGRAPH 4.1, and that might, otherwise, be lost in the flood of redundant information.
- There is arcane language: In the first sentence in PARAGRAPH 4.1, "establish" is used in the context of governments and institutions.
- There is ambiguity: What does "determine" mean? What does "identify" mean? How do these relate to documentation and communication?

Exhibit C-1 substantiates the assertion in Chapter 2 of this volume that most of the requirements of PARAGRAPH 4.1 are satisfied as a result of satisfying requirements in other paragraphs. The column titled "Conclusions" describes how the authors of this volume suggest implementers and auditors treat each requirement stated in PARAGRAPH 4.1.

Exhibit C-1. Finding the requirements of PARAGRAPH 4.1

	Shall	Where in 4.1	Where addressed—comments	Conclusion
1	Establish a QMS IAWRIS	¶4.1 first ¶	See ¶5.3 *b*, ¶5.5, ¶5.6, ¶8.1, ¶8.2, and ¶8.5 Rationale Institutionalization of the QMS is accomplished through the quality policy (¶5.3 *b*)—which makes following the QMS mandatory—and the assignment of responsibility and authority (¶5.5.1). Ensuring the establishment of the QMS is the responsibility of the management representative (¶5.5.2 *a*). Compliance of the QMS is measured (¶8.1), in particular as part of the internal audits (¶8.2.2). Problems with establishment are the subject of corrective action (¶8.5.2) and are reported in management review (¶5.6).	Fully addressed in the referenced paragraphs. This requirement statement is not discretely implemented or audited.
2	Document a QMS IAWRIS	¶4.1 first ¶	See ¶4.2 Rationale ¶4.2 lists the specific requirements associated with documentation (which includes records)—from both a content and a control point of view.	Fully addressed in ¶4.2. This requirement statement is not discretely implemented or audited.
3	Implement a QMS IAWRIS	¶4.1 first ¶	See all paragraphs and ¶5.5, ¶8.1, ¶8.2, and ¶8.5 Rationale Throughout ISO 9001:2000, every verb that specifies an action to be carried out is part of implement. Ensuring the implementation of the QMS is the responsibility of the management representative (¶5.5.2 *a*). Compliance of the QMS is measured (¶8.1), in particular as part of the internal audits (¶8.2.2). Problems with implementation are the subject of corrective action (¶8.5.2) and are reported in management review (¶5.5.2 *b* and ¶5.6).	Fully addressed throughout. This requirement statement is not discretely implemented or audited.

4	Maintain a QMS IAWRIS	¶4.1 first ¶	See ¶4.2, ¶5.6, ¶8.1, ¶8.2, and ¶8.5 Rationale Maintenance and the associated mechanisms are described in various paragraphs of ISO 9001:2000. Documents that define the QMS are updated as necessary (e.g., procedures are kept current) (¶4.4.3 b). Ensuring the maintenance of the QMS is the responsibility of the management representative (¶5.5.2 a). Compliance of the QMS is measured (¶8.1), in particular as part of the internal audits (¶8.2.2). Problems with maintenance (e.g., out-of date procedures, and inadequate processes) are the subject of corrective action (¶8.5.2) and are reported in management review (¶5.6).	Fully addressed in the referenced paragraphs. This requirement statement is not discretely implemented or audited.
5	Continually improve its [the QMS'] effectiveness IAWRIS	¶4.1 first ¶	See ¶8.5 Rationale ¶8.5.1 repeats and elaborates on "continually improve."	Fully addressed in PARAGRAPH 8.5.1. This requirement statement is not discretely implemented or audited.
6	Identify processes needed for the QMS throughout the organization	¶4.1 a	See ¶4.2, ¶7.1, and ¶8.1 ¶4.1 a and ¶4.1 b combine to define requirements for essential attributes of processes: what is to be done (¶4.1 a), who is to do it (¶4.1 a), when it is to be done (¶4.1 b), and what interactions or dependencies must be considered (¶4.1 b). Rationale One problem in dealing with this requirement is that identify is ambiguous. It has a large number of meanings (list, know, name, enumerate, and define), which lead to a vast selection of possible solutions (from list to define). Identification can range from a one-line title to a detailed, multipage procedure.	Between the processes identified in ISO 9001, the various plans, and the quality manual, all of the needed processes are identified. This requirement statement is not discretely implemented or audited.

Note: IAWRIS = in accordance with the requirements of this International Standard; QMS = Quality Management System; ¶ = PARAGRAPH.

Exhibit C-1 (continued). Finding the requirements of PARAGRAPH 4.1

Shall	Where in 4.1	Where addressed—comments	Conclusion
		The second problem is that although process is defined in ISO 9000:2000 as a set of interrelated or interacting activities, there is no way of distinguishing between an activity and a process. One organization may choose to identify the process as business acquisition (one activity is proposal preparation). Another organization may identify proposal preparation as a process and identify business acquisition as a phase of the business.	
		Problems with not identifying needed processes arise if they are either not implemented or if management is inadvertently unaware of what is going on. A needed process that is not identified as such is at risk—they may not be consistently implemented and applied, resourced, monitored, and improved.	
		Needed processes are identified throughout ISO 9001:2000 (document control [¶4.2.3], records control [¶4.2.4], management review [¶5.6], requirements review [¶7.2.2], customer communication [¶7.2.3], purchasing [¶7.4], internal audits [¶8.2.2], etc.).	
		Various paragraphs provide identification-related requirements:	
		¶7.1 requires that organizations plan and develop (as required) the processes needed for product realization.	
		¶8.1 requires that the organization plan monitoring, measurement, analysis, and improvement processes (including the determination of methods). Identification of other specialized processes not identified in ISO 9001:2000 is the responsibility of the organization (e.g., product realization, ¶7.1 *b* and ¶7.1 *c*).	

| 7 | Identify the application of processes needed for the QMS throughout the organization | ¶4.1 a | Although "plan" is not defined, "quality plan" is defined as a document that specifies applicable procedures (e.g., names) and resources.

In documenting process interactions in the quality manual (as specified in ¶4.2.2 c), some, though not necessarily all, processes are identified since they are at least listed or named.

In the context of ¶4.1 a, identify processes requires that management identify, in some appropriate level of detail, the activities that should be enacted in the organization. Where and when these processes are enacted are the subjects of subsequent requirements. | See ¶5.5, ¶6.2, ¶7.1, and ¶8.1
Rationale
As discussed in conjunction with the previous line item, identify is doubly ambiguous. Identify the application is doubly ambiguous.

In the context of ¶4.1 a, identify the application requires knowing where in the organization (and, perhaps, by whom) the processes are exercised, utilized, employed, and so forth.

This requirement can be addressed through various standard plans (¶7.1 and ¶8.1) that identify resources and applicable processes. The processes to be applied by an individual or organization may also be identified in job descriptions and organizational objectives or charters (¶5.5).

PARAGRAPH ¶4.1 a requires that organizations define the scope of application of each process included in the quality management system (e.g., each procedure identifies who is expected to follow it). The definition of scope of application is the basis for assigning responsibility and authority (¶5.5), for internal communication (¶5.5.3), and for establishing training content (¶6.2.2). | This requirement is assessed discretely by ensuring that, for each process identified as needed for the QMS, there is some identification of who is supposed to apply the process.

This identification is the basis for determining who can be interviewed to verify awareness and implementation of the applicable processes. |

Note: IAWRIS = in accordance with the requirements of this International Standard; QMS = Quality Management System; ¶ = PARAGRAPH.

Exhibit C-1 (continued). Finding the requirements of PARAGRAPH 4.1

	Shall	Where in 4.1	Where addressed—comments	Conclusion
8	Determine the sequence of these processes	¶4.1 *b*	See ¶4.2, ¶7.3 Rationale Determining the sequence of processes adds a dimension that may be omitted when individual processes and interactions (¶4.2.2 *c*) are defined. When the output from one process is an input for another, there is a natural order, which cannot be violated (e.g., unit test follows coding). The processes for which ¶4.1 *b* is most useful are those processes for which there is no natural order (e.g., code review before or after unit test), processes which may overlap (e.g., start coding before the design is complete), and management or administrative processes (e.g., product release occurs after all unit tests, integration tests, and system tests have been completed satisfactorily and reports have been submitted and approved). While project plans identify the sequence in which a specific cycle of processes are executed, permissible sequences are determined separately (e.g., in product and engineering life cycle descriptions [¶7.3.1]).	This requirement is assessed discretely by ensuring that, for each process identified as needed for the QMS, there is a determination of predecessor and successor processes. This sequence becomes the basis for planning process-based auditing and for determining what processes should have been completed and what artifacts should be available for a work product or project.
9	Determine the interaction of these processes	¶4.1 *b*	See ¶4.2 Rationale The interaction of the processes is documented in the quality manual. Documenting interactions requires that the interactions be determined.	Fully addressed in ¶4.2.2 *c*. This requirement statement is not discretely implemented or audited.

224

#	Requirement	¶	Reference / Rationale	Status
10	Determine criteria to ensure effective operation of these processes	¶4.1 c	See ¶5.3, ¶5.4 Rationale ISO 9000:2000 offers no definition of criteria beyond the common definition of criteria as "standards, rules, or tests on which a judgment or decision can be based." ISO 9001:2000 contains criteria the organization has adopted to ensure effective operation of its processes. The quality policy and quality objectives as they relate to the results of processes are the required criteria. These criteria are typically expressed in terms of stakeholder requirements: customer, employee, and shareholder satisfaction; profitability; field defects; share price; return on capital employed; staff turnover; budget performance; on-time delivery; waivers processed; and so forth.	Fully addressed in ¶5.3 and ¶5.4. This requirement statement is not discretely implemented or audited.
11	Determine criteria to ensure effective control of these processes	¶4.1 c	See ¶5.3 and ¶5.4 Rationale The quality policy and quality objectives as they relate to the implementation of the processes are the required criteria. ISO 9001:2000 contains criteria the organization has adopted to ensure effective operation of its processes. These criteria are typically expressed in terms of ongoing process performance: integration tests completed, passed, failed; defects at intermediate milestones; project staffing levels; on-time completion of milestones; weekly spend. The control criteria are typically closely related to the operational criteria but are at a level of detail suitable for process control.	Fully addressed in the referenced paragraphs. This requirement statement is not discretely implemented or audited.
12	Determine methods to ensure effective operation of these processes	¶4.1 c	See ¶8.2, ¶8.4, ¶8.5 Rationale The methods for ensuring effective operation are distinct from the methods for operation. Methods for ensuring effective operation include those methods associated with determining whether the criteria for effective	Fully addressed in the referenced paragraphs. The requirement statement is not discretely implemented or audited.

Note: IAWRIS = in accordance with the requirements of this International Standard; QMS = Quality Management System; ¶ = Paragraph.

Exhibit C-1 (continued). Finding the requirements of PARAGRAPH 4.1

Shall	Where in 4.1	Where addressed—comments	Conclusion
		operation (as discussed in line 10, above) are satisfied. These methods are • Measurement and analysis methods associated with operational criteria—particularly, customer satisfaction (¶8.2.1, ¶8.2.3, and ¶8.4). Project "lessons learned" reviews are a typical method for ensuring that the processes for projects operate effectively. • Internal audit methods (¶8.2.2) • Methods for taking corrective (¶8.5.2) and preventive action (¶8.5.3).	
13 Determine methods to ensure effective control of these processes	¶4.1 c	See ¶8.2, ¶8.4, ¶8.5 Rationale The methods for ensuring effective control are distinct from the methods for operation. Methods for ensuring effective control include those methods associated with determining whether the criteria for effective control (as discussed in line 11, above) are satisfied. These methods are • Measurement and analysis methods associated with control criteria—(¶8.2.3, ¶8.4). Periodic progress reviews and phase reviews are typical methods for ensuring effective control. A well-defined, effective project life cycle—from requirements engineering (elicit, analyze, document, validate, manage) to test, release, and support—is required before any control can be effective. • Methods for taking corrective (¶8.5.3) and preventive action (¶8.5.3).	Fully addressed in the referenced paragraphs. This requirement statement is not discretely implemented or audited.

14	Ensure availability of resources necessary to support operation and monitoring of these processes	¶4.1 *d*	See ¶6.1, ¶7.1 Rationale ISO 9001:2000 requires that adequate resources be provided for all processes associated with the quality management system (¶6.1), which includes any planning, measuring, and monitoring processes. In addition, ISO 9001:2000 specifically references resources for those processes associated with product realization (¶7.1).	Fully addressed in the referenced paragraphs. This requirement statement is not discretely implemented or audited.
15	Ensure availability of information necessary to support operation and monitoring of these processes	¶4.1 *d*	See ¶4.2, ¶5.5, ¶7.1, ¶7.2, ¶7.3 Rationale ¶5.5.3 requires that appropriate communication processes be established. In addition, • ¶4.2.2 requires that the organization create any documents needed by the organization to ensure the effective planning, operation, and control of its processes. • ¶7.1 specifies the content of product- or project-specific plans. • ¶7.2.2 requires that relevant personnel be made aware of changes to customer requirements. • ¶7.3.1 requires that the organization – Develop and maintain plans – Manage the interfaces between different groups involved in design and development to ensure effective communication. ¶7.3.4 elaborates on this requirement for intergroup coordination by requiring that design and development reviews include representatives of functions concerned with the design and development stage or stages being reviewed (e.g., hardware engineering, test, publications, customer support, regulatory engineering, and operations).	Fully addressed in the referenced paragraphs. This requirement statement is not discretely implemented or audited.

Note: IAWRIS = in accordance with the requirements of this International Standard; QMS = Quality Management System; ¶ = PARAGRAPH.

Exhibit C-1 (continued). Finding the requirements of PARAGRAPH 4.1

	Shall	Where in 4.1	Where addressed—comments	Conclusion
16	Monitor these processes	¶4.1 e	See ¶8.2 Rationale ¶8.2.3 details the activities related to process monitoring.	Fully addressed in ¶8.2.3. This requirement statement is not discretely implemented or audited.
17	Measure these processes	¶4.1 e	See ¶8.2 Rationale ¶8.2.3 details the activities related to process measurement.	Fully addressed in ¶8.2.3. This requirement statement is not discretely implemented or audited.
18	Analyze these processes	¶4.1 e	See ¶8.4 Rationale ¶8.4 details the activities related to process measurement.	Fully addressed in ¶8.4. This requirement statement is not discretely implemented or audited.
19	Implement actions necessary to achieve planned results	¶4.1 f	See throughout and ¶8.2 Rationale The actions referred to in this requirement statement fall into two categories—those associated with operation, monitoring, and control and those associated with recovering when achieving planned results becomes problematic. Starting with ¶4.2, ISO 9001:2000 requires that the organization implement its quality management system—the operation, monitoring, and control processes necessary to meet requirements and achieve customer satisfaction. ¶8.2.3 states the requirement to take action when results are not achieved based on process measurement. ¶8.2.4 states the requirement to take action when results are not achieved based on product quality measurement.	Fully addressed in numerous paragraphs. This requirement statement is not discretely implemented or audited.

#	Requirement	¶	Reference / Rationale	Status
20	Implement actions necessary to achieve continual improvement of these processes	¶4.1 *f*	See ¶8.5 Rationale PARAGRAPH ¶8.5.1 states the requirement to continually improve the effectiveness of the quality management system.	Fully addressed in ¶8.5.1. This requirement statement is not discretely implemented or audited.
21	Manage these processes IAWRIS	¶4.1 ninth ¶	See throughout and ¶5 Rationale ISO 9000:2000 defines management as "coordinated activities to direct and control an organization." Based on this two-part definition, ISO 9001:2000, in its entirety, is about process management. Direction is provided through policies, process definition, and planning. Control is provided through monitoring and measurement and, as appropriate, through corrective and preventive action. ¶5 defines requirements for management responsibility, including planning (¶5.4) and management review (¶5.6).	Fully addressed in ¶5 and throughout ISO 9001:2000 This requirement statement is not discretely implemented or audited.
22	Ensure control over outsourced processes that affect product conformity	¶4.1 tenth ¶	See ¶7.4. Rationale According to ISO 9000:2000, product encompasses services. However, neither ISO 9002:2000 nor ISO 9004:2000 offers a definition of outsource. The conventional definition is "to farm out (work, for example) to an outside provider or manufacturer to cut costs." For the purposes of this discussion, two assumptions can be made: • The work is done on behalf of the party sending the work out (i.e., the customer's relationship is with the party sending the work out). • The party sending the work out compensates the outside provider for the work. ¶7.4.1 requires that the organization control all suppliers and supplied products. It goes on to state that "the type and extent of control shall be dependent on the effect of the purchased product on subsequent realization or the final product."	Fully addressed in ¶7.4. This requirement statement is not discretely implemented or audited.

Note: IAWRIS = in accordance with the requirements of this International Standard; QMS = Quality Management System; ¶ = PARAGRAPH.

Exhibit C-1 (continued). Finding the requirements of PARAGRAPH 4.1

Shall	Where in 4.1	Where addressed—comments	Conclusion
		What Is Not an Outsourced Process Services offered directly by other parties to the primary organization's customers are not "outsourced processes." In some cases, a primary organization provides its customers with referrals to other organizations for related services under joint marketing agreements, certification programs, compatibility lists, and so forth. These are not outsourced processes. The primary organization's responsibility extends only to any representations it makes in the referral, which is why referrals are frequently wrapped in extensive disclaimers.	
23 Identify outsourced processes that affect product conformity within the QMS	¶4.1 tenth ¶	See ¶7.4. Rationale ¶7.4.2 requires that the outsourced processes be fully described, which satisfies the requirements for identifying these processes. It should be noted that outsourced processes require close attention to specification and monitoring to ensure that they are coordinated and compatible with in-house and other outsourced processes.	Fully addressed in ¶7.4. This requirement statement is not discretely implemented or audited.

Note: IAWRIS = in accordance with the requirements of this International Standard; QMS = Quality Management System; ¶ = PARAGRAPH.

Appendix D
A Template for Procedures

This appendix is presented in the form of a "procedure for procedures" for a fictional company called Product Development, Incorporated (PDI). PDI uses its company Intranet as the vehicle for promulgating procedures. This procedure is intended to create a minimum level of uniformity in any of the organization's procedures, whether the procedure is issued by the vice-president of engineering (to be followed by all engineers) or by the test manager (for use within the test department).

To streamline its documentation, PDI has created a template that allows policies and procedures to be combined in a single procedural document. The template, presented in Exhibit D-1, can also be used for a stand-alone policy or a stand-alone procedure, which is why the procedure and the policy sections are both labeled as optional. In addition, sections (like attachments) can be included as hyperlinks. The template is part of the procedure; it is also available on the PDI Intranet as a separate document.

The "procedure for procedures" conforms to its own rules.

Exhibit D-1. A procedure for procedures.

Title: Procedures			Policy: PDI24	Issue: 3
Author:	Application:	Authorized by:	Date Authorized:	Date Effective:
Joseph Rogers	Companywide	J. O. Cabot	12 January 2004	14 January 2004
Summary: Each employee of PDI can draft a new department-level policy or procedure. The policy or procedure is authorized by the manager of the department, who updates the department index.				
Revision history:				

Date	Issue	Reason for Change (most recent issue only)		
7 December 2001	1			
15-Jan-02	2			
12 January 2004	3	A new format is adopted *Records* added as a new, optional section in the Procedure *Changes Since Last Release* is eliminated as a separate section in the procedure (the information appears in *Revision History* in the procedure heading).		

Exhibit D-1 (continued)   A procedure for procedures.

Purpose	This policy and procedure ensures that policies and procedures are documented in a uniform manner, to facilitate understanding by all individuals affected by the policies and procedures and to ensure that policies and procedures are properly reviewed and approved prior to use.
Policy	All departments within PDI create, implement, and maintain policies and procedures to supplement existing policies and procedures when the existing procedures do not provide appropriate detail to address the requirements of the department.
Related documents	None
Review and distribution	This procedure is reviewed by the quality manager and by all department managers. It is distributed as part of the PDI Quality Manual.
Comments	Submit comments on this policy and procedure to the author
Procedure	The creation, release, control, and maintenance of department-level procedures.

Step	Responsibility	Action
1	Any employee, author, authorizing manager	DRAFT AND APPROVE **Any employee:** Draft a policy or procedure that includes at least the elements identified in Attachment 1 in the order listed. **Procedure author:** Draft a revision of an existing policy and procedure. The draft is created with the current version of Microsoft Word. To facilitate drafting procedures, a Word template is available as PTPLT.DOT in S:\PDI\FORMS on server PDI_QUALITY. 　　The draft is submitted to the manager who will authorize the policy and procedure for implementation. This manager initially approves the draft for review. For a new procedure, the manager assigns a number and a two- to four-letter prefix from the index. In revising an existing procedure, if more than one individual is listed as authorizing the procedure, the draft is submitted to the first individual listed. 　　When appropriate, others involved in or affected by the policy or procedure and those who support or receive the outputs from the process are consulted and involved in drafting and revising policies and procedures

2	Authorizing manager	REVIEW
		Circulate the approved draft for review and comments to all individuals identified in the review list. The request for comments includes a specific date by which comments are due, the person to whom comments should be addressed, and what happens if no comments are received.
		    For matters regarding Human Resources (HR) policy (e.g., terms and conditions of employment, leave, vacation), the draft will be circulated to the department HR representative for approval before authorization.
		    When a draft policy or procedure proposes actions not conforming to an approved policy or procedure that has a broader organizational scope, the author of the existing policy or procedure reviews the draft policy or procedure; the individual listed as authorizing the existing policy or procedure is also listed in the draft as an authorizer of the new policy or procedure.

3	Author	REVISE Incorporate comments Clarify or resolve conflicting comments
4	Authorizing manager	AUTHORIZE AND RELEASE Authorize and release the policy and procedure. When authorization by other individuals is required, the authorizing manager listed first in the procedure determines an appropriate method or methods of requesting, submitting, and retaining the authorization. Distribute the new procedure (e.g., place it in the appropriate network directory). Create or modify the procedure index (see Attachment 2).

5	Authorizing manager	Regular management review meetings include a review of the effect on policies, procedures, and standards of changes in
		   • Organization
		   • Technology
		   • Process—especially those associated with corrective action and customer complaints

6	Internal audit team	As part of the internal audit process, the auditors assigned to an area examine the current index, spot check documents in use, and examine minutes from recent management review meetings.

Records	Record	Method of control	Retention and disposition
	Department Index	Determined by manager	Until superceded. Previous version is overwritten by current version.
	Records of authorization by other individuals	Determined by manager	At least until procedure is released. Disposal of records is at the discretion of the manager.

Exhibit D-1 (continued)   A procedure for procedures.

Attachment 1	Required and optional sections of policies and procedures
	Each procedure contains the following clearly identified elements. Elements identified as optional are omitted if they do not apply. Elements appear in the order listed below.

Element	Description
Procedure number	AAAAnn, where "AAAA" is a four-character designator for the department. The quality manager assigns department designators to prevent duplication. "nn" represents a number assigned before the procedure is authorized. In drafting a new procedure, until a number is available, use the actual letters "nn."
Title	A brief, descriptive name for the procedure.
Issue	The revision level of the procedure. This is included in the procedure so printed copies can be easily checked to ensure that they are current. In drafting a new procedure, use 0 as the release level. Indicate the draft by a letter following the release level (e.g., 0A, 0B). The new procedure is released as Issue 1. When an existing procedure is undergoing revision, indicate the draft by a letter following the release level (e.g., 2A, 2B). The revised procedure is released at the next level (e.g., with all appropriate review comments incorporated, Draft Issue 3A is presented for authorization as Issue 4).
Application	The employees, departments, or activities to which this procedure applies.
Effective date	The earliest date on and after which the procedure is to be followed.
Summary	A brief description of the process governed by this procedure.
Authorization	The name of the individual who authorizes the procedure for implementation. Note that all HR-related procedures (e.g., attendance, decorum, dress, vacation, and leave) are authorized by the department manager and the department HR representative.
Author	The individual responsible for drafting the current revision.
Date	The date on which the procedure was authorized.
Revision history	The list of numbers under which the procedure has been issued and the dates issued; include a brief statement of the reason the most recent issue was created.

Purpose	The specific management objectives for creating the policy and procedure
Policy (optional)	A statement of policy
Related documents (optional)	A list of any documents that are directly or indirectly referred to in the procedure.
Review and distribution	A list of the titles of the individuals who review the procedure draft before release; a list of the individuals who are notified or to whom copies are distributed when the procedure is released. This list includes all or a representative sample of the employees expected to abide by the procedure, of the individuals who provide input for the process described by the procedure, of the individuals who receive the outputs of the process described by the procedure. Note that all HR-related procedures (e.g., attendance, decorum, dress, vacation, and leave) are reviewed by the department HR representative.
Equipment and facilities (optional)	Any equipment (hardware or software), reference manuals, standards, supplies, or facilities required to perform the procedure. All items are identified by the issue or revision level or levels with which the procedure had been verified.
Special skills (optional)	Any special skills required to perform the procedure.
Comments	Contact ifnormation for the individual to whom comments should be addressed.
Terms and definitions (optional)	Definitions of any new terms introduced by this procedure
Procedure (optional)	A detailed description of the process: the steps, circumstances, individuals responsible, and the criteria for completion. For complex procedures, consider including a flow diagram in the attachments to support the procedure definition. The procedure can reference other procedures, but the total information supplied must be sufficient for a qualified employee to execute the procedure.
Records (optional)	The title, method, and duration of retention for each type of record created by the activities described in the procedure
Note (optional)	Any comments or points of emphasis. This section should not introduce any new information regarding the steps in the procedure.
Attachments (optional)	Any sample forms or other attachments.

Page footer	The procedure number, title, issue, and page number in the form "x of y" (e.g., "2 of 3") appear at the bottom of each page.

Attachment 2

Required elements of department indexes

For each department-level procedure currently in effect in the department, the index provides the information listed below. Note that the index may be a home page on the Intranet.

Entry	Number	Title	Issue	Issue date (optional)
Description	The number of the procedure	The title of the procedure	Issue of the procedure that is currently in effect	Date on which the current issue became effective

Appendix E
A Case Study: One Approach to Life Cycles

This case study describes one organization's successful approach to defining life cycles. The material in this case study is drawn from the organization's engineering handbook, which serves as a quality manual for engineers. The description of the life cycle is provided in three formats:

- In a text-based procedure format, in Exhibit E-1
- As a process map in Exhibit E-2
- As a table of responsibilities and deliverables in Exhibit E-3

The material in this case study is intended to convey the level of detail and style of presentation of the life cycles. It has been extracted from a larger document that conveys additional information to new employees at ABC—and that is presented in a two-hour orientation course for new engineers. In addition, a library of detailed procedures, forms, templates, and examples ensure that the activities assigned to the phases are consistently understood and performed.

About the Company: ABC Systems

ABC Systems develops standard systems for warehouse automation. ABC develops, manufactures, and integrates hardware including bar code readers, optical recognition systems, shelving, carousel-mounted bins, conveyers, and servers. ABC develops software that controls all of the devices and schedules warehouse personnel. The ABC software product includes an optional inventory management and procurement system, BuyTrak. It also provides seamless interfaces to most commonly used procurement systems.

This case study describes activities from three of ABC's primary functional groups as they affect engineering:

- Marketing, which includes sales, product line management, sales engineering (supports demos, answers technical questions), marketing communications

- Engineering, which includes a number of disciplines in hardware engineering, software engineering, systems engineering, and project management
- Manufacturing, which includes inventory planning, procurement, logistics (warehouse, shipping/receiving, inventory control, stock room), and operations (assembly, test, repair)
- Professional services, which includes field service (installation and repair), telephone technical support, and project management (subcontractors who provide a full range of services including designing facilities, managing installation, transfer of inventory to new facilities, and turnkey installation of ABC systems).

The Product Life Cycle as a Text-Based Procedure

The top level life cycle is divided into stages, most of which conclude with a Stage Review at which executive management reviews progress and determines whether to authorize the project to move to the next stage. Responsibility for each stage of the project is assigned to the group that owns the bulk of the activities in the stage. Exhibit E-1 describes all eight stages of the project life cycle in a text-based procedure format.

The Product Life Cycle as a Process Map

Within the Product Life Cycle, the engineering organization maintains detailed, technology- and domain-specific life cycles that it applies, with or without tailoring, to specific projects. These life cycles include engineering activities in all stages of the product life cycle.

Exhibit E-2 summarizes the relationship between top-level engineering life cycle activities and the first three phases of ABC's product life cycle. Activities from manufacturing and support that have the greatest impact on engineering activities are also portrayed.

The following notation and conventions are used in Exhibit E-2:

- Time and activity flow from left to right. Activities that align vertically (e.g., one above the other) are performed in parallel.
- Some activities are represented by a stack of three boxes (e.g., "develop hardware unit" in Stage 3). This indicates that multiple instances of the activity may occur simultaneously (e.g., multiple hardware units are designed and developed concurrently).
- Gray-shaded areas indicate permitted, risk-based early-starts.
- The boxes with black shadows (e.g., "PHASE 1 REVIEW") represent decision gates that consider the results of the activities in the phase and authorize the project to continue. The outputs of activities that flow horizontally into the gates are the basis for the decision.

Exhibit E-1. The eight stages of the product life cycle.

Stage	Primary owner	Summary of activities
1 Concept	Marketing	Marketing describes a business opportunity, with general product capability, potential market, time frames, profit margins, effect on current products, competitive information, and risks. Marketing management selects the most beneficial candidates and requests an engineering review of the opportunities. Engineering provides an assessment of the technology-based risks associated with the proposal. Engineering consults with and represents professional services and manufacturing for issues of supportability and manufacturability. If an accurate, timely assessment of a technology-based risk exceeds the current capability of the organization, engineering provides a detailed plan (e.g., a small project) for assessing that risk—including the early start of in-house development and the evaluation of procurable components. Marketing prepares a proposal that incorporates the business opportunity and the technology-based risks associated with schedule, cost, and content. **Stage 1 review:** Senior management reviews the proposal and approves the project to proceed to feasibility.
2 Feasibility	Marketing	A project team is formed to determine whether the proposed functionality, margins, and time frames are feasible. Any technology-based risk-assessment activities proposed in Stage 1 are executed by engineering. Detailed requirements are defined jointly by marketing and engineering. Based on the requirements, engineering creates an initial system design and a high-level plan for the system solution. Marketing updates the business proposal and reissues it as a project proposal. **Stage 2 review:** Senior management reviews the project proposal and approves the project to begin design and development.
3 Design and development	Engineering	The system design and interface requirements are completed. The system design is reviewed against the requirements to ensure that each • Requirement is traceable to one or more elements of the design (reviewers look at requirements and ask, "Where is this?").

Exhibit E-1 (continued).   The eight stages of the product life cycle.

Stage	Primary owner	Summary of activities
		• Element of the design is in response to one or more requirements (reviewers look at design elements and ask, "Why is this?").

The work is allocated to engineering teams, which begin detailed design and planning, coordinated with the overall project plan. The plan describes the engineering life cycle or life cycles employed by the project and specifically includes, if necessary, multiple levels of integration and integration testing and preliminary releases to the factory system test team.

Hardware and software development are coordinated to the greatest extent practical, based on the risks and technologies selected for the solution. However, ABC recognizes that effective testing in software development may require a stable version of the target platform. As a result, once the hardware design and development completed the planned hardware development tests, a Stage 3A review occurs.

Stage 3A review: Senior management reviews progress and any changes that affect the project proposal and approves the project to begin preproduction manufacture of hardware units required for engineering system test.

Preproduction manufacturing is planned and may be performed by Manufacturing or Engineering.

To minimize risk, procurement of components begins as late as possible in project, but ABC recognizes that lead times may require an early start to the procurement of components.

Software development bypasses the Stage 3A review and continues as planned until the necessary hardware is available for completing the software development unit and integration tests. Once the tests are completed, the project team meets to review the test results and to approve the software for release to engineering system test.

Engineering uses the factory system laboratory to conduct the engineering system test, combining the released software and the preproduction hardware.

Stage 3 review: Senior management reviews progress and any changes that affect the project proposal, and approves the project to begin factory system test.

Exhibit E-1 (continued).   The eight stages of the product life cycle

Stage	Primary owner	Summary of activities
4 Factory system test	**Phase 1:** System test **Phase 2:** Marketing support	The factory system test is conducted in the factory simulation laboratory and passes through two distinct phases.
		In the first phase, only in-house personnel participate. Professional services personnel (field service, technical support, and project management) are trained and any final integration defects and usability issues are identified and addressed. Developed hardware is supplied by manufacturing (e.g., preproduction build).
		Stage 4a review: The product manager approves the project to begin Phase 2 of Stage 4.
		In the second phase, customers identified as beta partners send representatives to the factory simulation laboratory for training and to identify any final operational issues that need to be addressed.
		Stage 4 review: Senior management approves the project to begin beta partner deployment.
5 Beta partner deployment	Professional services	The product is deployed at beta partners' sites by professional services (with engineering support) as prescribed by the beta partner agreements. On the basis of the agreement and the customer's organization, the beta deployment may include
		• Installation in a customer laboratory
		• Installation at a customer warehouse (for operation)
		• Training of customer personnel and customer training personnel.
		Stage 5 review: The product manager approves the project to begin controlled introduction.
6 Controlled introduction	Marketing	As the manufacturing, marketing/sales, and professional services organizations complete their new product introduction activities, the product is approved for sale to customers.
		Controls may be by geographical region, market segment, and so forth.
		There is no Stage 6 review. Once the last of the controlled introductions is completed, as defined in the new product introduction plan, the marketing product manager announces that the product has achieved general availability. Progress during Stage 6 is reported in the monthly general product line business reviews.

Exhibit E-1 (continued).   The eight stages of the product life cycle.

Stage	Primary owner	Summary of activities
7 General availability	Marketing	The product is available for revenue shipment to all intended customers and markets.
		Activity during this stage is reported in the monthly general product line business reviews. Based on performance or the arrival of a planned replacement, the product manager (marketing) prepares a sunset plan, including the market impact, upgrade paths, sources of authorized third-party support, and so forth.
		Note that "sunset" applies only to major versions of products (e.g., 7, 8), not to incremental releases (e.g., 7.1, 7.2), which are discontinued at the discretion of the Product Manager.
		In some cases during Stage 7, there may be planned transitions to third parties (e.g., for service and support) to release ABC internal resources to work on new products.
		Stage 7 may also include planned ramp down in volumes, anticipating markets' requirements.
		Stage 7 review: Senior management reviews the sunset plan and approves its implementation.
8 Sunset	Professional Services	The plan to terminate availability and end all support for the product is announced in an appropriate manner to the installed base.
		Stage 8 review: Senior management and the project team meet separately and jointly. Successes and failures are analyzed. Opportunities for improvement associated with the product life cycle are identified, documented, and reported to the affected organizations for action. The results of Stage 8 reviews are monitored by the director of quality in engineering and are presented for review in the monthly general product line business reviews.

The Product Life Cycle as a Table of Responsibilities and Deliverables

Exhibit E-3 is taken from a larger table that appears in the engineering handbook. The complete table summarizes the deliverables associated with all phases of the product life cycle. Documents referred to by title are supported by templates that include requirements for review and approval. The larger table contains entries for other groups and functions.

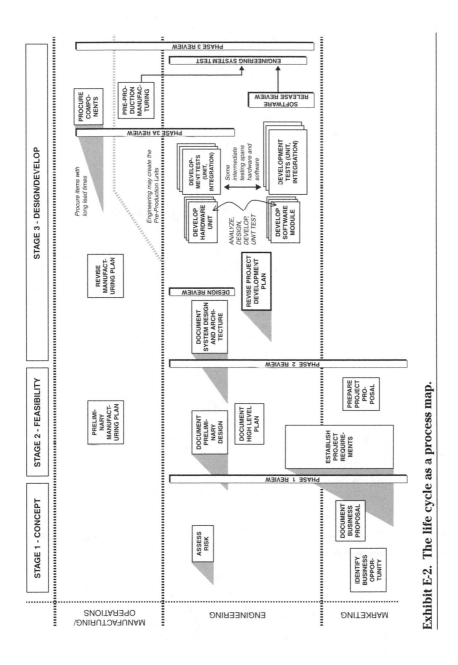

Exhibit E-2. The life cycle as a process map.

Exhibit E-3. Identifying responsibilities and deliverables.

Stage	1	2	3	4
	Concept	**Feasibility**	**Design and development**	**Factory system test**
Marketing	Business case business proposal	Project Requirements Document Project Proposal New Product Introduction Plan Beta Deployment Plan		
Engineering	Risk analysis report and plan (if required)	Project Requirements Document System Design Document (preliminary) System Development Plan (high level) Regulatory Impact Assessment Risk Assessment Report	System Design Document (complete) System Development Plan (complete) System Architecture Document Interface Specification or Specifications Component Detailed Design Document or Documents Engineering System Test Plan and Report Hardware and Software Development Integration Test Plan or Plans and Report or Reports Factory System Test Plan Regulatory Approval Plan	Factory System Test Report Regulatory Approval Report or Reports Defect Reports in BugTrak Defect Reporting and Tracking System
Professional services	(Contribute to risk analysis)	(Contribute to new product introduction plan)		
Manufacturing	(Contribute to risk analysis)	(Contribute to new product introduction plan) Procurement Plan (preliminary)	Operations Introduction Plan Procurement Plan (complete)	

Appendix F
Implementation as a Managed Process

This appendix is structured to serve as a stand-alone guide for teams implementing any types of systems. It contains the following subdivisions:

Exhibit F-1. Defining three key terms.[1]

Procedure	Process	System
1. A manner of proceeding; a way of performing or effecting something 2. A series of steps taken to accomplish an end 3. A set of established forms or methods for conducting the affairs of an organized body	1. A series of steps, changes, or functions bringing about a result 2. A series of operations performed in the making or treatment of a product	1. A group of interacting, interrelated, or interdependent elements forming a complex whole ... 8. An organized and coordinated method; a procedure

Introduction to the Elements of a System

There are three key words associated with systems. These three words are delineated in Exhibit F-1.

Note that the definitions overlap, which creates significant confusion and fuels many debates about the difference between a process and a procedure. For the purposes of this discussion, the following definitions pertain:

- A system is a set of elements, which when assembled, produce a defined, predictable, result. A system encompasses operators, training, documentation, facilities, equipment, processes, procedures, and policies.
- A process is a set of steps or actions, executed in a specific order to produce a defined, predictable result. A system may represent part of a process, a complete process, or multiple processes.
- A procedure defines the ways in which the steps or actions in a process are intended to be carried out; it communicates in some form (e.g., in pictures or words on paper, computer messages, or signs), the way in which the actions are performed to produce the specified result. Some procedures or some steps in procedures define activities that ensure that the results are correct. These activities involve verifying the integrity of the result (e.g., testing and inspection), verifying the integrity of the process, and verifying that the specified steps have been completed (e.g., progress reports, audits). Appropriate verification activities are inserted in the overall work flow to catch problems and misunderstandings as early and as frequently as practical. The decision on where to insert these steps is based on management's assessment of the level of risk associated with the process:
  - Complexity of the process
  - Confidence in the operators
  - Cost of verification versus the cost of the range of possible errors
  - Prior experience.

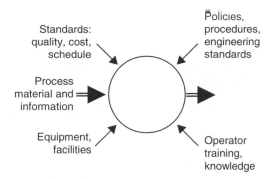

Exhibit F-2. The Crosby process model.

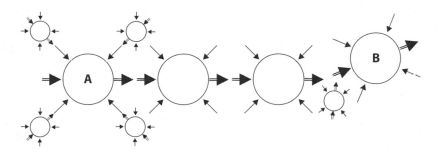

Exhibit F-3. Linked process models.

As an effective definition, a procedure provides all the information required by qualified operators to perform their assigned tasks in the actual work environment. The level of detail and direction in the procedure is determined by the amount of training, experience, and judgment specified for qualified operators. Training, experience, the nature of the process (e.g., complex, critical), and procedure content are balanced to ensure the timely completion of the process.

Philip Crosby represents the relationships among the elements of a process in what he calls a Process Model,[2] portrayed in Exhibit F-2.

To facilitate analysis, operation, and management, complex systems are divided into subsystems; processes, into subprocesses.

As illustrated in Exhibit F-3, the output from one process becomes the process material or information input to another. More than one process may provide input to another (as at B). Even the supporting inputs (e.g., training, facilities, procedures, standards) are the outputs of other processes. In addition, the output from a process may provide input to more than one other process.

The Implementation Process

The implementation of any system follows a process that can be defined with the same precision and operated with the same control as the development and introduction of a new product. Implementation starts with the management decision to introduce or to modify a system. Implementation concludes with the successful introduction of the new or modified system into the workplace. Employee involvement as early and as often as possible is a critical factor in the success of any implementation. In many cases, it is the experienced employees, the senior or master line operators, who bring the opportunity for a new system to the attention of management, and who are able to provide valuable input to the design or redesign of the system.

Managing the implementation as a process or project ensures that the new or enhanced system is in place on time, within budget, and that the new or enhanced system performs exactly as expected. Systematic implementation allows management to

- Plan for and maintain productivity and customer service levels during the implementation
- Minimize the stress on the organization.

Successful implementation of a new or enhanced system requires completion of a sequence of activities, typically grouped into phases to facilitate monitoring and control. The degree of change determines the importance and duration of the phases.

The activities and stages of the implementation process are summarized in Exhibit F-4.

When the scope of the implementation is sufficiently small, Phase 3, Test, and Phase 4, General Implementation, can be combined.

Each of these phases is further described in the following paragraphs.

Phase 1: Define Requirements

Requirements definition encompasses two activities. First, identify and document the requirements of the organization. The documented requirements are reviewed and confirmed by management. For example, there are typically requirements for

- The duration of the requirements definition; when the initial plan is required
- The duration of the whole implementation (e.g., a target for completion)
- Resources (head count, equipment, budget for direct and indirect expenditure)

Exhibit F-4. Implementing a system.

Phase	Typical activities
1 Define requirements	• Assign a team to define requirements and develop an implementation plan; the team leader or one of the members becomes the implementation project manager • Create a plan for the first phase • Educate and train team (team techniques, research techniques, identification and use of experts, technology and methods, etc.) • If appropriate, define methods and begin measurement of current processes to develop a baseline for determining improvement; involve and educate appropriate members of the organization • Identify or create governing policies • Define requirements • Assign responsibilities for implementing systems that meet the requirements • Create a brief summary of how each requirement will be met • Plan for the remaining four phases • Approval by management to begin design and development • Communicate progress to entire organization
2 Design and develop	• Continue to educate and train team • Involve additional people as required (experienced operators) • If appropriate, continue measurement of current processes • Acquire samples of any new tools required; draft new or revised procedures, documentation, and training material • Verify tools and draft material • Improve tools and draft materials • Estimate level of improvement, productivity, or yield • Maintain plan; communicate progress to entire organization • Approval by management to advance to the pilot implementation
3 Test	• If appropriate, continue measurement of current processes • Educate and train pilot team with draft materials (policies, procedures, documentation, training material) • Install new tools • Operate the system with close monitoring and support from the implementation team • For major changes to or replacement of complex or critical systems, consider operating the new and old systems in parallel, comparing outputs • Validate tools and materials • Verify estimated levels of improvement, productivity, or yield • Fine tune tools and draft materials • Maintain plan; communicate progress to entire organization • Approval by management to advance to the general implementation

Exhibit F-4 (continued). Implementing a system.

Phase	Typical activities
4 General implementation	• Educate and train operators with final materials (policies, procedures, documentation, training material) • Continue to monitor and provide additional support for the new process for a predefined period of time • Install tools • Measure achieved levels of improvement, productivity, or yield • Operate the system with decreasing levels of monitoring and support from the implementation team • Maintain plan; communicate progress to entire organization • Recognition by management of completion of implementation
5 Implementation review	• Review all implementation activities and metrics • Define areas of strength and weakness • Define improvements that could be made to the implementation system • Record results

- Priority of the implementation with respect to existing activities (e.g., any critical activities that must not be impacted by the implementation)
- Specific functional requirements or restrictions the new or improved system must meet (e.g., must work with existing MIS systems)
- Objectives for improvement or new capability that must be achieved to justify the expenditure of effort.

The success of the project depends on both management and the process operators being satisfied with the outcome. As these two groups often have different objectives, mutual satisfaction will not be achieved if only one party's requirements and perceptions are considered. Through careful communication, education, and employee involvement in the implementation process, the implementation team can build the broadest possible base of support and achieve the highest level of perceived and actual satisfaction.

The team must place a high priority on reconciling requirements that appear to be mutually exclusive. For example, reducing errors, improving productivity, and creating a more employee-responsive environment may appear to be in conflict until priorities and additional explanation are provided. This reconciliation must begin with education and communication. When all parties understand the intentions and background of the apparently conflicting objectives, the perceived conflict may no longer exist, the objectives may be modified, or one or more objectives may be discarded.

The second step in defining requirements is to break down the initial, high-level objectives into successive levels of detailed objectives. These objectives communicate, requirements to the individuals who will create the procedures, identify the tools, and so forth. The level of detail, the number of levels through which the original organizational objectives must be broken down, cannot be defined *a priori*. The initial breakdown is complete when the team members (or appropriate individuals) feel they have sufficient information to prepare a brief description of the system as it will be implemented and an initial draft of the plan. The plan, described in detail in Exhibit 7-6, addresses all of the components of the system:

- Policies
- Procedures, measurements, and standards
- Facilities
- Equipment capability and capacity
- Operator capability, capacity, and training
- Requirements for process materials (including information) required as input to the system
- A description of the outputs, including targets for overall yield and productivity
- Projected direct and indirect cost of the implementation; list areas for which costs cannot be projected
- Significant risks that may affect the cost or success of the implementation (e.g., technology, competition, and other projects planned or in progress that may divert resources)
- Significant assumptions and dependencies (e.g., other projects that must be completed as prerequisites for the implementation)
- Initial metrics—methods to monitor the success of the system through all or part of the implementation
- Ongoing metrics—methods that are part of the new system to provide the feedback required to monitor and control the system effectively
- An initial set of milestones with target completion dates

With management approval, the team should be ready to begin Phase 2, Design and Develop.

As with all nominally linear processes, the actual activity entails a number of iterations. The more complex the new system, the more iterations occur. Objectives are defined. A brief summary is produced. As a result, the objectives and the summaries are refined. When the initial plan is produced, the objectives and the summaries may be further refined.

In addition to repeating steps, the steps frequently overlap. To compress the cycle time, before the objectives are completely defined, individuals begin to draft portions of the implementation summary. The clear definition and maintenance of the functional requirements and objectives is a critical factor in the efficiency and the success of the implementation.

Phase 2: Design and Develop

As the implementation team members take the activity back to their groups, an additional level of requirements definition may be required before derivative and more-detailed plans can be created. The members of the implementation team coordinate their groups' efforts with the overall efforts.

The implementation manager monitors and facilitates the critical path activities as reported by each group participating in the implementation.

The final part of the design and development phase is to verify the tools, processes, procedures, and other new material through reviews and experimentation. This is usually done in a laboratory environment, with individuals who have been involved in the implementation. This minimizes the investment in and exposure of processes and tools at a time when they are still potentially subject to significant change.

Phase 3: Test

The test is conducted in an actual work environment with individuals who have not previously been involved in the implementation. The test phase ensures that the procedures, training and support mechanisms, and interfaces with other organizations and systems function as expected. For complex systems, the test is an opportunity for management to assess the operation of the new or modified system in a live environment for a specified period of time before authorizing the general implementation of the system.

Because this is the first operational test of the new system, the implementation team is on call to provide additional expert support, which will not be available or required for the general implementation.

Phase 4: General Implementation

With management approval based on the results of the test, the implementation procedures perfected and proven in the test are repeated as the new system undergoes each subsequent implementation.

Intensive measurement, monitoring, and support continue for the period of time specified in the plan. After that period of time, the operational metrics and standard support and reporting mechanisms built into or associated with the new system will be sufficient to maintain the system.

Phase 5: Implementation Review

The implementation review allows the company or the organization to derive the last bit of benefit from the implementation. By reviewing the implementation and the areas of strength and weakness, and by recording opportunities for improvement in both areas, the groundwork is done for improving the next implementation.

Implementation Planning

Planning is a key activity that occurs throughout the implementation; it involves individuals at all levels of the organization. The plan is initially drafted in the first phase; details are added and modifications made as the implementation progresses.

Each plan or element of the plan can be traced to a clearly specified goal, which includes:

- A tangible or measurable result
- The means and criteria for measuring completion
- Any time, budget, and resource constraints
- Any time-related requirements (e.g., for completion)
- Resource requirements—any limitations on the amount of effort that can be applied to each task
- Dependencies created by resources (e.g., parallel tasks cannot usually be assigned to the same person) or deliverables (e.g., the output of one task may be required as the initial input to another task)

The plan includes:

- A description of the process that will be followed to meet the objectives and goals of the implementation
- Specific deliverables associated with each step in the process—both as inputs and outputs—and the source of each deliverable
- Estimates of the effort required to complete each step, the skills required to perform the activity, and the availability of people with the specified skills
- A schedule—the tasks arranged in chronological order—reflecting all aspects of the time estimates and dependencies
- A complete delineation of dependencies between steps, all of which must be accounted for in the schedule and process definition
- A list of any risks and contingency plans for dealing with the risks
- A description of the process used to manage the implementation (e.g., weekly meetings, department representatives empowered to make commitments for their organizations, report formats, distribution of information; change request escalation, approval, notification)
- A description of the method and criteria on which the management decision to advance from step to step is based

At the conclusion of each phase, there is a formal mechanism for recognizing completion. To provide clear direction and to avoid the cost and stress of last-minute surprises, define and publish the criteria for completing each step as far in advance as possible. Defining the criteria in advance encourages a more objective assessment of the realities of the completed task. The criteria may be changed, but the degree of change and the reason for the change can be documented and agreed to.

Acceptance criteria describe all measurable expectations held by management; the plan includes the method for determining that each criterion is satisfied. The criteria must be agreed to by all groups involved in the implementation. To the extent that any criteria are unilaterally imposed or assumed to be understood, there is a risk of misunderstanding.

To succeed, the plan must be:

- Agreed to—by management and by the individuals responsible for carrying out the plan.
- As detailed as is appropriate to eliminate bias and to provide confidence that most factors have been considered.
- Realistic—all individuals and organizations involved confirm that there is minimal risk in following the plan within time frame, budget, and resource constraints.

Implementation of even a simple system requires careful planning to ensure that cost, schedule, and quality requirements are all satisfied. Perhaps the most important part of complex or long-duration plans is the ability to accommodate change. Not only must the plan clearly communicate requirements, it must also clearly communicate changes. The planning methodology must be congruent with the rate of change of requirements and schedules. For example, if schedule changes occur daily, a planning methodology (policies, procedures, tools, and resources for planning) that requires several days to update the plan cannot be completely effective.

Forward Planning

For each implementation activity, the initial schedule for a task should be based on effort required and resources available. If management's targets for completion require it, the schedule can be shortened in two ways, by modifying:

- The way the tasks are accomplished to reduce the effort
- The resources available

The schedule cannot be shortened by edict. The implementation manager's task is to challenge proposed schedules by examining assumptions:

- Sequential activities that can be overlapped
- Competing priorities (e.g., "I have to do this other thing first.")
- Resource limitations that can be overcome
  - Equipment (e.g., more, faster, other)
  - People (e.g., additional help, overtime, manual activities that can be automated)

Duplicate activities that can be effectively consolidated
  - Unnecessary activities that can be eliminated without affecting the quality of the final output (e.g., implementation of unnecessary features, creeping elegance, rubber-stamp approvals, frequently waived approvals or administrative requirements)
- Overstated or nonimmediate requirements
  - Negotiation ploys (e.g., "I said January so it wouldn't go past March.")
  - Requirements that can be phased in with system maintenance and enhancement (e.g., "We'll need it, but not until...")

Plans become more accurate as they evolve—and as they move toward completion. They should always be based on best estimates and experience. To ensure that planning inputs are as accurate as possible, the implementation manager must eliminate the cultural pressures and the opportunities to provide unrealistic estimates: both high (sandbagging—just in case something goes wrong) and low (milestone chicken—someone else will be late first).

The project manager performs key activities that improve the accuracy of the estimates. The estimation process is reviewed to ensure that all known tasks are accounted for and that known risks and dependencies are identified with contingency plans in place. Progress in the implementation is monitored and communicated to identify necessary schedule changes as early as possible. Finally, when schedule changes must be made, they are a cooperative effort to adapt to previously unknown circumstances.

Quality, Cost, Schedule, and Content

Cost and schedule are traditionally inversely linked. Increase one to decrease the other. Reduce duration by adding resources and increasing cost; reduce cost be deferring certain activities and increasing duration. Under no circumstances can quality—meeting requirements—be adjusted to control cost and schedule. If a product does not perform as required, it does not matter how little it cost or when it arrived.

in some circumstances, cost and schedule can both be reduced by adjusting content (e.g., decommitting or deferring functionality).

Effort, Method, and Resources

Estimation of effort is related closely to method and resources. Working alone, the right person may be able to complete specific tasks in a relatively brief time. In implementing systems, even if an experienced individual contributor may be able to draft a procedure quickly, time must be allocated for gathering initial input, tools and methods selection, review of the final procedure, and any training required for new tools or techniques.

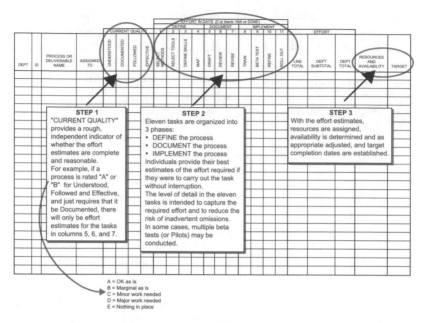

Exhibit F-5. Form for gathering effort estimates.

Exhibit F-5 illustrates a standard method for gathering effort estimates from team members. The effort estimates are gathered in three steps. *First*, the individuals completing the form list the projects, processes, or deliverables and estimate the current quality of each. *Second*, effort estimates (in days) are provided for 11 tasks. Not all the tasks apply in every case. The estimates of current quality and of effort are compared and discussed until a consensus is reached. *Third*, with baseline effort estimates in hand, resource availability is analyzed to determine a target completion date for each project, process, or deliverable. By reviewing the proposed dates with all team members, dependencies are identified and adjustments made to optimize the implementation for the team. A planning form is included in Exhibit F-9.

Another factor affecting the accuracy of effort estimation is management expectation expressed in deadlines and schedule targets. Even when management is clear in its commitment to forward planning, any target tends to influence gross estimates. Although conventional wisdom is quick to point out (usually with a choked laugh) that work expands to fill the time available, the most pervasive problem in planning is underestimating the effort required. The tendency to underestimate resources can be offset by:

- Making forward planning an explicit requirement
- Defining the process for completing the activity at a sufficiently granular level to offset even subconscious bias; as each step progresses, it is decomposed into substeps to improve the accuracy of the estimate
- Working in units of time appropriate to the level of detail of the plan; for example, the initial plan may be in weeks—as each step progresses and is further decomposed into substeps, time can be specified in days or hours
- Involving the people who will do they work to validate estimates
- Monitoring progress so that inevitable adjustments may be made in a timely manner

The planning process balances the degree to which the process being planned is understood with the precision and accuracy of the input requested. In planning to implement a new process, if the activities span months, it may be a waste of effort to create a plan that times activities in hours. In addition, even with highly effective planning, the first version of a plan for implementing a new process may underestimate effort and schedule by more than 40 percent.

Benefits of a Standard Methodology

Standardized project planning and project management methodologies provide significant benefits to everyone involved with the project:

- Prior experience in systems implementation management and in implementation-related activities is transferable, which increases efficiency and minimizes stress.
- Control procedures are well-defined and understood.
- Standard documentation minimizes learning time and facilitates communication both within and without the project team.

The Implementation Plan and Project File

This section describes a format for an implementation plan that provides the information required to assess the validity and viability of the initial plan. There is no reason that the plan be constructed or maintained as a single document. Once the plan is approved, and at periodic checkpoints, the plan can be updated and reissued; between those checkpoints, only the schedule is typically updated. Minor modifications to other portions of the plan can be communicated in meeting minutes.

The project file is a repository of the information that was and is required to manage the project. It can comprise one or more notebooks or file folders. It can be on paper or online. It can be maintained in one or more locations by one or more people. When the project is completed, selected portions of the project file are archived to serve as a corporate memory for reference in assessing planning performance or in planning a similar project.

The implementation plan and project file are discussed in the following paragraphs. All of the examples are drawn from the plan for a fictional company, Product Development, Incorporated (PDI), to obtain ISO 9001 registration.

The Implementation Plan

The implementation plan typically provides the information described in Exhibit F-6.

Reporting Progress

Exhibit F-7 illustrates a standard method for progress reporting that allows a team member's detailed input on progress to be readily consolidated into the project manager's progress report.

A report template is included as Exhibit F-8.

The Project File

A project file contains current and relevant historical information on the progress of the implementation and on the system to be implemented. A project file can be maintained in more than one location by more than one person. It can be a paper or an electronic document, or it can be in a combination of media.

The purpose of the project file is to provide a defined source for information about the implementation. It typically contains:

- Plan (current and prior)
- Schedule (current and prior)
- Minutes of meetings in which decisions were made or actions assigned
- Records of progress in completing assigned tasks
- Records of review meetings, of reviewers' comments, and of the disposition of these comments
- Records of tests (e.g., pilot sites) as specified in the plan, of test results, and the disposition of all reported problems

The project file contains the information that the project manager requires to ensure that plans are followed and commitments are met. In addition, the project file provides historical data that can be analyzed to control ongoing implementation activities (e.g., address potential delays before they have a significant effect on the success of the project) and to plan future implementations.

Exhibit P-0. The contents of an implementation plan.

Item	Description
Summary	A one- or two-sentence description of the overall purpose of the project. For example,
	"This plan defines the activities and resources required to prepare PDI for ISO 9001 registration. The effectiveness of this investment will be tested by an audit by an accredited registrar in March of 1993."
Scope of application	A list of the organizational units affected by the plan and how they will be required to participate in the plan. For example,
	"All functional areas of PDI, including both line and staff/support are addressed by education, planning, and implementation activities described in this proposal. All functional areas will be required to support and implement the provisions of this proposal through
	• The evaluation and analysis of current business practices for efficiency and competitive advantage • The modification and reimplementation of existing procedures • The definition and implementation of new procedures."
Author	The name, title, and contact information for the individual responsible for the draft of the plan. This is typically the project manager.
Approvals	This section contains two lists: reviewers (those who see the plan to make comments) and those who approve the plan for execution. Reviewers typically include all groups affected by the plan.
Comments	The name, title, and contact information for the individual responsible for controlling changes to the plan. This is also typically the author or project manager.
Document control	How to obtain copies of the latest version of the plan. This section may not be necessary if there is a standard method for controlling plans.
Changes from previous issue	An aid to the reader in identifying substantive changes.
Changes anticipated	When the plan is issued or reissued, this section alerts the reader to portions of the plan that may be subject to change.
Related documents	Any other plans, standards, documents (e.g., specifications or procedures) that are referred to directly or indirectly in this plan.
Contents	A table of contents—if the plan is more than ten pages in length
Abbreviations and acronyms	A table expanding or explaining any abbreviations or acronyms used in the plan. This is especially important for readers who are external to the implementation team.

Exhibit F-6 (continued).   The contents of an implementation plan.

Item	Description
Background and objectives	A brief (one or two page) summary of prior activity and specific objectives for the project. This section can describe the inspiration for the project (customer or competitive pressure, government regulation), the primary benefits or objectives sought from the project, the reason behind the target completion date, any high-level phases envisioned by the requester (e.g., immediate versus intermediate versus long-term requirements). This section sets a tone and direction that keeps the project on track.
Critical success factors	Activities within or without the implementation process that are critical to the success of the implementation. Although all factors are important, this section defines the key activities that must be monitored and executed. For example, in achieving ISO 9001 registration, the PDI plan identifies internal audits, broad-based involvement and awareness, management commitment, and education as critical success factors.
Implementation process overview	This section of the plan describes the activities that will be undertaken to execute the plan. They should be those that the implementation manager/project manager reports to senior management. as such, there may be 10 or 12 high-level steps, listed in approximate chronological order. From a project management perspective, these steps are broken down into as much detail as is necessary to manage the project in the company culture. For example, the PDI plan lists the following steps:

- Selection of consultants
- Awareness
    - Senior management awareness
    - Ongoing awareness
- Registrar selection
- Audit team selection
- Preassessment
- Analysis of preassessment report
- Internal and external audit policies and procedures
- Definition of quality system documentation requirements
- Team facilitator training
- Skills training
    - Quality-system implementation
    - Analyzing and optimizing processes
    - Documenting procedures
    - Value-added auditing for ISO 9001
- Process definition, modification, and (re)implementation
- Internal audits
- Corrective action
- Registrar audit.

Item	Description
Costs, resources, and funding	All known direct and indirect costs associated with the plan. In some cases, ranges of costs may be given. The costs can be organized by associated major step identified in the implementation process overview. Specific budget and resource constraints (e.g., existing head count) should be recorded. If appropriate, the business case for waiving some of those constraints can be made (e.g., increase head count by one for 6 months; reduce duration of implementation by 2 months).
Risks	This section lists significant areas of unusual risk (e.g., fire and earthquake are not usually included). For each risk, a fallback strategy should be briefly outlined. For example, if a person is completing another project that inspires a low confidence of on-time completion, an alternative resource might be identified.
Dependencies	This section lists the key, unusual assumptions on which the plan is based (e.g., availability of a new technology, completion of another project; continued availability of the e-mail system is not usually included). This notifies individuals not directly involved in the implementation that they have a new customer to consider.
Human factors	Every change has an effect on the people involved. This section summarizes the current readiness of the organization to make the change and what, if any, steps are planned to prepare the organization. For example, the PDI plan contains the following in the human factors section:

There are two primary areas of concern.

The first concern is overcoming skepticism based on the quality improvement programs PDI has launched and abandoned in the past. This is addressed initially in the awareness training:

- *Customers require this activity as a condition of doing business with PDI*
- *The required surveillance visits bring the registrar back at least twice a year*
- *Market pressures make it essential that PDI be proactive in simplifying and optimizing its internal processes and in adopting a methodology for continuous improvement.*

The second concern is in overcoming the reluctance engineers have about ISO 9001 based on concerns that the resulting system is inevitably bureaucratic and overly restrictive. Team involvement and strict adherence to the goal of building responsive, supporting systems will prove over time that the resulting quality management system will be beneficial to all levels of the organization and to the company as a whole.

Exhibit F-6 (continued). The contents of an implementation plan.

Item	Description
Contacts	The list of individuals who are actually involved in the implementation and who represent their organizations. This may be a roster of the implementation team, but it frequently lists individuals who are performing parallel, independent activities.
Planning milestones	The complete list of milestones the project manager will monitor and the team members will collectively report on. This typically expands the major milestones listed in the implementation process overview.
	For each milestone, there is a person responsible, an assessment of effort required (in days of labor), and a target for completion. In initial versions of the plan, although some activities may not be sized or assigned to an individual, there must be some mechanism (e.g., a note or a comment section) for defining when all "to be determined" (TBD) tasks will be assigned and sized.
	This method of presenting milestones can be integrated easily in a format for reporting progress. A suggested format is presented at the end of this section.

For critical projects and processes, the project file also contains the evidence that management and customers may require to be confident in the progress of the implementation.

Supporting the Implementation

The preceding sections assume that mechanisms are in place for two systems required to support the implementation process: corrective action and management responsibility. If they are not, the implementation process will have to allow for their creation.

Corrective Action

Successful implementation requires a means for requesting changes to systems and processes. These requests can address a number of objectives: elimination of existing problems, prevention of potential problems, and improvements to increase product or process performance, yield, or capability.

As organizations transition from reacting to customer problems to preventing potential problems from occurring, the corrective action system expands to handle all types of requests. The corrective action system provides for recording and processing requests and for providing feedback to the requesters. In addition, the system defines the prioritization, routing, monitoring and aging, and if necessary, escalation of requests. The one mandate is that a request can never be lost.

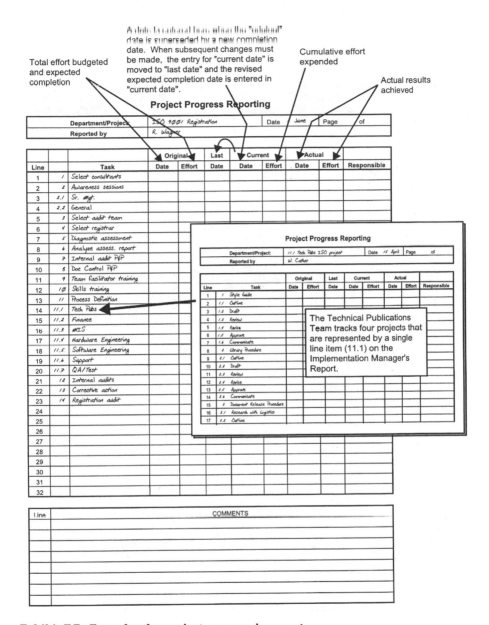

Exhibit F-7. Form for the project manager's report.

To ensure that policies and procedures remain current, corrective action typically involves regular review of all policies, processes, and procedures. This can be accomplished by external review or audit of procedures as well as by internal review by process operators and the managers responsible for the processes.

263

Project Progress Reporting

Department/Project:		Date		Page	of
Reported by					

Line		Task	Original		Last	Current		Actual		Responsible
			Date	Effort	Date	Date	Effort	Date	Effort	
1										
2										
3										
4										
5										
6										
7										
8										
9										
10										
11										
12										
13										
14										
15										
16										
17										
18										
19										
20										
21										
22										
23										
24										
25										
26										
27										
28										
29										
30										
31										
32										

Line	COMMENTS

Exhibit F-8. Blank progress report form.

Management Responsibility and Authority

Because systems implementation involves change and expenditure of company resources, the extent of the implementation team's responsibility and authority must be clear. In the event that the implementation exceeds the team's level of authority, there must also be a clearly defined route for involving managers with additional responsibility and authority. For the implementation of significant systems, a senior management representative may be assigned to the team as a participant or a mentor. An alternative is to provide the implementation/project manager with direct access to senior management through a steering committee.

Profile of an Implementation Manager

The implementation manager is the project manager designated to see the implementation through — from defining requirements to general rollout of the new system. The project manager coordinates and monitors the key activities that affect the success of the implementation. Other individuals are typically responsible for the planning, management, and control of tasks and subtasks, but the project manager incorporates their individual plans and maintains control of the implementation as a whole.

The goal of the project manager is to deliver on schedule and within budget a system that meets or exceeds management's expectations.

A project manager's success is based on the system's success in satisfying the needs of the end users—those individuals who operate the system in their daily work environments. The project manager's job requires demonstrated concern for the end user; it also requires a significant time investment in helping users understand how the system benefits them and their organization.

Typically, the project manager facilitates solutions for a large number of diverse issues. These solutions often require compromises to be reached between cost, performance, and schedule. Careful planning and project management minimize the need for these compromises and the resulting sacrifice of some aspect of the projected benefits to be derived from the system.

Responsibilities

As a project manager, the job of the implementation manager is to:

- Recommend and secure management agreement on individual implementation responsibilities and plans
- Ensure the documentation of acceptance criteria and tests that demonstrate that each deliverable meets the specified requirements
- Coordinate testing of all elements of the system

- Ensure that implementation responsibilities and procedures are fully documented and understood
- Verify that formal, closed-loop reporting channels are available
- Verify that all problems are reported to and addressed by the appropriate authorities in a timely manner and that feedback to individuals reporting problems is provided in a timely manner
- Monitor and coordinate critical process design and development activity that directly affects the quality of the overall implementation
- Ensure that all required communication occurs among the groups participating in the implementation
- Keep management and the user community informed of progress achieved against the plan
- Maintain a project file containing project plans, minutes of meetings, problem reports, change requests, and current and historical supporting documentation

A project manager's success is based on a number of criteria, most of which involve ensuring that others execute assigned tasks:

- To ensure that users and management agree on the required levels of performance, quality, and cost
- To create and monitor a project plan establishing the goals and objectives of the project and identifying the resources, time scales, and schedules required to meet these goals
- To identify, secure, and monitor the resources necessary to meet commitments
- To coordinate the use of resources
- To prioritize elements of the implementation

Knowledge, Skills, and Abilities

The most important activities a project manager undertakes are those related to facilitating communication. The project manager is the primary contact among all the groups involved in the implementation and with management.

The project manager's involvement is most critical whenever tasks change or when deliverables change hands. For example, some of the critical points requiring the project manager's attention are:

- The initiation of the project
- Approval to progress from one step to the next
- Test
- Beginning of general implementation

A project manager typically works without any permanent staff, relying on an understanding of the organization, the support of management, and the ability to influence others.

The project manager requires a comprehensive knowledge of the organizational objectives for the new system and of all of the systems that will interact with the new system.

Project planning and control skills are also essential. These include the ability to analyze tasks, to define work breakdown structures, and to design and maintain schedules, incorporating data regarding progress and delays.

Personal Attributes

The successful project manager has personal attributes that reflect requirements to facilitate communication, to resolve disputes, to manage change and large volumes of data, and to influence individuals:

- Awareness and empathy
- Personal energy
- Maturity and experience
- Ability to solve problems
- Leadership
- Judgment and initiative
- Interpersonal skills
- Independence

The current level of performance, before any changes are introduced, becomes a baseline against which progress is measured and managed. All levels of the organization expect improvements. The project manager's task is to build consensus on how improvement is to be measured.

Samples

The following pages contain the following samples:

- A sample progress report form. This is a copy of the form illustrated in Exhibit F-7.
- A sample effort estimation form. This is a copy of the form illustrated in Exhibit F-5.

The sample progress report form can be provided as a document, as a spreadsheet, or as a report from a project management or database tool. A sample progress report form is found in Exhibit F-8.

The sample effort estimation form can be provided as a document, as a spreadsheet, or as a report from a project management or database tool. A sample estimation form is found in Exhibit F-9.

The Implementation Model

Exhibit F-10 is a process map for achieving ISO 9001:2000 registration, and Exhibit F-11 describes each step in the process map in Exhibit F-10.

								EFFORT IN DAYS (0 or blank =NA or DONE)															
				CURRENT QUALITY				DEFINE				DOCUMENT			IMPLEMENT				EFFORT				
								1	2	3	4	5	6	7	8	9	10	11					
DEPT	ID	PROCESS OR DELIVERABLE NAME	ASSIGNED TO	UNDERSTOOD	DOCUMENTED	FOLLOWED	EFFECTIVE	SELECT METHODS	SELECT TOOLS	DEFINE SKILLS	MAP	DRAFT	REVIEW	REVISE	TRAIN	BETA TEST	REFINE	ROLL OUT	LINE TOTAL	DEPT SUBTOTAL	DEPT TOTAL	RESOURCES AND AVAILABILITY	TARGET

Exhibit F-9. Blank effort estimation form.

Development Processes and Procedures

List of Suggested Procedures To Support a Software Engineering Life Cycle

The following procedures support the phases in a typical software engineering life cycle:

- Project requirements document
- Project development plan
- Software engineering procedures, standards, conventions (for life cycle phases; i.e., feasibility, design, implementation, validation, support, maintenance), to include
    - Software requirement specifications
    - Software functional specifications
    - Software design specifications
    - Test plan
    - Test report
    - General release and support (handovers, release criteria checklists, replication, rollout, corrective action)
    - Maintenance

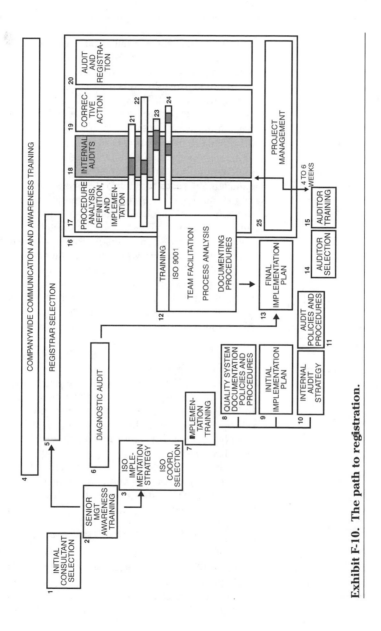

Exhibit F-10. The path to registration.

Exhibit F-11. The Path to Registration.

Number	Title	Description
1	Initial consultant selection	Any organization can implement ISO 9001 without the involvement of a consultant. However, the initial senior management awareness training (2) and the diagnostic audit (6) require the participation of one or more individuals who have experience in both the requirements of the standard and in the diverse ways in which similar organizations have successfully addressed these requirements. The consultant can be an independent expert or he or she can be from another division of the same company.
2	Senior management awareness training	Although a realistic estimate of the cost of the implementation will not be available until the initial implementation plan is completed (9), senior management needs to make a decision to fund at least the planning portion of the implementation. In addition, even when market pressure makes the decision moot, senior management needs to understand that ISO registration is an extended commitment that will have a profound effect on the way in which the organization is managed. Senior managers need to understand their role in the implementation and the ongoing processes, that ISO registration is not something the quality department does, and that ISO registration is not a one-time event.
3	ISO implementation strategy, ISO coordinator selection	The implementation strategy determines a scope (e.g., what parts of the company or organization) and the methods by which the processes will be defined, documented, and implemented. For example, will the organization adopt industry best practice or will it try to develop processes that reflect its way of doing business and preserve the organization's unique culture and values? Will processes be developed by a small core team or by a team of representatives from the affected organizations? The ISO coordinator is at least the project manager, responsible for planning and overseeing the activities that lead to ISO registration. The ISO coordinator may be the management representative. The ISO coordinator may also be a project manager and a team of representatives from the affected organizations.
4	Companywide communication and awareness training	Throughout the implementation, the whole organization is kept informed of decisions, progress, and strategies. If the implementation team is perceived (whether or not it is true) as working in a closed room, issuing edicts, the roll-out will have to overcome unnecessary resistance.

Number	Title	Description
		It should also be noted that only the implementation team and the internal auditors need in-depth familiarity with the requirements of ISO 9001. Everyone else focuses on the organization's policies, procedures, and standards—and on ensuring that the organization's products meet customer requirements and satisfy management's goals for time to market and cost.
		The whole organization needs to know enough about ISO 9001 and the implementation to achieve a level of confidence and comfort that prevents the spread of rumors.
5	Registrar selection	Although the registrar is, of necessity, an independent third party, the repeated, periodic visits mean it also becomes a partner. It is the organization's responsibility to find a registrar that is acceptable to its customers or market, that has experience in the organization's technology and type of business (so audit findings will be relevant and useful), that has views on how to interpret the standard that are compatible with those of the organization, and that has an acceptable fee structure and approach to its customers for scheduling, cancellation, and reconciliation of findings.
		In addition, new levels of standardization in the registration process mean that registrars are willing to assume responsibility for a certificate issued by another registrar—picking up the surveillance process without requiring a full reassessment.
6	Diagnostic audit	The diagnostic audit is performed by a consultant who can not only identify deficiencies but also prioritize and suggest solutions. The diagnostic assessment in combination with the implementation training (7) provides the information the implementation team needs to create an initial implementation plan (9). Because organizations vary in their level of process sophistication and discipline, the diagnostic assessment is an essential first step in answering management's concerns (and fears) about what ISO registration will cost.
7	Implementation training	Implementation training provides the implementation team with in-depth knowledge about the standard and about the types of activities and deliverables associated with an implementation. By incorporating the results of the diagnostic assessment, the training becomes a workshop that establishes the majority of the content of the next four items: quality system documentation policies and procedures (8), initial

Exhibit F-11 (continued).   The Path to Registration.

Number	Title	Description
		implementation plan (9), internal audit strategy (10), and audit policies and procedures (11).
8	Quality system documentation policies and procedures	These policies and procedures establish how procedural documentation is issued and maintained. An example of an approach is found in Appendix D.
9	Initial implementation plan	The implementation plan is a detailed plan that addresses at least the elements of the road map in Exhibit F-10. It is as detailed and rigorous as a product development plan. At this point, senior management is given an opportunity to review and approve the plan, with appropriate adjustments (e.g., spread it out over 18 months), up to and including canceling the project.
10	Internal audit strategy	Alternative strategies are discussed in conjunction with Paragraph 8.2.2. Frequently, the members of the implementation team are best qualified to perform the initial internal audits. In cases where members of the implementation team are representatives from the affected organizations, the auditor training (15) provides additional reinforcement of the information in the implementation training (7) and also enhances the abilities of the representatives to go back to their organizations to provide effective, accurate, and forceful guidance on proposed procedures (17 and 18).
11	Audit policies and procedures	These policies and procedures address the requirements of ISO 9001:2000 PARAGRAPH 8.2.2 (e.g., for sampling, reporting results, corrective action, etc.)
12	Training	This training is provided for the core team and for any additional people from the affected organizations who are to be pulled in to execute the implementation (e.g., running teams, writing procedures). It addresses the requirements of ISO 9001 and three additional topics that are frequently taken for granted: facilitation, process analysis, and documenting procedures. The complete training can be accomplished in three to four days; in some cases, individuals may require only part of the training (e.g., process analysis and documenting procedures) or team facilitation.
13	Final implementation plan	With a thorough understanding of the requirements of the standard as they pertain to the organization, and with detailed estimates in hand from the individuals who will actually be executing the implementation, a detailed plan is created. As with the initial implementation plan, at this point, senior management is given a second opportunity to review and approve the plan, with appropriate adjustments (e.g., spread it out over 18 months), up to and including canceling the project.

Exhibit F-11 (continued)   The Path to Registration.

Number	Title	Description
14 15	Auditor selection Auditor training	Auditors are selected based on the criteria in the audit policies and procedures (11) and trained at least four weeks before they are expected to audit. If the auditors are also implementation team members, the training can be provided earlier so they can have a chance to experiment with and refine their knowledge and skills as the implementation progresses.
16–24		The implementation progresses nominally through four stages: analyzing, defining, and implementing processes (17); conducting an internal audit when there is enough evidence available (18); making any required changes (19); and finally, undergoing a similar audit by the third-party registrar (20). The four lines of boxes (21, 22, 23, and 24) illustrate that different parts of the organization progress at different rates. In each of these lines, the first white box corresponds to "procedure analysis," the gray box is "internal audit," and the second white box is "corrective action." The lines of boxes at 21, 22, and 23 represent groups that had different implementation starting points and varying implementation and corrective action times. The line of boxes at 24 represent a group that underwent two internal audits and two cycles of postaudit corrective action. Internal audits can start well before everybody is ready. The earlier they start (subject to the availability of evidence), the more time is available to recover from problems. The final step (20) is to undergo a similar audit by the registrar. This is scheduled after at least one complete round of internal audits and corrective action has been completed.
25	Project management	The ISO project is managed against the implementation plan (13) with the same rigor and diligence the organization applies to its product development projects.

Areas To Consider for Supporting Procedures and Standards

Consider procedures and standards for the following activities, which support the life cycle within the department:

- Reviews (code, design, test)
- Coding practices and standards
- Tools
- Management of incidents (bugs, enhancements)
- System backup, archive, and recovery
- Configuration management (change review and control, source control and document control)

Procedure Definition and Construction: The Seven Key Elements

When developing procedures to support processes, the following key elements should be considered and defined:

- Responsibility
- Action
- Inputs
- Outputs
- Performance criteria for the process operator (e.g., schedule, capacity, error rates)
- Control mechanisms (e.g., verification, review, and approval)
- Standards, e.g., applicable and associated standards and procedures

References

1. *The American Heritage Dictionary of the English Language,* 4th ed., Houghton Mifflin, Boston, 2000.
2. Crosby, Philip B., *Quality Education System for the Individual,* Philip Crosby Associates, Inc., Winter Park, FL, 1988, p. 37.

Appendix G
Mapping the Standard to Core Competencies

As described in Appendix F, based on the organization's core capabilities and processes and defined sequence of activities, a logical work breakdown structure is developed, dependencies and priorities are established, resources are identified, and a detailed plan for achieving ISO 9001 compliance is prepared.

Mapping the standard to the organization's core processes identifies the requirements of ISO 9001 against which the success of the implementation will be measured. Although the unique needs of the organization determine the processes and procedures, identifying the applicable requirements of ISO 9001 allows the implementation teams to anticipate possible issues and self-assess their work. In some cases, citing these requirements and explaining the benefits and logic behind the implementation can open lines of communication and facilitate the work of the team in overcoming institutional inertia and resistance to change.

Core Processes and ISO 9001

The following paragraphs suggest the relationships between selected core processes and the paragraphs of ISO 9001:2000. The authors of this volume have selected those relationships that offer the organization the greatest opportunities and leverage for solving problems and improving processes.

*Requirements Engineering**

Exhibit G-1 describes the activities and related paragraphs of ISO 9001:2000 as they apply to requirements engineering.

Project Management

Exhibit G-2 describes the activities and related paragraphs of as they apply to project management.

* Requirements engineering is also discussed in Chapter 7 in conjunction with PARAGRAPH 7.5.2 under "The five activities of requirements engineering."

Exhibit G-1. Requirements engineering.

Typical activities	Related paragraphs and opportunities
Elicit needs from internal (e.g., marketing) and external customers	As one aspect of customer communication, the processes for eliciting needs are effective (7.2.3) to the extent that the identified needs are complete (e.g., nothing missing), correct (e.g., nothing extra), clear, and unambiguous.
	By defining the analysis, review, and capture processes that transform needs into requirements, the organization can position marketing, product management, and sales organizations to communicate needs in an efficient and effective manner.
	Critical components of the elicitation process are to ensure that it remains free of premature commitment (as the elicited needs have not yet been analyzed for feasibility, 7.2.3 *c*) and that it captures and communicates the elicited needs and changes to the elicited needs to the reviewers.
	As part of the communication process, in organizations that produce standard or off-the-shelf products, requirements elicitation is a continuous process, identifying new needs and changes in currently identified needs that can become new requirements and require changes (7.3.7) to plans (7.3.1) and other design and development outputs (7.3.3) and activities.
Analyze elicited needs against a set of predefined criteria	Analysis is the first form of review (7.2.2). One of the most significant challenges to organizations is to ensure the availability of experts (6.2 and 7.1) for analysis. Because the timing of opportunities is frequently beyond the control of the organization, and as the experts are assigned to perform other project- or product-related activities, performing effective analysis may require the organization to replan (7.1, 7.3.1, and 7.5.1) current activities. The vicious circle to be broken begins when the organization does not have enough people to do an adequate job of analyzing needs. Inadequate analysis leads to commitments that are not well understood and that inevitably take more effort than planned. Resource overruns on these prior commitments tie up people needed to analyze new needs as they are received, which results in continuing over commitment, and so forth.
	In addition, it is important that downstream organizations (e.g., test, support, and manufacturing) be represented in the analysis, to ensure that:
	• Interfaces between groups are managed (7.3.1)
	• Transitions occur smoothly (e.g., acceptance criteria are well defined and satisfied; 8.2.4)
	• Design and development outputs derived from the require-ments provide appropriate information for those functions (7.3.3 *b*).
	Defined criteria related to *complete* (e.g., nothing missing), *correct* (e.g., nothing extra, free from unnecessary constraints), *clear*, and *unambiguous* to ensure that the organization is both interested in (e.g., from a business perspective) and capable (7.2.2 *c*) of meeting the requirements that evolve from the needs.

Exhibit G-1 (continued)   Requirements engineering.

Typical activities	Related paragraphs and opportunities
Capture requirements and the results of the internal analysis and discussion	The output of the analysis is a baseline set of requirements, assumptions, and decisions, which are placed under document control (4.2.3) once they begin verification (e.g., review by all affected parties, including, potentially, the customer; 4.2.3 and 7.2.2).
Verify the captured requirements to ensure that there is nothing missing and nothing extra	In organizations that provide off-the-shelf products and services and that work in integrated teams to analyze needs and capture requirements, the verification is a relatively straightforward, final review of the complete set of requirements developed by the team. In contractual situations, the verification can become a lengthy, resource-intensive negotiation.
Manage requirements • Communicate • Change • Monitor contracts and commitments	Proposals to change requirements undergo the same analysis and review described above. In addition, requirements changes become inextricably linked with design and development changes (7.3.7). Part of the review of requirements changes is an assessment of the effect on current commitments and on current work products so that those commitments and plans (7.3.1) can be renegotiated and revised as required to ensure that the organization continues to be able to meet its commitments (7.2.2 *c*).

Integrated, Interdisciplinary Teams

Exhibit G-3 describes the activities and related paragraphs of ISO 9001:2000 as they apply to establishing and managing integrated, interdisciplinary teams.

Product Engineering

Exhibit G-4 describes the activities and related paragraphs of ISO 9001:2000 as they apply to designing and developing products.

Third-Party Development

Exhibit G-5 describes the activities and related paragraphs of ISO 9001:2000 as they apply to managing third-parties designing and developing products and product components and providing product-related services.

Quality Assurance

Exhibit G-6 describes the activities and related paragraphs of ISO 9001:2000 as they apply to quality assurance.

Quality Control: Verification and Validation

Exhibit G-7 describes the activities and related paragraphs of ISO 9001:2000 as they apply to verification and validation (quality control).

Exhibit G-2. Project management.

Typical activities	Related paragraphs and comments
Plan • Work Breakdown Schedule (WBS) • Organization Breakdown Structure (OBS) • Estimate effort • Skills inventory and acquisition • Schedule	Plans ensure both the availability of resources (6), including trained personnel (6.2.2), and the proper application of processes for a specific project or product (7.1). Because the plan is an attempt to predict the future, improving future plans (8.5.1), reviewing proposed plans (4.2.3 *b*), and controlling approved plans is enhanced by recording assumptions and the estimates and parameter values that are the basis for the plan. The successful transformation of requirements into delivered product requires coordination (7.3.1), planning (7.3.1), and communication (5.5.3 and 7.3.3 *b*) to ensure the readiness of all functions from engineering and manufacturing to marketing, sales, order administration, and customer support. The life cycle, expressed as stages of design and development (7.3.1 *a*) becomes the basis for the work breakdown structure, the assignment of responsibilities (7.3.1 *c*), and the development of the schedule.
Manage and monitor the plan • Risk management	The plan itself is the primary vehicle for ensuring that roles, responsibilities (7.3.1 *c*), and processes (7.1) are documented and understood, and, in particular, that verification and validation occur as planned, to prevent defects from propagating and to minimize the cost of correction (7.3.1 *b*). Management monitors progress against the plan (8.2.3) and takes appropriate steps to manage risks and prevent slippages (8.5.3) and to correct problems that occur (8.5.2).
Revise/adjust the plan	To the extent that the plan is an essential communication and coordination vehicle, updating appropriate portions of the plan is required (7.3.2).
Report progress—internal and external	Periodic progress reviews (5.6.1 and 7.3.4) allow management at all levels to determine and maintain an effective and efficient strategy for the investment of the organization's resources and to ensure that the organization's performance remains consistent with the defined objectives (5.4.1).

Configuration Management and Document Control

Exhibit G-8 describes the activities and related paragraphs of ISO 9001:2000 as they apply to configuration management.

Manufacturing and Logistics

Exhibit G-9 describes the activities and related paragraphs of ISO 9001:2000 as they apply to manufacturing and logistics.

Exhibit G-3. Integrated teams

Typical activities	Related paragraphs and comments
Meetings	Teams that include representatives of all affected functions reduce the time to communicate, discuss, and decide. Meetings serve as planning sessions (7.3.1), requirements (7.2.2) and design reviews (7.3.4), and verification activities (e.g., code reviews, document reviews; 7.3.5).
Meeting reports— action items	Many of the activities that are performed in meetings are required to produce records (7.2.2, 7.3.1, 7.3.4, 7.3.5, and 4.2.4). One useful technique is to require that every working meeting produce a report documenting action items and decisions. In some cases, the report may be a printed copy of a document on which the author has captured comments from a review meeting. When actions are assigned to a number of people, an e-mail or memorandum summary reminds people of their commitments and supports follow-up at subsequent meetings. The meeting reports can be filed in the project folder to provide historical information on the project, which is especially useful for lessons-learned sessions aimed at improving future activities (8.5.1).

Service and Support

Exhibit G-10 describes the activities and related paragraphs of ISO 9001:2000 as they apply to service and support.

Organizational Change

Exhibit G-11 describes the activities and related paragraphs of ISO 9001:2000 as they apply to managing organizational change.

Functional Priorities

The following suggest priorities for core processes as they apply to typical functional organizations seeking to derive the greatest benefit from ISO 9001.

Business Acquisition

Business acquisition includes sales and marketing functional organizations, typically responsible for finding and growing the organization's customer base and for managing product evolution.

1. Define interfaces with internal organizations
2. Requirements analysis—capability
3. Requirements definition
4. Requirements change management

Exhibit G-4. Product engineering.

Typical activities	Related paragraphs and comments
Design and develop	Whatever techniques, methods, and processes are used the design outputs are under change control (4.2.3 and 7.3.7). In specifying the requirements for the approval of changes, the organization can increase the degree of control as a work product progresses through the process, achieves wider distribution, and is the basis for other work products.
Test	As part of the life cycle definition and the plan, each review (7.3.4), verification (7.3.5) and validation (7.3.6) activity is called out and planned.
Release	Based on the defined review, verification, and validation activities, product quality (8.2.4) and process execution (8.2.3) are monitored and the results, when compared with the defined acceptance criteria (8.2.4) become the basis for determining when a product can be promoted from one stage of the life cycle or activity to another. A documented procedure defines responsibility, authority, processes, and appropriate criteria for determining the disposition of products with known defects (8.3).
Maintain • Enhance • Correct	Whether maintenance is treated as a new project or as a phase in an ongoing, never-ending project, the proposed requirement (e.g., enhancement request or incident report) is analyzed, documented, verified, planned, and implemented. The ability to trace (7.5.3) between approved change requests (7.3.7) and product changes (in either direction) ensures that the organization maintains the integrity of the product content (e.g., no missing changes, no unauthorized changes). Traceability supports the interface between development and the test organizations (7.3.1), ensuring that no changes sneak through untested (8.2.4) because the test organization was unaware of the change. When incidents are determined to be legitimate defects, the organization is responsible for taking appropriate action to eliminate the detected nonconformity (8.3 *a*) and to eliminate the source of the problem (8.5.2) so that it does not reoccur. As defects are detected and corrected in previous versions of products, part of preventing reoccurrence (8.5.2) or preventing occurrence (8.5.3) is evaluating the defect against other versions of the product in which the defect may not yet have been discovered (or in which the cause of the defect may have been inadvertently eliminated).
Tools/ automation	Establishing and maintaining the organization's infrastructure (6.3) is an essential enabler of modern engineering processes, from the communication's network to project management tools, to configuration management tools, to editors, debuggers, and compilers.

Exhibit G.4 (continued). Product engineering.

Typical activities	Related paragraphs and comments
Knowledge management and transfer	Knowledge management and transfer, the ability to capture, recall, and reuse experience, contributes to the accuracy of initial plans (7.1 and 7.3.1), the readiness of downstream organizations (7.3.2 *b*), and the ability to maintain effective communications with external customers (7.2.3), particularly those who report defects (8.5.2) and those who demand feedback and visibility into the organization's response (8.3).

Product Development

Product development includes systems, hardware, and software engineering, as well as systems test, project management, and possibly, a software quality assurance (audit and review) function.

1. Engineering life cycle definition
2. Requirements management
3. Planning and project management
   - Development
   - Verification and validation
4. Configuration management
   - Controls for change
5. Maintenance
   - Life cycle scalability
   - External problem resolution

Manufacturing

1. Define interface with engineering/development
   - Planning to ensure capability to meet commitments
   - New business (resources and training)
2. New types of service (process engineering)
3. Integrate quality functions (self-checking, failure-proofing, continuous in-line inspection by peers)
4. Automate systems to greatest extent practical

Service and Support

1. Define interfaces with internal organizations
   - Product introduction and service planning to ensure capability to meet commitments
   - New business (resources and training)
2. New types of service (process engineering)
3. Automate systems to greatest extent practical

Exhibit G-5. Third-party development.

Typical activities	Related paragraphs and comments
Make-buy decision/plan, specify requirements, solicit, select	Successful make-buy decisions are based on assessment of both technical and business capabilities. As part of the initial solicitation and selection process, technical feasibility is determined by engineering representatives, closely supported by purchasing or supplier relations specialists who focus on the feasibility of establishing mutually successful business relationships. The successful decision-making process coordinates the two sets of criteria to mitigate the risks associated with many make-buy decisions. As solicitation and selection overlaps design and development, an established process ensures that an appropriately detailed statement of what is required is available (7.3.3 *b* and 7.4.2), that the right resources are available (6.2) on the business evaluation side, and that the roles and responsibilities are clearly defined (5.5.1) for each phase of selection, from determining initial feasibility to creating a short list and soliciting commitments, to awarding the contract. To ensure that the selected supplier budgets for and supports the expected levels of coordination and communication, the specified requirements include all of the deliverables, including progress and project reporting, meetings, technical planning and information exchanges, and so forth.
Monitor and manage (coordinate and control), change, correct	Monitoring and managing a selected supplier who is developing a product or supplying a service (e.g., who is not providing a standard product or service) entails continuing the same close cooperation and coordination (7.3.1) between those responsible for the business management and those responsible for the technical management. In many cases, the project team, with a supplier management representative, and sometimes with a representative from the supplier, is responsible for ongoing coordination and planning of the outsourced development or service (4.1). Changes, costs, commitments, and plans (7.3.1) are adjusted in real time. Product components delivered by the supplier are folded into the configuration management system (7.5.3 and 7.5.5) to preserve their integrity and are subject to the review (7.3.4), verification (7.3.5), and validation (7.3.6) specified in the requirements agreed to by the supplier (7.4.2).

Exhibit G-6. Quality assurance

Typical activities	Related paragraphs and comments
Plan, review, report, take action and follow up	Quality assurance refers to the audits (8.2.2) and oversight function that verifies that processes are followed (8.2.3) and that products complete all of the required steps (8.2.4) before they advance to subsequent stages of the product life cycle.
	Deficiencies are the responsibility of management to correct (8.2.2 and 8.5.2), with appropriate follow-up by the quality assurance function.
	Whether the personnel performing quality assurance have other responsibilities or are full-time quality assurance, whether they are part of the project team or are from a separate organization, their obligation is to provide an objective view of the project. Results are reported not only to the line manager who is responsible for correcting any problems but also, at an appropriate level of abstraction, to top management (5.6.2 *a*), whose concerns for the health of the organization transcend allegiance to a specific project.

Exhibit G-7. Quality control: verification and validation.

Typical activities	Related paragraphs and comments
Plan	The verification and validation activities that are appropriate (7.3.2 *b*) for each stage (7.3.1 *a*) of the standard development life cycle are determined. In addition, any verification or validation specific to the product is also determined (7.1 *c*). Necessary resources, including personnel and hardware and software that are to be procured or developed, are identified and scheduled. In many cases, test plans are integrated with project plans (7.3.1) to further communication and coordination.
Specify	At each stage of development, design outputs, which become inputs to the next stage of development, include or reference the acceptance criteria (7.3.3 *c*), which define the scope of the subsequent verification activities (7.3.5). The testing procedures specific to the product are defined in sufficient detail to ensure that personnel performing the verification and validation are required to demonstrate that the acceptance criteria are satisfied (8.2.4) and to produce the required records.
Test	Verification and validation is executed as planned at each stage of development. Defects are identified, corrective action is taken (8.5.2), and the tested product is controlled to ensure that it is not inadvertently used (8.3). To accelerate design and development, product is frequently released with lists of known defects so that subsequent stages of the life cycle can begin or continue. When appropriate, a product with known defects is approved for release to customers (8.2.4) so that they can begin to use the parts of the product that do work correctly (8.3).
Report	Requirements for records of testing specific to the product (7.1 *d*) are determined, including, in particular, the content, the method of storage (and retrieval), and the period of time for which the records are to be retained (4.2.4).
Retest	When defects are corrected, the product is retested to ensure that it does satisfy the input requirements (8.3). The extent of the retest depends on the nature of the product and the ability of the engineers to isolate or predict the effect of changes.
Tools/automation	The tools required for testing are part of the organization's infrastructure (6.3). When systems used for testing are shared with support or development because of cost or scarcity, careful planning and coordination (7.3.1) ensure that adequate resources are available. Particularly when test systems are shared, the test hardware and software are controlled to ensure that the specified configurations are available and used (7.6) and that the tests produce valid results. The traditional horror story involves software product intended to run under version X of an operating system. At the same time, software developers were exploring Version X+1 of the operating system. Extensive testing was inadvertently done on a system configured with Version X+1 of the operating system, resulting in a significant delay as the testing was restarted.

Table G.1. Configuration management

Typical activities	Related paragraphs and comments
Identify	Identification applies to all configuration items, including documents, drawings, specifications, bills-of-material (4.2.3), and hardware and computer software (7.5.3).
Control • Review and analyze effect • Prioritize • Approve • Plan	Changes to configuration items are reviewed for content (feasibility, clarity, validity, etc.) and for effect on work that has already been completed (7.3.7). Once a proposed change is approved, plans are updated as appropriate to reflect the new scope of work and to ensure that the change is correctly implemented (7.3.1). The updated plans address the verification and validation necessary to ensure that the change is implemented correctly (7.3.5, 7.3.6, 8.2.4) and that the change does not introduce unintended side effects that adversely affect the previously established capability of the product (7.5.5). Configuration management tools automate the notification, review, tracking, and approval processes associated with configuration management.
Status accounting	Recording and reporting the status of product and product components enables activities to be coordinated (7.3.1) and provides information that is required to ensure that • Planned activities are completed before products and components are released to subsequent stages of design and development (8.2.4) • Incomplete or otherwise defective product is not inadvertently released to subsequent stages of design and development (8.3) Configuration management tools automatically track and report status and changes in status to affected individuals.
Audit	Configuration management tools automatically perform a continuous audit by ensuring that • Changes in product can be traced back to approved change requests • Approved changes can be traced forward to the appropriate product changes (7.5.3) • Required activities (e.g., tests, reviews, approvals) take place before the associated configuration management activities (e.g., release and promotion) In some cases, the system test group manually verifies the integrity of delivered builds before beginning validation. Periodic internal audits (8.2.2) confirm that configuration management processes are effectively implemented and maintained and that activities take place as specified in plans and in procedures (8.2.2).
Tools/automation	The tools required for configuration management are part of the organization's infrastructure (6.3). When licenses for the use of configuration management tools are limited because of cost, careful planning and coordination (7.3.1) ensure that adequate resources are available.

Exhibit G-9. Manufacturing and logistics

Typical activities	Related paragraphs and comments
Introduction planning	Coordination and planning for the introduction of new and modified products into manufacturing begins early in the product life cycle (7.3.1) and ensures that the organization has the capability to deliver on commitments related to manufacturing (7.2.2). These commitments range from testing to quantities and delivery lead times. As appropriate, requirements for manufacturability are included in the product requirements (7.2.1 *d* and 7.3.2 *d*), and supplied requirements are reviewed (7.2.2) for implications related to manufacturability.
	Manufacturing is kept informed of progress (7.3.1) and changes (7.3.7). The information required by manufacturing is included in the outputs from design and development (7.3.3 *b*). This information may include training (e.g., as part of preproduction or prototype production), as well as bills-of-materials, assembly instructions, product certification (e.g., UL, FCC), and other required documentation.
	In some organizations, manufacturing engineering may represent the interests of manufacturing during the design and development phase of the product life cycle and may have a process for the design and development of manufacturing processes and capability. For organizations that provide manufacturing services (e.g., contract manufacturers), the provisions of design and development (7.3) can be applied to the manufacturing engineering processes.
Operation	Manufacturing operation is planned (7.5.1) to ensure the availability of all resources (6), including measuring equipment (7.5.1 *d*) and information (7.5.1 *a*, 7.5.1 *b*), and to ensure that processes are followed.
	Plans range from periodic, formal resource plans (e.g., for raw materials, components, etc.) to team meetings held at the beginning of a shift to assign work orders.
	Suitable methods are applied to monitor and measure product characteristics (8.2.4) against acceptance criteria and process performance (8.2.3) against plans.
	Procedures (7.5.1 *b*), suitable equipment (7.5.1 *c*), and trained personnel (6.2.2) ensure that materials and products are not inadvertently damaged. In particular, procedures (7.5.5) ensure that components that are susceptible to damage from electrostatic discharge are properly handled (e.g., grounded floors and workstations, operator heel straps, and wrist straps).
	Nonconforming product discovered at any stage of manufacturing is identified and controlled (e.g., segregated) to ensure that it is not inadvertently used in subsequent manufacturing operations (8.3) or delivered to customers for use. A material review board or similar function determines the disposition of the nonconforming product (8.3).
	The progress of product through the manufacturing process is recorded (7.5.3) both to ensure that all specified steps, including testing (8.2.4) are completed and to secure any required records (4.2.4).

Exhibit C.0 (continued). Manufacturing and logistics

Typical activities	Related paragraphs and comments
Inventory	The organization inspects, tests, or otherwise confirms that incoming purchased material conforms to the organization's purchase specification (7.4.3). Suitable storage facilities (6.3), procedures, and appropriate packaging and transportation methods (7.5.5) preserve the conformity of received material and finished goods until product is delivered to the customer.
Purchasing/ supplier management	Whether the organization manufactures its own products with purchased materials or outsources all or part of its manufacturing activities (4.1), the selection of qualified suppliers involves specifying the requirements to be met by the supplier (7.4.2) and then evaluating candidates' technical capabilities and business relationships against those requirements (7.4.1). The organization ensures that qualified personnel are available to perform those evaluations (6.2), which, on the technical side, may entail site visits, reference checks, procurement and testing of samples, and abbreviated pilot runs.
	Once the supplier is selected, periodic progress and technical reviews, audits, and so forth are conducted, as documented and agreed to in the purchase specification. These reviews and audits ensure that activities are coordinated (7.3.1, 7.4.2) and that the organization receives as much notice as possible about changes in the products and services provided by the supplier.
Change management	A systematic process for reviewing and approving engineering change proposals (ECPs) and implementing them as engineering change orders (ECOs) minimizes the effect on inventories and disruption in manufacturing.
	A change control board, representing sales or marketing, engineering, manufacturing, purchasing, support and other affected parts of the organization is responsible for the review and approval of ECPs and ECOs.
Tools and automation	The tools required for manufacturing are part of the organization's infrastructure (6.3) and are typically the domain of a manufacturing or operations engineering group.
	For extensive or specialized manufacturing processes, the plans, policies, and procedures followed by manufacturing engineering are as rigorous, detailed, and important as those applied to product engineering. Design and development of new manufacturing processes is followed by appropriate piloting (7.5.2), adjustment, and systematic, planned rollout through training (6.2.2) and the deployment of new procedures and equipment (7.5.1).

Exhibit G-10. Service and support.

Typical activities	Related paragraphs and comments
Introduction planning	Coordination and planning for the introduction of new and modified products into service and support begins early in the product life cycle (7.3.1) and ensures that the organization has the capability to deliver on commitments related to service and support (7.2.2). These commitments range from response times for on-site or remote technicians to providing seven-day-a-week, 24-hour-a-day (7 x 24) facilities management. As appropriate, requirements for supportability (e.g., remote diagnosis and licensing) and serviceability (e.g., installation, repair, and management) are included in the product requirements (7.2.1 *d* and 7.3.2 *d*), and supplied requirements are reviewed (7.2.2) for implications related to support and service. Service and support organizations are kept informed of progress (7.3.1) and changes (7.3.7). The information required by service and support is included in the outputs from design and development (7.3.3 *b*). This information may include training (e.g., as part of product validation and initial deployment), as well as user documentation and internal, technical documentation. Careful planning of the transition from engineering to support and service ensures the availability of required resources (6) and preserves the organization's ability to meet its commitments to customers (7.2.2 *c*), especially during periods when engineering may be providing support and service at the same time it is ramping up for the next project. In some organizations, service and support may have a process for the design and development of services, especially when third parties are involved (e.g., outsourcing, dealers, and distributors).
Incident handling • Analyze • Resolve • Escalate • Track	Service and support is frequently the first line of communication with customers (7.2.3). Service and support's handling of customer-reported "incidents" results in corrective action (8.5.2) through the identification of defects in products (8.3). Whether an incident identifies a defect or is an enhancement request, the result is an input (7.3.2) for future development and for changes to in-process development (7.3.7). Access to information regarding individual service agreements (7.5.1 *a*) enables service and support personnel to respond in a way that meets the organization's commitments to each customer and restores or enhances customer satisfaction.
Reporting and knowledge management	In addition to forwarding individual defects and enhancement opportunities, automated service and support systems for call handling and tracking capture data that can be analyzed to identify trends (8.4 *c*) related to both product performance (8.2.4) and customer satisfaction (8.2.1). Careful analysis of incidents closed with "no-trouble-found" (e.g., customer error or misunderstanding) can originate suggestions for reducing cost of ownership and cost of service and for improving customer satisfaction.

Exhibit G-10 (continued). Service and support.

Typical activities	Related paragraphs and comments
	Coordination between service and support and engineering allows service and support personnel to provide appropriate information to customers on the status of the resolution of previously reported incidents (7.2.3).
	The service and support system also facilitates the efficient exchange of information among service and support personnel about customer status and previously reported and resolved problems.
Professional services • Support • Consulting • Installation • Outsourcing	Planning and management (7.5.1) ensure that the organization is able to meet its commitments related to professional services, which include services offered with the product (e.g., warranty) as well as services that are purchased separately (e.g., consulting, installation, and facilities management).
	In some cases, commitments to support products require that the organization archive development tools and the associated hardware and that the organization take steps to ensure the availability of third-party components.
Tools and automation	The tools required for service and support are part of the organization's infrastructure (6.3) and are typically the domain of service and support management and, perhaps, an information technology group.
	For extensive or specialized service and support processes, detailed plans, policies, and procedures are supplied. Design and development of new service and support processes is followed by appropriate piloting (7.5.2), adjustment, and systematic, planned rollout through training (6.2.2) and the deployment of new procedures (7.5.1).

Exhibit G-11. Organizational change.

Typical activities	Related paragraphs and comments
Downsize, layoff, merge, acquire, transform, reorganize, reengineer	When organizational change is planned, it is the responsibility of senior management to ensure that "the integrity of the quality management system is maintained" (5.4.2 *b*). At a minimum, these changes invoke a review of current commitments (7.2.2 *c*), to ensure that the organization retains the capability to meet them, and any appropriate communication with customers (7.2.3) in the event that changes to commitments are required.
	As soon as is practical, new responsibilities are communicated to personnel (5.5.1), plans are revised, and affected procedural, project, and product documentation is updated. The management representative is responsible for ensuring that these revisions are implemented (5.5.2 *a*).
	If the organization has an ISO 9001 registration, the responsible individual (typically the management representative) may also be required to communicate the changes to the registrar.
	When two registered organizations merge, there is no requirement that the registrations be consolidated (e.g., in a single certificate, from a single registrar) or that both organizations operate under the same quality management system. When management objectives require that the merged organizations follow common processes, the best practices captured in the two quality management systems can simplify the communication, education, discussion, and evaluation necessary to define and adopt a new, single, quality management system.

Appendix H
A Sample Questionnaire for Registrar Selection

Exhibit H-1 indicates questions that can be adapted to any organization's needs and provided to candidate registrars for submission before any lengthy interviews.

Exhibit H-1. Registrar questionnaire.

Questionnaire	Comments and rationale
1. How long has your company been an ISO 9000 registrar?	Experience is an indicator of the quality of the registrar's services. It also provides confidence that the registrar will be in business for as long as the organization needs its services.
	Because all registrars adhere to the same rules of operation, a newer registrar that is building market share may be more responsive in scheduling and competitive in cost.
2. What accreditation has your company received directly? What is the accreditation body (e.g., RAB, UKAS) and what is the scope of each accreditation (e.g., 9001, AS9000, TL9000, EAC codes)?	Determine what accreditation is relevant to the organization's markets and products. Ensure that the registrar's scope is relevant to the organization's products and services. Because the EAC classifications and the North American Industry Classification System codes are relatively vague, further information on the registrar's capability is solicited during further contacts with the registrar.

Accreditation body	Scope

Questionnaire	Comments and rationale
3. If you operate under a Memorandum of Understanding (MOU) or other arrangement with an accredited registrar (e.g., you perform assessments on their behalf), what is the name of that registrar? What accreditation body accredits that registrar? What is the scope of that registrar's accreditation (e.g., EAC codes)? What are the terms that govern your activity?	In some cases, a registrar may have an agreement with another registrar to perform audits in a specific geographic region or industry sector. The goal of this question is to ascertain the accreditation body that will be identified on the registration certificate.

Registrar	Accreditation body	Scope	Terms

Exhibit H-1 (continued). Registrar questionnaire.

4. What are your policies for assigning auditors (e.g., substitution)? What policies govern the behavior of the assessment team you send (e.g., published code of conduct)?	As part of the accreditation process, the registrar is required to have auditors who are certified to act as lead assessors in the designated industries. The question may be answered with references to ISO standards and to the quality manual the registrar is required to maintain.
5. Will you send the same team each time? If not, how do you ensure continuity and consistency from audit to audit?	Although auditors are professionals, trained and experienced in the appropriate industries, familiarity with the organization's nomenclature and personnel enhances the efficiency, effectiveness, and depth of each successive audit. The frequency of the audits and the number of intervening audits at other companies make it extremely unlikely that excessive familiarity will lead to inadvertently overlooking nonconformities. In some cases, the registrar's audit team leader may be assigned to the organization, with team members assigned based on availability. In the event that the audit team changes completely, what preparation and handover does the registrar implement to ensure consistency?

Exhibit H-1 (continued). **Registrar questionnaire.**

6. What is your method for determining the size of the assessment team?	The size of the team affects travel and lodging costs. It also determines the number of guides the organization is required to provide (one guide per auditor). Registrars typically adjust the number of auditors to keep the on-site time at a single site to less than a week.
7. What companies with businesses similar to ours have you registered? What are the scopes of their registrations? Please provide contact information. <table><tr><th>Company</th><th>Scope</th><th>Contact</th></tr><tr><td></td><td></td><td></td></tr><tr><td></td><td></td><td></td></tr></table>	Registrars are required to keep a list of firms they have registered and certificates they have issued. For each firm and certificate, the scope statement is provided. These are the references that are checked as part of the selection process.
8. Based on what you know of our company, what do you consider viable alternatives for scope of registration (e.g., product, site)?	The organization can provide a summary of its structure and of registration certificate or certificates it intends to apply for (e.g., for a product line, for a site).
9. *(If appropriate)* How do you approach companies with multiple locations?	The organization can provide a summary of the activities at its locations. For example, if all of the field locations follow the same procedures, the registrar may be able to issue the certificate by auditing "headquarters" and one or two nearby field offices. Other field offices are audited as part of the surveillance process—when the registrar is in that area for another audit.

Exhibit H-1 (continued). Registrar questionnaire

10. Do you subcontract any registration-related activities to other organizations? If so, indicate to whom.	Although the use of subcontractors should have no effect on the quality or confidentiality of the audit, it provides an indicator of the registrar's ability to ensure consistent audits. In addition, some organizations are reluctant to provide information to consultants, even under the most stringent nondisclosure agreements.

Activity	Subcontractor(s)
(a) Preassessment	
(b) Documentation review	
(c) Initial assessment	
(d) Surveillance visits	
(e) Software assessments	
(f) Other	

(g) If applicable, what processes do you have in place to assure the quality of subcontracted services?	The registrar may have a policy and procedure to provide. At a minimum, the results of the subcontractor's work are reviewed by the registrar.

11. What is your registration process? What do you provide or require for:	The registrar typically has a document or Web site that describes the process.

(a) Preassessment (coverage, on-site duration, number of auditors, report format and availability)	
(b) Additional support during preparation for the initial assessment	Although the registrar cannot also consult, it can provide training and references to relevant publicly available standards and documents.
(c) Review of quality system documentation (duration, documents required to be provided, format [electronic, paper], and availability [remote access, e-mail attachment, etc.])	

Exhibit H-1 (continued). Registrar questionnaire.

(d) Initial assessment (on-site coverage, duration, number of auditors, exit meeting, report format and availability)	The registrar's auditors typically issue a preliminary report and a recommendation for registration at the conclusion of the audit; the report must still be approved by the appropriate management personnel at the registrar. Although it is possible, the auditors' recommendation is rarely if ever reversed.
(e) Follow-up to initial assessment (review of corrective action plan and corrective action implementation, on-site coverage, duration, number of auditors, report format and availability)	
(f) What is the application process? What forms, etc. are required?	
12. What are your criteria for issuing a certificate after the initial assessment? A provisional certificate? Define any terms such as major and minor nonconformity. Please provide examples from our industry.	At this time, the traditional clause-based definition of major and minor, derived from the 20 sections of ISO 9001:1994, has not been translated to the process-based format of ISO 9001:2000. Even with the clause-based definitions, there is a wide range of ways in which registrars determine when a certificate can be issued—ranging from, "on receipt of a corrective action plan for all nonconformities, no matter how severe," to, "after a reaudit of certain areas in which major nonconformities were found." Some registrars do not "fail" clients except in the most egregious cases.

Exhibit H-1 (continued).   Registrar questionnaire.

10 During assessments do you require us to provide knowledgeable guides to accompany each auditor during interviews?	If the answer to this question is not an unqualified "yes," the candidate is dismissed from consideration. The registrar may have a guideline defining what is expected from guides.
14 What is your reassessment or ongoing surveillance process?	Registrars typically reaudit on a semiannual basis, according to a general plan developed in conjunction with the initial registration. Planning for a specific surveillance audit typically starts at least a month in advance of the audit.
(a) Review of quality system documentation (coverage, duration, report format and availability)	
(b) Surveillance/reassessment visit (coverage, frequency, duration, number of auditors, exit meeting, report format and availability)	
(c) What sections of the standard are reviewed at every reassessment (e.g., internal audit process)?	
(d) Follow-up to surveillance visits (review of corrective action plan and corrective action implementation, on-site coverage, duration, number of auditors, report format and availability)	
(e) What are your criteria for maintaining the certificate after each surveillance visit?	
(f) How do you handle changes? In clients' organizations? In quality system documentation? What are the notification processes?	What notification is the organization expected or required to provide? How?
(g) During reassessments will you allow us to provide knowledgeable guides to accompany each auditor during interviews?	

Exhibit H-1 (continued).   Registrar questionnaire.

15. What records do you maintain? Are there any written records of audit results other than those we receive?		The registrar typically retains the auditors' notes and any follow-up recommendations for the next audit. When the auditors realize they have insufficient evidence to issue a nonconformity, they will flag it for the next audit. The auditors may identify these as observations, for the use of the organization and the next audit.
16. What provisions do you have for companies producing software or specialized or regulated products? For example: – Are your auditors familiar with the Software Engineering Institute's Capability Maturity Model or Capability Maturity Model Integrated for assessing the capability of software development organizations? – Are your auditors familiar with the European and U.S. regulatory requirements applicable to our products (e.g., FDA, NRC, UL)?		Familiarity with regulations and other models allows the registrars' auditors to understand the organizations business processes. In some cases, the registrar may be qualified to perform a single audit addressing the requirements of more than one standard (e.g., "combining an ISO 9001 audit and …").

17. What fees, expenses, or other charges are typically associated with registration and surveillance visits?

	Initial assessment	Surveillance visit
Deposit		
Application fee		
Review of quality system documentation		
Preparation and assessment		
Cancellation and rescheduling		
Follow up to verify corrective action?		
Cancellation and rescheduling		

Related information you should receive:
- Is the deposit refundable?
- Is the application fee refundable?

At what point does the registrar add auditors and reduce the duration?

Exhibit H-1 (continued). Registrar questionnaire.

Expenses			How are travel and lodging arrangements managed? Do you share travel expenses with multiple clients? Do you have local personnel?
Certificate fee			
Other			

18. What are your scheduling requirements?

(a) What is the lead time to schedule a preassessment?	
(b) What is the lead time to schedule an initial assessment?	
(c) How far in advance of the initial assessment to do you require quality system documentation?	
(d) What is the lead time to schedule a surveillance visit	
(e) How far in advance of surveillance visits do you require current quality system documentation?	
(f) What notice do you expect to provide for rescheduling the initial assessment?	
(g) At what point is the assessment schedule firm except for circumstances beyond your control?	
(h) What notice do you expect to receive for rescheduling an initial assessment?	
(i) What notice do you expect to provide for rescheduling surveillance visits?	
(j) At what point is the surveillance schedule firm except for circumstances beyond your control?	
(k) What notice do you expect to receive for rescheduling surveillance visits?	
(l) How far in advance do you plan audits?	
(m) How far in advance do you announce or plan surveillance visits?	

Exhibit H-1 (continued).   Registrar questionnaire.

19. What if the review of the quality system documentation indicates that the initial assessment should be deferred? What charges would we incur? What would be the minimum delay we could expect? How would you communicate the results of the documentation review to us?
20. Additional information and comments

Comments and Questions

The greatest advantages of a book are its portability and persistent availability. For the authors, it provides an opportunity to draft, review, revise, and clarify. The greatest drawback to a book is the separation of author and audience, the lack of real-time feedback from which to gauge how well a concept has been communicated, how well it is received, and the level of interest.

Your comments and questions are appreciated and will be carefully considered for subsequent revisions of this volume and of our conclusions. We will make every effort to respond to questions.

Regards ,

Bob Bamford

Robert Bamford

William J. Deibler

William J. Deibler

**SS
QC**

Software Systems Quality Consulting
San Jose CA
Phone: 408-985-4476
Fax: 408-248-7772
www.ssqc.com
e-mail: 9001book@ssqc.com

About the Authors

William J. Deibler II and **Robert Bamford** founded SSQC in 1990 to support software development organizations in Software Engineering Life Cycle Definition, Software Quality Assurance and Testing, Business Process Reengineering, ISO 9000 Registration, and CMM implementation. Bill and Bob have developed and published numerous courses, auditing tools, research papers, and articles on interpreting and applying the ISO 9000 standards and guidelines and the SEI Capability Maturity Model for Software. They were principal authors and editors of *A Guide to Software Quality System Registration under ISO 9001* and have been active members of the United States Technical Advisory Group for ISO/IEC JTC1 SC7—Software Engineering Standards subcommittee, which is responsible for the development and maintenance of ISO 12207 and ISO 15504.

Their clients range from Silicon Valley–based organizations to large government subcontractors. Their clients have successfully achieved ISO registration and advanced maturity levels based on the Capability Maturity Model for Software from the Software Engineering Institute at Carnegie Mellon University.

William J. Deibler II has an MS in Computer Science and 20 years experience in the computer industry, primarily in the areas of software and systems quality assurance, validation, and development.

Robert Bamford has an MA in mathematics and, in a career spanning 35 years, has served as an instructor and staff writer and managed training development, technical publications, professional services, and third-party software development.

As founding partners in SSQC, Bill and Bob have accrued extensive experience in managing and implementing CMM- and ISO 9001–based process improvement in software and hardware engineering environments.

Index